Managing the Public Sector

Managing the Public Sector

A Comparative Analysis of the United Kingdom and the United States

Andrew Massey

Lecturer in Politics, Queen Mary and Westfield College, The University of London

Edward Elgar

Published by
Edward Elgar Publishing Limited
Gower House
Croft Road
Aldershot
Hants GU11 3HR
England

Edward Elgar Publishing Company
Old Post Road
Brookfield
Vermont 05036
USA

A CIP catalogue record for this book is available from the British Library

A CIP catalogue record for this book is available from the US Library of Congress.

ISBN 1 85278 333 8

Printed in Great Britain at the University Press, Cambridge

Contents

Preface and Acknowledgements

Over the last few years the teaching of public administration has undergone as radical a transformation as its subject matter. In some universities it no longer exists, but has been transformed into 'management studies' and transferred to the business school. I disagree with these changes, not out of any nostalgia for the old order, and certainly not out of some misplaced academic conservatism, but because I think they are wrong. The study of a country's public administration is integral to understanding its political system; as Don K. Price (1983) so eloquently argued, administration is the 'seamy side' of politics. But it is more than that, it is also profoundly different to mere management. The belief that governing a sophisticated industrial democracy in the late Twentieth Century can be equated with retailing has been one of the more pernicious myths of the New Right.

My aim in writing this book has been to chart the impact of the changes on the public sector in Britain and the US, asking the questions: What has happened? Why did it happen? How did it happen? I have concentrated, therefore, upon the activities of the New Right, but also provided alternative perspectives, where appropriate. I have sought to give the readers a wide appreciation of the subject, introducing them to as much of the literature as the subject will stand, but without mechanistically listing all the different approaches. In this respect, the text flows with its subject, but with 'signposts' off to the other perspectives available. I have not tried to write an ideologically inspired critique of the changes, or a standard textbook which lists all of the critiques, preferring to aim for a measured review of the reforms and including within each chapter some conclusions based upon the evidence. Much of the existing literature is partisan, advocating further liberalisation, or excoriating the changes that have occurred. I have attempted to discuss the debate, but not joined either side; in my view many of the reforms were necessary and even laudable, but there have also been costs resulting in avoidable harm being inflicted upon the public sector. The latter was often due to the malignant effect of ideology being implemented as dogma. The book is based on a mix of documentation and literature scans combined with original research, which was mainly in the form of large-scale interviewing in Britain and the US of politicians, political appointees, serving public sector officials and former officials.

I chose to concentrate on Britain and the US because it is here that long-standing New Right governments, indeed explicitly anti-state administrations, have attempted to implement similar policies. The two countries have close historical and constitutional links and during the period covered (from the late 1970s) there was also a personal empathy between the leaders, as well as a flow of ideas in both directions across the Atlantic regarding the best way for government to tackle its problems. It is my hope that people will find this comparative approach a useful one for understanding the subject. Accordingly, the book begins with an examination of the role of the public sector and the corpus of the subject, discussing the reasons why Britain and the US evolved their respective systems and looking at the core political values of the two countries.

Chapters 2 and 3 then chart the impact of New Right reforms upon the British civil service, showing the historical background to the present structure and discussing the reasons why the Conservative Government of Mrs Thatcher found this an unsatisfactory inheritance and the methods she employed to reform it. Chapter 4 continues this theme with an analysis of the reform of the US federal civil service, contrasting the reasons why under Reagan and Bush this has been less successful or far-reaching than the British version. The tenor of analysis then shifts to privatisation and a series of chapters charts the ideological motivations and managerial dynamics for privatisation at the federal level in the US (Chapter 5), the UK (Chapter 6), which includes a case study of the Electricity Supply Industry, and the sub-national level in both countries (Chapter 7). Chapter 8 is a general conclusion, but it must be stressed that the analysis of each chapter includes a set of observations relevant to that subject and the links it has with the rest of the book. I should note that an article in Government and Opposition, 1992, Vol. 27 is based upon some of the sections in chapters 2–7.

Throughout the book I have used English spellings, except where direct quotation made this inappropriate. I have also left all my interviewees anonymous. Some of those who agreed to answer my often impertinent questions expressed no wish to remain anonymous, the majority of civil servants, however, did not want to be directly quoted. For the sake of continuity I have, therefore, avoided personal identification.

All books are collective efforts to a greater or lesser extent, and this has been no exception. I owe a great debt of gratitude to many people in both Britain and the US, particularly the more than one hundred people who agreed to my interviewing them in Los Angeles, Sacramento, San Diego, Santa Barbara, Washington DC, London, Winchester, and Birmingham. I was fortunate enough to spend some time visiting the Department of Political Science at California State University, Los Angeles, in 1989. Whilst there I conducted over sixty interviews with people involved in the public sector at national, state, county and city level. I wish to record my gratitude to the faculty there for their extraordinary kindness and generosity toward me during this period. I am particularly indebted to Professor J.T. 'Ted' Anagnoson and Professor Harry Hall, for their superb academic and logistic help. I would also like to thank Professor Gene Dvorin, and Randy and Fran Altenberg. Whilst in Los Angeles I was privileged to meet and discuss the nature of change in the American public sector with Professor Joel Aberbach of UCLA, Professor Bill Lamner and Professor Larry Berg, of USC, and Graham Kannon, of Representative Berman's staff. All of these people helped to shape my views on the subject. I am also indebted to Professor James Pfiffner, of George Mason University, who enlivened my trip to Washington DC in 1989 with some invigorating debate, and considerable documentary support. He helped to shape my interviewing profile whilst in the capital. It is difficult for an outsider to gather the 'flavour' of American politics and I have not sought to write a textbook on American government. My goal has been the more modest one of simply examining a policy common to both countries and seeking to discover what has happened during the process of implementation. The natural kindness and generosity of spirit displayed by so many Americans greatly aided me in my task.

In Britain I also have many people to thank. The first to be mentioned must be those who part-funded this project. They include the Nuffield Foundation, the Political Studies Department of Queen Mary and Westfield College (under the successive charge of Mr David Black, Professor James Dunkerley and Professor Ken Young), and the Public Policy Research Unit of QMW, whose Director, Dr Wayne Parsons provided considerable support for the American research. I must also register the kindness and patience of Edward Elgar; his courtesy in extending deadlines was unwavering. There were a large number of people who agreed to be interviewed in Britain; they ranged across a number of Whitehall departments at often very senior levels, the new auditing and regulatory agencies and local authorities. Most people expressed a wish to remain completely anonymous. While respecting this request, I still thank them for their time and advice. I am grateful to Mrs Jenny Barnes of HCC for helping me to establish the case study of Hampshire's reforms, and Keiran Walsh of INLOGOV for his comments on the British local government changes. I am also indebted to Dr Wayne Parsons for his ideas and suggestions over the years and his generous comments on the draft of this book. Other people who have kindly given their time to comment on the draft are Professor Trevor Smith, Vice Chancellor of the University of Ulster (who also helped to establish my visit to Los Angeles), Major L. Cousins (RAOC), and Professor Ken Young, who read and commented upon chapters 1 and 5. None of these people can be held accountable for errors appearing in the final version, much as I might like to blame them; I have sole responsibility there.

My profoundest thanks are reserved for Gill Massey, who has borne the burden of my writing with fortitude and only occasional outbreaks of annoyance. She has also conspired to ensure that the arrival of one Peter James Massey, in the middle of the project, delayed the final version only minimally, despite Peter's best efforts to the contrary. It is with gratitude and relief that I dedicate this book to her.

1 The Question of Governance: An Epidemic Malady of Constitutions

> What then made us to differ? Why was it that, in that epidemic malady of constitutions, ours escaped that destroying influence; or rather that, at the very crisis of the disease, a favourable turn took place in England, and in England alone? It was not surely without a cause that so many kindred systems of government, having flourished together so long, languished and expired almost at the same time.
> (Thomas Babington Macaulay, 1854, p.70)

A COMMON HERITAGE: BRITISH AND US APPROACHES TO ADMINISTRATION

Some questions are as old as scholarship. It is the answers to them that are the product of fashion, though even fashion often appears to be a carousel, delivering the same answers, but in a different sequence to those perennial questions. In his review of Hallam's *Constitutional History* (1828), from which the foregoing quotation is taken, the young Macaulay addresses the central issues which have vexed those involved in writing, interpreting, amending and implementing constitutions since the English revolutions of the Seventeenth Century. Stripped of legal and philosophical verbosity these themes render down to debates about the nature of the relationship between a government and those it governs: in particular, the definition and boundaries of the state and civil society; the rights of individuals within the polity; the mode by which the state executes the decisions of the policy-makers; and the methods by which they take decisions and are held accountable for the entire policy process from formation through to evaluation.

Those who struggle with the problems of drafting, or exploring, the limit to government and the accountability of the polity to its members are confronted with the struggle of devising a system which is flexible enough to cope with alternating periods of calm and conflict, whilst reconciling its practice to some *a priori* guiding principles of their (given

1

or prescribed) society. A multiplicity of constitutions have been written that attempt to achieve this. Many have 'languished and expired'.

American constitutionalising has led the US to the other extreme from that which exercised the fears of Macaulay and his predecessors. An extreme, moreover, to which they felt driven by the very European autocracy about which Hallam and others were writing. Don K. Price argues that:

> from colonial days, Americans have sought to escape even responsible authority by various automatic formulas for salvation or for secular perfectibility. It began with the confidence that depraved humanity would reach the millennium by the grace of God, and since then at various times various elites – eager to escape the burdens of political responsibility – have put their faith in endless technological progress or the free market or some even less plausible dogma. But the contemporary world is complex enough so that even those who disapprove of politics and distrust government on principle must grope for some system of disciplined organisation. (1983, p.129)

Price's diagnosis of the problems inherent to America's attempts to reconcile the eternal contradictions of government traces the threads of the colonial inheritance in the formal and also in what he calls the 'unwritten' constitution; the formative ideas which shaped the political and cultural systems of the US. Of these, the negative attitudes towards authority carried by the religious dissenters fleeing the autocracies of the Old World are of fundamental importance as they shaped lasting attitudes towards government.

In Britain and the US the events of the Seventeenth and Eighteenth Centuries were of profound importance for enshrining the foundation of an established system of checks and balances upon unfettered royal/executive authority. It was a separation of power which 'originated in fundamental beliefs', especially that of the Puritans in 'the depravity of mankind', which prevented the establishment or maintenance of an institutional structure 'with absolute political authority' (ibid., p.150); but it effectively 'depended on institutional habits' becoming entrenched in the constitutional practice of both countries which would hold the exercise of political power accountable to external authority (ibid.).

While the American Revolution ended the formal constitutional ties between the UK and the US, continuities remained in the form of close philosophical links between the two administrative systems. These reflected their rejection of a traditional establishment 'or a theology that justified authority' and therefore 'politically inoculated' the two systems against the kind of political tyranny found on continental Europe and elsewhere (ibid., pp.151–2). In both countries it is Protestantism, which allowed the relationships first between public administration and theology, then that between public administration and science, to develop differently from the models found in other countries (ibid., p.60). In short:

> In this approach, the Americans and the British were closer to each other than to continental Europe. Both came to believe in the most fundamental kind of separation of powers in their political systems, namely, the separation of the institutions that wielded political power from those concerned with the search for truth, whether on a religious or scientific basis. (Ibid., p.150)

In both countries, the public sector came to regard itself, to a greater or lesser extent, as a neutral layer between the government and the governed. Unlike Weber's Prussian counterpart, however, the administrators saw themselves not as the unfeeling implementors of executive orders, but as an essential check upon arbitrary rule. The evolving American federal service and the British ideal personified by Trevelyan (Hennessy, 1989, pp.17–52) characterised the civil servant as a neutral guardian of the people's rights. The atavistic concept of a Lockean Natural Law sprang from a deep well, from which was drawn the public ethic of those who served in the central administration. They were imbued with a sense of duty which recognised government's proper monopoly of coercion, but understood the need to fetter it with full accountability. That is, government must appear to behave in the public interest. A logical concomitant of this is the clear difference between public and private sector management, a topic returned to in a later section.

THE THREAT TO THE PUBLIC SECTOR

These constitutional settlements are again being undermined by the current political and social developments in both countries. The challenge is in part manifested as an attempt by both Right and Left to undermine the administrative process. In the US the relationship between the three main branches of government is constantly debated, but the difficulty of establishing coherent control in policy-making and reconciling the demands of leadership with those of accountability are what provoked

Price to write his treatise (also, Pfiffner, 1988). There is policy drift and an immobilism at the centre that has been the subject of criticism leading to calls for yet more constitutional amendments, noticeably to balance the federal budget, a move which hits at the heart of the day-to-day workings of America's current political process. Whilst, in Britain, the membership of the European Community and the steady accretion of Community law with direct applicability to the administrative process, is gradually supplanting the traditional public administration of that country with the formal European administrative legal codes and laws which it has hitherto explicitly shunned (Jowell and Oliver (eds) 1988).

These external threats to the settlement are combined with an internal disaffection which is deadlier in its potential and has contributed in profound ways to the external calls for reform (see for example, Charter 88 in Britain). In both countries throughout the 1980s the election of governments committed to an anti-state stance has wrought drastic changes upon the perceptions of the relationship between the public and private sectors. The phrase 'anti-state' should not be confused with 'anti-system'. Both conservative administrations have been vocal in their support of liberal democracy (with the emphasis being on 'liberal' in its traditional economic sense rather than its contemporary US usage as 'left-wing') and maintain a steadfast opposition to avowed opponents of the political system *per se* (Gamble, 1988).

Their anti-state bias has been directed at the enemy within: the bureaucracy, the activities of civil servants, indeed at the apparatus of the state, but not at the state itself. The servants of the state have been perceived as usurpers of the prerogatives of the executive and the result has been a series of reforms to check their power. Flynn traces the growth of these ideas via the work of influential writers like Samuel Brittan (*Capitalism and the Permissive Society*, 1973), Bacon and Eltis (1976), Seldon (1977) and many others on both sides of the Atlantic Ocean (1990, pp.10–12). The impact of these ideas has been characterised by Hood as a new public management (1990) and by Pollitt as neo-Taylorism (1990).

Extensive work by the Public Choice school of writers has led to considerable revision by the New Right of their view of the role of public servants. The more influential writers include Buchanan and Tullock (1962), Niskanen (1971, 1973) and (also with regard to inter-governmental relations) Olson (1982). These writers adopt a neo-classical economic view of political behaviour and argue that the perspective of 'rational economic man' should be applied to politicians and bureaucrats (Alt and Chrystal, 1983). That is, they are self-interested, personally maximising actors within the political process.

Dunleavy has distilled the essential 'rational actor' model:

> at the heart of all public choice accounts [which] assumes that:
>
> people have sets of well-formed preferences which they can perceive, rank and compare easily;
>
> their preference orderings are transitive or logically consistent, so that if someone prefers socialism to liberalism, and liberalism to fascism, then they will also prefer socialism to fascism;
>
> people are 'maximisers' who always seek the biggest possible benefits and least costs in their decisions. They act rationally when they pursue their preferences in an efficient manner and maximise benefits net of costs. On this formal definition, someone behaves 'rationally' if they optimise their preferences in a consistent fashion, however substantively ill-advised we may judge their preferences to be; and
>
> people are basically egoistic, self-regarding and instrumental in their behaviour, choosing how to act on the basis of the consequences for their personal welfare (or that of the immediate family). (1991, p.3)

This leads bureaucrats, as economically rational actors, to seek to maximise their personal wefare (and massage their own egos) by manipulating their often dominant positions with regard to politicians, gained by virtue of their permanent status, to increase the size of their agencies and budgets (ibid., pp.154–6).

The growth of the public sector in terms of personnel and expenditure has been the New Right's focal point of attack upon it. Gray and Jenkins show how Public Choice writers 'adopt a reforming zeal' arguing that administrators are merely budget maximisers (1985, pp.58–62). Often an 'iron triangle' evolves between the administration, politicians and powerful interest groups, which by-passes the electorate and leads to waste and inefficiency as cosy deals are negotiated between these players. It is a view which elevates the power of bureaucrats close to that of the politicians and suggests that the political process consists of quasi-corporatist (or even fully corporatist) cartels which subvert the national democratic interest. The political reality, therefore, belies the constitutional theory and can even threaten individual liberty, as well as the national budget. In this interpretation the administrators are seen as 'having monopolies of given services' where to all intents they are able to increase the size of their budget to meet their goals; 'most of their goals, such as income, status, prestige and power, are related to the size of their budget' (ibid., p.59).

Yet, as the succeeding sections of this chapter will illustrate, any theory based upon viewing the public and private sectors as being possessed of similar dynamics, or even applying the analysis of the firm to that of government, is in real danger of misinterpretation, although Self's peremptory dismissal of them as 'simply crude' (1977, p.11) is itself lacking in refinement. Critiques of Public Choice by Goodin (1982), Dunleavy and O'Leary (1987), and Dunleavy (1990, 1991) have made this point forcefully, whilst Flynn notes that often 'the reason for having public provision at all is that a purely market arrangement would produce an unacceptable outcome' (1990, p.97). Politically unacceptable, that is, in that a market solution to basic social, educational and health needs would place the provision of those services beyond the ability of a large minority of people. Much of the theoretical foundation for Public Choice theory, therefore, (and thus also for the New Right generally) is decidedly shaky. As a market-based critique it has a natural conservative bias, but its biggest flaw is what Dunleavy calls the:

> uncritical adoption of a line bureaucracy paradigm; their use of fuzzy and soft-edged accounts of bureaucrats' utility functions; their inability to come up with method-ologically legitimate supply-side variations in bureaucratic behaviour; and their use of crude generalisations to move from explanations of a single bureau's behaviour to that of systems of bureaus ... thus achieving a level of explanatory crudity which not even conventional Marxists any longer aspire to reach. (1991, pp.172–3)

Oversimplicity can itself lead to confusion. Hood has argued that in order to understand the impact of the New Right upon the public sector it may be helpful to think in terms of a 'new public management', that takes into account the trends of the past decade within public adminis-tration towards internationalisation, automation, privatisation and attempts to peg back growth (1990). Such a study would use an analysis suggested by the 'new' public management(s) to examine the problems of waste, malversation and catastrophe, whilst attempting to reconstruct 'who we teach', 'what we teach' and 'how we teach' (ibid.). Gray and Jenkins (1985), however, attempt to construct a model that recognises bureaucratic politics, a process that takes account of organizational history when analysing administrative decisions.

Yet, whichever theory is used to understand the place of the public sector there has to be an acceptance that politics and administration, although constitutionally separate, are a single process (Derlien, 1987, pp.129-40). Thomas encapsulated the differences succinctly when she argued that:

> the British Philosophy of Administration promoted the doctrine that politics and administration are fused processes, while the traditional American doctrine concentrated on a separation between the two processes. (1978, p.33)

Her belief, however, that the American doctrines derived from business administration 'are not relevant to an understanding of the development of British administrative thought' (ibid., p.1) has clearly been superseded by events. Indeed, the history of public administration in this century illustrates the interaction between the two systems. It has to be admitted though that her arguments with regard to the British being more influenced in the early years of the century by ethics and a strong moral approach to society, which was reflected in the writings of such English Idealists as T.H. Green, whilst the Americans were more concerned with the application of science to administration, reflect the work of Price and do show a relatively unimportant divergence between the two countries (ibid., pp.236–7). This divergence is unimportant because it is difficult to see why that should mean the American theories are not applicable to a study of European systems; indeed, quite the contrary case could be made. Where she is on stronger ground is with her belief that there is a need to 'attach an ethical, as well as an economic cost to goods' (ibid., p.243), something that can be seen to be lacking in several other approaches, most noticeably in cost benefit analysis (see Self, 1970). It is this ethical cost which so infuriates those dedicated to unravelling the protective cloak of the welfare state and has led them, when in power, to institute a series of major reforms.

The reforms have had several goals, indeed each new activity has taken place within a welter of minor targets such as privatisation, greater efficiency, or a reduction in the size of the national civil service. The often unstated elemental threads intrinsic to all of them, however, have been:

1. to reduce the role and extent of the 'state' in order to enhance that of the private sector;
2. to facilitate the acquisition of entrepreneurial skills and activities within society generally;

3. to prevent future expansion of the public sector, often through the creation of a powerful coalition of interests to counter the perceived welfare-demanding coalitions which have linked their interests to those of the bureaucrats;

4. to de-politicize many (mainly economic) policy decisions and their being entrusted to professional experts, rather than the whim of politicians and bureaucrats perceived to be in the thrall of self-serving interest groups;

5. to inculcate public sector organisations with the best techniques of private sector practice in order to bring the discipline and inherent efficiencies of the marketplace to the activities of the state;

6. to entrench the divisions between the private and the public in such a way that individual civil liberties are protected by inalienable property rights, which act as a flexible bulwark against the power of the state and the temptations of state employees and elected politicians to behave in an arbitrary and capricious manner, abusing their power, power loaned to them in trust by the citizenry.[1]

Clearly it is not possible, within the confines of this book, to deal with the entire set of changes in both the UK and the US. That would require a magnum opus of several volumes and many hundreds of thousands of words. The boundaries of this work must of necessity, therefore, be drawn narrower than the totality of the subject and that inevitably requires a selective approach to the subjects tackled. Consequently, the following chapters will take the stated aims of the reformers as the guiding theme and examine them in relation to control of the central bureaucracies; the relationship to the periphery (local and sub-national government); attempts to enhance the scope and power of the private sector, and moves to resuscitate areas of economic decay. This approach provides an analysis of the changes that includes a representative review of their effects, without engaging in the tedium of attempting an unmitigated description of all the individual activities pursued.

Before this can attempted, however, it is necessary to define some of the terms that will be used and explain the use of theoretical perspectives. The remaining sections of this chapter, therefore, discuss the nature of the public sector, then proceed to review the different perspectives and theories relevant to the study of it, before concluding with an introduction to the European and American approaches to public administration which expands the comments of the opening section.

THE SCOPE AND NATURE OF PUBLIC ADMINISTRATION

In their introduction to a bibliographical guide to the literature on US public administration, Caiden *et al.* discuss the arguments regarding the boundaries of public administration (1983). Like Thomas, in her review of the *British Philosophy of Administration* (1978), they show that the minimalist view restricts public administration to the confines mapped out by Woodrow Wilson in his 1887 essay which concentrated attention on the practical issues of 'how governments should operate' and the 'most efficient ways of doing business' (1983, p. xii). They argue that studies of public policy have been kept separate or distinct despite increasing attempts to fuse the study of public policy with public management. Clearly this distinction is no longer valid and there is much recent work that uses policy studies to inform the analysis of public management (or to use its more traditional term, 'public administration').[2] Price eloquently argues for the demise of the old academic barriers by noting that 'the old studies of public administration have begun to be supplanted' by policy analysis, an approach with 'greater scientific depth', which, although it originated in the other social sciences, has helped academics and practitioners understand 'some of the complex issues involving the interaction of government programmes' (1983, p.4).

Caiden *et al.* have performed a valuable definitional service, however, in that they have provided a list of headings under which the generic constituents of American public administration theory and practice can be found. They include:

1. the ideological roots of public institutions, including social contract, federalism, separation of powers, representative government, and civil rights;
2. theories of public administration and administrative norms;
3. contextual influences on public administration in society;
4. the functions of administration;
5. the role of public administration in society;
6. the history of the public sector;
7. institutional arrangements of public service delivery, forms and structures, administrative organisation;

8. public and administrative law, public controls, and administrative discretion;
9. behaviour of government organisations and government officials, codes of conduct;
10. relationship between public organisations and between them and other social organisations;
11. relations between public officials and the people;
12. citizens' images and opinions of the public sector and officials' attitudes towards the public;
13. public sector productivity and performance, measurement and evaluation;
14. public planning and forecasting;
15. policy formulation and implementation;
16. management of government organisations, including leadership and supervision;
17. public finance and budgeting, accounting and auditing;
18. public personnel management and labour relations;
19. professional development: education and training for the civil service;
20. public enterprise;
21. comparative public administration;
22. the anthology and sociology of the field;
23. biographies of civil servants;
24. research methods;
25. public information, accessibility. (1983, pp.xiv–xv)

Despite the overlap of some of the elements in this seemingly comprehensive list, any work that takes place within Europe must now add to it a section that takes cognisance of European Community (EC) administrative law, a small but increasingly important element in the management of the public sector in Britain. With this caveat the twenty-five headings of American public administration are easily translated to the United Kingdom and the reference to federalism has a special relevance for a Europe which is groping towards some closer political union in the train of its economic success.

Obviously any comprehensive attempt to review the literature under each of these headings would be a perpetual labour, such is the nature of the output in the field. An added benefit of the list, and one that even a cursory review of the literature reveals, is its confirmation that the minimalist approach to public administration is wrong. Like political theory it is clearly a field within political science (Waldo, 1984, p.x) and attempts to construct 'best practice' guides in the style of the Woodrow Wilson school (or for that matter some modern business schools) that do not integrate an appreciation of political theory with the management of decision-making are destined to be devoid of much practical utility. At best they are simply irrelevant. Peter Self's analysis illustrates that attempts to separate administration from policy/politics are flawed (1977, pp.48–52, 149–91). He argues that:

> The almost obsessional wish of such (administrative/management) theorists to spell out the duties of posts explicitly, and to systematise relations between superiors and subordinates, runs quite contrary to the actual practices found in the higher branches of public administration. (Ibid., p.51)

In other words, the administration of political decisions, which is the role of the public service, is itself a political activity and is indivisibly linked to the political decision-making process. To attempt to hive out decision-making to an accredited group of experts, whether these are business people, economists or of any other quasi-professional occupation, is a de-politicising activity (Massey, 1988). It is akin to the professionalising of policy-making which can be deeply undemocratic and (ironically) often inefficient in its use of resources when implementation takes place.

The reason that Wilson (and indeed the US) attempted to keep public administration and politics separate was to reduce the effect of the 'spoils system', but the belief that public administration is 'not comfortable leaving the solid ground of process to embrace objectives' (Caiden *et al.*, 1983, p.9) is simply not credible. To fail to take account of these things is to miss the important developments in third sector organisations (McGill and Wooton, 1975), the voluntary sector and mixed enterprises, all of which intrude upon the role of the bureaucrat at central and sub-national levels.

Waldo captures the sense of this when he argues that in attempting to understand the essence of American public administration it is essential to have a view of American history, 'the lessons of Confederation, the constitutional framing and writings' and early governmental and local governmental experience (1984, p.xxv). Furthermore, that this should be set alongside an analytical history of the "business civilization" of the US and a discussion which shows the influence of ideas and individuals (ibid., and p.xxvii). Yet in many university departments there has been a 'migration of public administration out of political science' to other foci such as 'social psychology, sociology, economics, business administration', and similarly related disciplines (ibid., p.liv). The foregoing classification of Caiden *et al.* suggests a requirement for inclusive approaches; to divorce the study of public administration from political science *per se* is to study management divorced from the political system which nurtured it. It is an exercise in futility, calculated to produce arid lawyers or accountants skilled at abstract manipulation, but devoid of insight into the ways of the world. Put at its bluntest, administration is 'the seamy side of sovereignty' (Price, 1983); it is what makes constitutions actually work.

PUBLIC ADMINISTRATION BECOMES PUBLIC MANAGEMENT

In many respects a discussion about whether public administration has become public management is a semantic nonsense, as to 'administer' something is to 'manage' it; to talk of turning administrators into managers is a tautology. The importance of the terms lies in the different emphasis given to them by the public and the private sectors and by the sententious lecturing of the former by the advocates of the latter. Generally 'administration' is something done by the public sector's bureaucrats, whilst those in the private sector 'manage'. Consequently, there is often an excited welcome given to the prospect of new management techniques being imbued by the administrators of the public sector (as in the example of the United Kingdom's *Next Steps*, 1988) and a feverish attempt to adopt the taxonomy of the private sector, even to the extent that this may infringe 'administrative process' or offend tradition; indeed, this may often be the reason for it. The work of Perry and Kraemer goes so far as to claim that public management represents a merger of the 'normative orientation' in public administration with the 'instrumental' orientation found in 'generic management' (1983, p.x, as quoted by Gunn, 1987, p.35). It is a perspective eloquently ridiculed by Pollitt (1990, pp.156–7, 161, 164).

The semantic confusion is partly caused by fashion and partly by novel approaches to problems within the public sector. Kooiman and Eliassen argue that, although shortcomings in public administration 'have always been with us', there 'is evidence that managing governments today is qualitatively different' than it was even twenty-five years ago, particularly in Europe (1987, p.1). The impact of New Right thinking is one reason for thinking this, whilst the difficulties of administering mature welfare states in periods of slow or negative growth are materially different to those of facilitating inchoate welfare structures within growing economies. Kooiman and Eliassen outline three levels of analysis at which public management can be considered:

> First at the level of the public sector as a whole, embedded in its social environment, secondly at the level of public organizations in their immediate social, political and administrative contexts, and thirdly at the level of the internal running of public organizations and the role of the public managers as leaders. (1987, p.5)

They might usefully have added that at all of these levels of analysis the perspective adopted is informed by the political theory of those being studied (both explicitly and implicitly) and also by the theoretical approach of the analyst, a fundamental lesson of political science dating at least from the early 1920s and the work of Karl Mannheim (Mannheim, 1954).

The confusion about the term 'public management' is the result of both polemical and academic analyses neglecting this explicit definitional point. As a result some observers have 'framed their definition in more theoretical and analytical terms. Others have outlined the concept on a practical basis and have given a stipulative definition' (Kooiman and Eliassen, 1987, p.8). Gunn captures the nub of the issue when he writes:

> Much seems to depend on where any particular preacher places the emphasis, whether on: (1) *public* management, implying that we can learn something from generic management but that the public sector is still much more dissimilar than similar to the business sector; or (2) public *management*, with the implication that management is management and the claims to uniqueness of the public sector are overstated. (1987, p.43)

Whilst his own view is that there are 'positive arguments for moving away from traditional public administration to a wider concern with public management' (ibid.) it is clear that there are fundamental differences between the public and private sectors. It is simply puerile to pretend that 'generic management' penetrates beyond the superficial level. Public sector management is the more complex of the two (an argument returned to throughout the following chapters).

Those who strongly oppose this proposition are most often found in the private sector, or are advocates of its extension into the traditional areas of public administration (Kooiman and Eliassen, 1987, p.12). To proclaim the difference, however, is not to decry the private sector, merely to point out the truism that the two are not the same, they have vastly different, if at points overlapping, constituencies and their roles are separate and unalike, even if again there is an overlap and occasional unity of purpose. There is nothing unusual in this: in a capitalist country the public sector will inevitably be broadly supportive of the goals of capitalism, but this does not mean that public sector managers are capitalists and nor should they be if they are effectively to discharge their wider duties. To state this is not to fall into the trap of adopting a version of functionalism, but merely to argue that to pretend there are no principal differences is facile. There may well be some universal principles of management, although it is probably safe to venture that they await discovery, but even though there are obvious areas of overlap, public sector management/administration is different to that of private sector management because the latter is defined by the former. It cannot be otherwise in an age of mass democracy that has not, as yet, adopted the formulae of libertarian anarchy propounded by some on the extreme wing of New Right thought (a point touched upon by Dahl, 1982; and Bekke, 1987). The private sector exists and functions only because the conditions for the exercise of private power and the accumulation of individual wealth are protected by the state. It is the state which lays down the parameters within which the private sector operates.

In a mass democracy the unfettered exercise of private accumulation is simply not practicably possible and therefore all activities are subjected to the control of the political process, tolerated, guided, licensed, and even promoted by the state. In such societies the vacuity of pretending the private and the public are one and the same is self-evident. They are two parts of the same whole, to be sure, but they are clearly separate parts. This analysis, whilst not subscribing to any explicit theory, is one that can draw from recent corporatist writings (Williamson, 1989), New Left work (for a discussion see Hoffman,1984 and 1988), and also High Tory views of the role of the state and society (see Beer, 1982; Gamble, 1988; Middlemas, 1979). Whilst many in the liberal (New Right) camp would, obviously, dissent from it, some liberal theorists are acutely aware of the limits on the private sector and the need to recognise the political dangers inherent in denigrating the public service to the extent that it cannot fulfil its proper role (Gray, 1986; 1989a and 1989b). In short the greatest danger to the private sector is its own success and the need for some redistributory mechanism, a need some liberal writers are acutely aware of, whilst excoriating the Western experiment in 'market socialism' (Gray, 1989b, pp.64–79).

To the extent that they are two parts of the same entity, or society (the nomenclature differs according to the theoretical perspective adopted), the major distinctions between the public and private sectors are reflected in Baber's list:

As compared with the private sector, government:
1. faces more complex and ambiguous tasks.
2. Has more difficulty implementing decisions.
3. Employs more people with different motivations.
4. Is more concerned with securing opportunities or capacities.
5. Is more concerned with compensating for market failures.
6. Engages in activities with greater symbolic significance.
7. Is held to stricter standards of previous commitment and legality.
8. Has a greater opportunity to respond to issues of fairness.
9. Must operate or appear to operate in the public interest.
10. Must maintain minimal levels of public support above that required in private industry. (1987, pp.159–60)

The argument, therefore, is that the public sector's managers are driven not by the profit motive, although that may be a subsidiary goal, but by the principles of accountability. Under some governments it may be that efficiency and profit are important motivations, but under all governments the fiduciary elements of the public sector combine with the symbolic elements and also goals such as the need for market compensatory mechanisms, redistribution activities, claims by disadvantaged groups for equal treatment, and response to demands by fund-authorising bodies for the redress of grievance before the granting of supply.

A useful addition to the preceding list is the argument that government properly has a monopoly on coercive sanctions and the use of violence (as argued amongst others by Gunn, 1987, p.38). Yet even this does not go far enough as, in the light of much privatisation activity, which has reached even into the field of penal controls, there is a need to add the caveat of a monopoly of state licensing of activities, rather than state activities *per se*. Gunn provides a useful categorization or, rather, spectrum of the various approaches to the question of defining public management, which can be summarised as: (a) public administration is unique; (b) public and private management are alike only in unimportant respects; (c) public management is the integrative paradigm between public administration and generic management; (d) there is a convergence between business and public management; (e) management itself is a generic study; (f) public administration is a less efficient form of business management (ibid., pp.37–42). Clearly this book tends towards the position of (b) in Gunn's list, as:

> public management is a dynamic and strategic process of interpreting the environment, struggling over the political agenda and handling public bureaucracy in accordance with possible or intended outcomes. (Bekke, 1987, p.26)

Also, whilst it may be overly harsh and contradicted by some firm European and American evidence, there is some truth in Metcalfe and Richards' acerbic observation that:

> The success rate of transplants from business to government is low both for techniques and individual managers. Successful businessmen rarely make the grade in the public sector. (1987, p.66)

The reverse view is that of Hoskins, a former adviser to Mrs Thatcher before becoming Director General of the Institute of Directors, who believed that few, if any, post-war cabinets could match the quality of most major company boards. Managing the public sector, however, is often considerably more complex than management within the private sector. As Flynn points out, it is about more than decisions to maximise profits and control markets, if it were not then a public sector organisation would be indistinguishable from a business (1990, p.86). It is, therefore, also about the realisation of the fundamental principles of the relationship between the government and the governed, discussed at the start of this chapter, principles with a considerably longer 'shelf-life' than 'generic' management techniques. It is useful, therefore, to return to these questions at this juncture in order to consider the part that public sector management has to play in the broader scheme of translating policy into practice. One of the functions of bureaucracy is, after all, merely to act as an organisational process by which the wishes of the centre are transmitted into action at the periphery.

PUBLIC SECTOR MANAGEMENT AND POLITICS

A 'great deal depends not on formal legal structure but on political habits and social context' in different countries (Price, 1983, p.8). The effects of their respective revolutions left both the UK and US deeply suspicious of dogma and the many types of government found in continental Europe (ibid., p.10). In addition to which the British intensely distrusted republicanism, whilst the Americans developed a distrust of any system that centralised power and neglected to enunciate the detailed rights and duties of the different levels of government to each other and to the citizenry.

A large part of administration, and the management of public sector administrations in liberal democracies, is about liberty and the pursuit of 'good' government whilst protecting and nurturing liberty. The study of it is the study of liberty and an attempt to answer the perennial questions associated with it and the conduct of government. Methods of analysis which aid this concern are an aid to learning *per se*, but also to the pursuit of better government itself. Macaulay's essay on Milton contains a short story which illustrates this basic concern:

> Aristo tells a pretty story of a fairy, who, by some mysterious law of her nature, was condemned to appear at certain seasons in the form of a foul and poisonous snake. Those who injured her during the period of her disguise were for ever excluded from participation in the blessings which she bestowed. But to those who, inspite of her loathsome aspect, pitied and protected her, she afterwards revealed herself in the beautiful and celestial form which was natural to her, accompanied their steps, granted all their wishes, filled their houses with wealth, made them happy in love and victorious in war. Such a spirit is Liberty. At times she takes the form of a hateful reptile. She grovels, she hisses, she stings. But woe to those who in disgust shall venture to crush her. (1854, p.19)

Yet a few years later he shifted from such a fixed position when his reading of Hallam led him to believe that at some periods 'it was now, therefore, absolutely necessary to violate the formal part of the constitution, in order to preserve its spirit' (ibid., p.73). A dilemma faced by leaders in a time of crisis; administrators caught between the executive and legislature; police officers and members of the security forces seeking to enforce the law or detect crime. Public sector management, therefore, is an integral part of the political process and its study an integral part of political science.

NOTES

1. Various sources, but see Ascher, 1987; Baber, 1987; Bennett and Johnson, 1981; Butler, 1987; Dunleavy, 1986; Grace, 1985; Hambleton, 1988; Hood, 1990; Letwin, 1988; Massey, 1988; Peters and Austen, 1985; Savas, 1987; Swann, 1988; Veljanovski, 1987; Wiltshire, 1987.
2. There are many examples, but see Batley, 1989; Harte, 1988; Stockman, 1986.

2 Value for Money and the British Civil Service

The attempt to impose a largely generic and neo-Taylorian model of management on the public services seems to have been either an act of culpable ignorance on the part of those concerned or an exercise in (possibly unwitting) ideological imperialism, or some mixture of the two. (Pollitt, 1990, p.144)

There is general agreement that the Next Steps initiative, launched three years ago, is progressing well. In the quest for public services which achieve the highest quality within the finance available, it has been the expressed policy of the Government to give the Next Steps Agencies the managerial freedoms and incentives necessary to deliver the improved performance which is the initiative's raison d'être. These aims have met with a large measure of support across the political spectrum. (Fraser (Efficiency Unit), 1991, Foreword)

Behold, we put bits in the horses' mouths, that they may obey us; and we turn about their whole bodies. (James 3. 3)

REASONS FOR CHANGE

More than a decade of conservative governments in the UK and the US have led to fundamental re-appraisals of the role of the state. The ideological imperatives for this were examined in the last chapter; it is the intention here and in the following chapters to map the result of those dynamics. Whether one shares the views of Pollitt or Fraser, as depicted in the foregoing quotes, depends upon the personal perspective adopted; the phrases 'ideological imperialism', 'culpable ignorance', and 'general agreement' are clearly value-laden expressions of the authors' own opinions. The important (value-free) point to make is that the liberal/conservative governments of the period were elected on explicitly ideological manifestos which had the remodelling of central state structures as a primary goal. It is philosophical liberalism which provided the snug saddle for Western Chief Executives, and institutional reform which provided the bit by which they sought to induce a cultural curvet.

This chapter first outlines the dynamics that led to change in the British civil service. These were technical, structural and ideological. The next two sections examine the ideological impetus that has structured those changes, a twin impetus that has grown out of New Right theory and the perspective of professionalising groups and their urge for autonomy. There then follows a discussion of the central bureaucracy inherited by the Conservatives upon their election to office in 1979, and the reasons why Mrs Thatcher and many of her colleagues were determined to implement a radical structural and cultural change. This establishes the framework for the next chapter, which explores many of those changes in more detail. Much of this analysis is then applied to chapter 4, which explores the situation in the US, where there have been similar government-inspired assaults upon the executive branch for over a decade.

Over time there is a constant pressure for institutional change within advanced societies. For the most part it takes the form of lobbying at the margins for incremental tinkering, at other times it is manifested as a strong challenge to the political/social status quo. There are a variety of sources from which the pressure may emanate, not all of them articulating the demands of recognised social groups. Technological innovation can provide an opportunity for the redeployment of resources or the overhaul of antiquated bureaucratic systems. The revolution in information technology brought about by developments in the utilisation of micro-chips is an example (Pitt and Smith, 1984). In Britain the computerisation of the Inland Revenue, the Police Forces, and the departments of state responsible for health, social security, national insurance, the collation of statistics, the licensing of drivers and vehicles, amongst others, has transformed the potential for organisational change. The professions play a crucial role in identifying, formulating and implementing change wrought through technological innovation (Dunleavy, 1986; Massey, 1988). Despite their public interest claims to objectivity, such activities are ideologically bound and directed, a point returned to later in this book. The potential for further technology-led change is an area that would benefit from more research (Taylor and Williams, 1991, pp.171–90).

Changes in fashion are linked to technological innovation and ideological shifts. The massive interventions and structures of the Welfare State are no longer the political vogue. An immense literature sprouted in the

1970s which claimed that governments were overloaded and that by attempting to regulate every aspect of the economy and society they were in danger of losing control.[1] Government emphasis has moved away from the collective, to that of the individual: the individual as consumer, client and citizen (OECD, 1987). Structural changes, therefore, have been designed to facilitate the 'shrinkage' of the state and reflect the goal of 'empowering' the citizen. Individuals are being encouraged to make provision for themselves as the ubiquitous Welfare State is honed back into a minimalist safety-net.

Technological innovation, ideological fashion, political passion, and electoral success combined in Britain in the early 1980s to provide a powerful momentum for changes in public sector management. Academic commentators variously identified the period as one which marked the end of the post-war consensus combined with disillusion with the Welfare State and the institutions identified with it. Their individual political perspectives on the subject determine their stated reasons for this, and include:

1. 'the guilty men of history' approach, an essentially nationalistic perspective which views the country as having been 'betrayed' by successive political leaders who squandered the nation's Victorian legacy;
2. the 'failure of Keynesianism' approach, which argues that the failure of economic policy to provide the promised full employment and high living standards resulted in a creeping alienation from the post-war structures. This is often linked to the neo-Keynesian analysis, which perceives the economic and industrial decline of Britain as a result of the failure to understand and fully implement Keynesian prescriptions;
3. liberal and neo-liberal approaches which have been transformed into the New Right analysis and are fully discussed elsewhere in this book. This analysis calls for the implementation of free-market solutions to the problems of the economy; it is ironic, however, that for social and political 'ills' greater state power and centralisation is part of the prescription;
4. radical left and New Left approaches. These see the problems as part of the inevitable contradictions of capitalism, as predicted by classical socialists, but so far forestalled by a constant stream of concessions from the bourgeoisie, via the Welfare State, designed to secure proletarian compliance with the existing relationships to the means of production.

These are admittedly broad and somewhat crude categories: one has only to attend a seminar containing political economists to be made aware of the infinite refinements possible on this theme. The main point, for any discussion of public sector management, is that the elements of the consensus have declined, for whatever reason, and there are some dominant common themes that have emerged in the drive to restructure the British central state apparatus.

THE IMPETUS OF THE NEW RIGHT

The dominant themes have been those of the New Right. This is not to say that the Left have not been critical of the civil service and central administration, to the contrary, left leaning politicians and academics have maintained a stream of criticisms aimed at the civil service (Benn, 1981; Dunleavy, 1991). Yet whilst the British Left have been influential at the sub-central level in British politics, indeed many local government reforms have been inspired by the Government's desire to limit their power, radical prescriptions for the central civil service have been utterly impotent. The ideological momentum has been that of the Government, the goals and the timetable have been set by it.

The broad themes of the New Right's general critique of the Welfare State are familiar. Flynn lists those which apply to the reform of the British civil service (1990, pp.10–15) as:

1. The arguments of Brittan (1973) who has called for markets 'as the best mechanisms for deciding what to produce and how to distribute the products' (Flynn, 1990, p.10). Brittan's work is an eloquent call for individualism against collectivism and for his belief that the defence of individual liberty is inextricably bound to the efficiency of free markets, private property and the pursuit of profit. It is an analysis which draws upon the works of what is variously known as the 'Austrian school', or sometimes (and not always correctly) as 'monetarism'.

2. The work of Bacon and Eltis (1976), who saw Britain's problems as stemming from too few producers overburdened by a parasitical state. Furthermore, the goods and services of the public sector are deemed to be inferior to those of the private sector because the former lack the incentive and discipline of the market (Flynn, 1990, p.11).

3. Finally there is the Public Choice school of thought, as discussed in the preceding chapter, which draws on the work of writers like Niskanen, Olsen, and Buchanan to argue the constructively wasteful nature of bureaucracy, a process facilitated by the corporatist tendencies of the Welfare State, whereby constituencies of interest build up around the services provided by the welfare system that defend collective action and public intervention, thereby preventing the implementation of market-led economies and rational appraisals of welfare provision.

The New Right has constantly sought the limits of government, and in his book of that title, Schmidtz has eloquently used game theory and an ingenious solution of the Prisoners' Dilemma to prescribe those limits (1991). He argues that:

> Society runs itself. As long as a system of property rights protects and gives meaning to people's right to be left in peace, individual initiative will produce the essential elements of human flourishing. The trouble is, this liberal insight presupposes the efficacy of markets, and markets can fail. In particular, the fabric of social harmony, woven by markets from threads of self-interested action, may prove too delicate when it comes to producing goods. (Ibid., p.1)

It is at this juncture that there lies a role for government. In his exploration of the foundations of consent, legitimacy and therefore government, Schmidtz re-evaluates the modern nature of social contract and justice, arguing that the reason for the existence of coercion in a just (that is, liberal) society is to force free riders to participate and avoid their evasion of responsibility. Public goods supplied through the public sector, therefore, are a way of overcoming market failure and individual recalcitrance.

Yet many on the libertarian New Right, and Schmidtz himself, argue that this perspective does little to prescribe the limits of government beyond pious exhortations for efficiency. He argues that as a result of this:

> the public goods argument is unsound. Its descriptive premise is that coercive public goods production makes each person better off from the person's own perspective … (t)he descriptive premise is, by and large, false … It takes a stronger, more controversial normative premise to derive the permissibility of coercion from the descriptive facts as they really are. (Ibid., p.84)

His solution is a system of 'assurance contracts' (ibid., pp.86–8). Thus he moves away from pure market solutions, but seeks instead a cooperative, voluntaristic society where 'reciprocity is the backbone' of society (ibid., p.156). In short he is looking for a justification for big government other than the perceived 'need' for public goods such as health, education, law and order and so forth. The difficulty of such solutions is that they are extrapolations from false or simplistic premises such as 'the loss of Eden' (ibid., p.20) or some similar metaphor. They then fail to take account of powerful anti-system groups; these may be, for example, ideological, ethnic, linguistic or religious minorities. In short, in any society a pragmatic recourse to the use of coercion to enforce rules is necessary. Private property can only exist because the majority of society allow it to exist. That still allows for (even encourages) cooperation and free markets, but it is all presupposed by the existence of state authority and its legitimate monopoly of coercion, exercised in the public interest, in order to enforce contracts and prevent violent disorder. In a democracy the state may reflect society, but it is also society's ultimate guarantor. The tapestry of history, culture, hierarchy, class and individual motivations is too sophisticated to be explained away by pretty fairy stories and liberal arguments about the nature of actual and hypothetical consent. Schmidtz's belief in teleological and emergent justifications for public goods is a useful addition to the analysis, but is still too close to the Hobbesean contractualism it claims to surpass.

Clearly most active national politicians seeking office would not advocate the dissolution of the state, but those on the liberal/conservative right do seek a re-evaluation which is largely informed by New Right thinking. Their belief in market solutions to the problem of providing public goods is summed up by Metcalfe and Richards:

> Governments in most advanced countries are in a process of reconsidering or revising basic assumptions about the boundaries between public and private sectors, the scope of regulation and the opportunities for deregulation. (1990, p.156)

In the end the choice is limited because private and 'public choice are interdependent elements of a total process, not alternatives' (ibid., p.158) and are therefore complementary elements of the same activity. It is notable that most of the New Right's ideas regarding the structures of the public sector have been articulated by economists, yet:

Economists typically have a one-dimensional approach to this. More competition is the only solution they give serious and systematic consideration. (Ibid., p.173)

This paucity of analytical alternatives has important repercussions when 'public management is a creative function of guiding change' (ibid., p.ix). Whatever their strengths, however, it has been the New Right's ideas that have provided the dynamic for public sector change.

A PROBLEM OF PROFESSIONS

The implementation of these ideas took the form of:

- constructing market mechanisms wherever possible;
- promoting competition between providers so that consumers should be allowed more choice;
- the pursuit of individualism and consumers' rights;
- attempts to cut back state provision to a minimum; with those able to opt out of (or 'top-up') state provision being encouraged to do so;
- a more managerial approach to administration to be introduced throughout the public sector. (Flynn, 1990, pp.15–16)

Critics of this approach charge that the implementation of these ideas became goals in their own right, with Pollitt in particular excoriating the movement as being mere 'managerialism' or 'neo-Taylorism', which, he argues is itself an ideology (1990).

In making his case, Pollitt outlines the main thrust of the 'managerialist' movement. He uses Hartley's definition of ideology to press his point (1983, pp.26–7, as quoted in Pollitt, 1990, p. 6), that is the:

essential characteristics of ideology are, first, that it consists of values and beliefs about the state of the world and what it should be. Second, these cognitive and effective elements form a framework. In other words, ideology is not simply a summation of a set of attitudes, but consists of some kind of relatively systematic structuring (though the structuring may be psychological rather than logical). Third, ideologies concern social groups and social arrangement – in other words, politics in its widest sense of being concerned with the distribution and ordering of resources. Fourth, an ideology is developed and maintained by social groups, and thus is a socially-derived link between the individual and the group ... Fifth, ideology provides a justification for behaviour.

This is one of the more succinct and straightforward definitions of ideology offered in political science; it recognises that ideologies are 'looser, messier and more contradictory creatures' (ibid.) than they are often thought to be. The first part could even be re-stated as: an ideology is simply a system of action-related ideas. In accepting Hartley's interpretation, Pollitt argues that managerialism is an ideology because (to paraphrase him):

1. Managerialism consists of ideas and beliefs and its 'most obvious valuation is of management itself – it is not only important, it is also good'. Thus it 'indicates how the world should be', it is prescriptive.
2. Managerialism is 'a systematically structured set of beliefs' in that the belief in the potential of better management. The 'favourable analysis of the achievements of the corporate sector over the last half century', the atavistic suspicion of the public sector, the distrust of politicians, the trusting acceptance that the public sector is shielded from competition, are all connected.
3. Managerialism is a vehicle by which some social groups are awarded privileges, whilst others are marginalised. The ideology justifies the authority of managers over the workforce and presents successful corporate chiefs as paragons. It is in the interest 'of managers themselves to promote a set of beliefs which highlight the special contribution of management and thereby justify management's special rights and powers'. (Pollitt, 1990, pp.7–10)

Managerialism has at its heart the 'seldom-tested assumption that better management will prove an effective solvent for a wide range of economic and social ills' (ibid., p.1). Thus managerialism contains within its ideology a belief in innovation and 'ever-more-sophisticated technologies' and their application through new procedures and a disciplined workforce. Management is a 'distinct organisational function' dependent upon a core of 'professional' managers, and to 'perform this crucial role managers must be granted reasonable "room to manoeuvre" (i.e. the right to manage)' (ibid., pp.1–2). Such arguments can be traced in a direct line from the classical management theorists such as Gulick and Taylor, through to the new corporate heroes like Sir John Harvey-Jones (Pollitt, ibid.; Thomas, 1978; Peters and Waterman, 1982).

It is easy to see how Pollitt can argue the case for managerialism as an ideology in its own right. It is more helpful, however, to view it as another manifestation of the ideology of professionalism. Pollitt's list, ticking off aspects of the definition provided by Hartley, emulates the behaviour of professionalising occupations in ticking off the traits they have identified within their own group which they believe resemble professionalism. That is, those occupations which seek the status and autonomy of professionalism for themselves often adopt the functionalist trait theory approach (a list of perceived traits which if acquired lead to professional status (Greenwood, 1965)) and then set out to prove that they satisfy the requirements necessary to be deemed professional (Johnson, 1972; Illich, 1972; Wilding, 1982; Massey, 1988). Managerialism displays this behaviour in that managers seek autonomy, establish professional bodies, claim a distinct corpus of knowledge, argue that they have technical expertise, hold positions of social importance, and claim to represent a 'better' way of proceeding towards social and economic goals. They also frequently display contempt for politicians and 'time-wasting' democratic processes, a facet of the Grace Report, which is discussed in the following chapters.

In this they are no different to any other occupation seeking professional status. The ideology of professionalism is itself aligned to and indeed part of the greater liberal ideology, despite having elements at odds with the free-market ethos of the New Right (Massey, 1988, chs.2–3). It supports the dominant ideology of the Western countries in which it is so powerful because professional status is licensed and indeed sometimes created by the state. Professions came into existence as a result of the state delegating to them certain important monopolistic activities. This either reflected the de facto autonomy and status of the social professions like law and medicine, or it was as a result of the massive extension of the Welfare State and the economic and industrial interventions of governments during the age of consensus in the decades after World War Two. For those technical professionals, such as engineering, and the newer professions like personnel management, there is not even that degree of autonomy found in law and medicine, they function within the hierarchies of the corporate sector, their power is provided by virtue of their employment. They display a dual allegiance; they profess fidelity to their 'profession', but primary loyalty is to their employer and thus to that organisation's goals, such as profits and private capital accumulation. These professionals believe that they properly discharge their professional obligations by serving their employers to the best of their ability (Massey, 1988). To this end, many of those most dedicated to the pursuit of managerialism, as deftly defined by Pollitt, are in fact people who hold 'professional' status within both public and private sector hierarchies.

Managerialism, then, is not an ideology, but a tool by which those possessing an ideology seek to achieve their goals. The junior and middle managers themselves are seeking autonomy, status and control over their subordinates, thus they will attempt to further the status of 'professional' management as a vehicle for this, presenting it to the politicians as a way in which they (the politicians) may achieve their aims. The New Right politicians will pursue managerialism as a method of controlling bureaucracies and implementing the cultural changes defined by their ideology of neo-liberal/conservatism. They are 'licensing' it, imbuing managers with elite status because they see them as powerful allies. Ironically, one of the goals the Government has had in enfranchising the new profession of 'management' is to use it to batter some of the entrenched privileges of the older professions, an example being public sector medicine and attempts to reform the National Health Service (Pollitt, 1990, ch.3; Milne, 1987). New Right academics will applaud managerialism for the same reason, whilst worrying lest it too seek restraint of trade in the form of monopolistic privilege, combining with the special interest groups benefiting from public provision in the way old-style bureaucrats are alleged to have reinforced their positions (Niskanen, 1973). Senior civil servants will see within it a tool for controlling their subordinates, whilst simultaneously claiming managerial/professional freedom from ministers and ridding themselves of routine activities, and indeed whole swathes of line functions into new executive agencies, an aspect touched upon by Dunleavy (1986).

By viewing managerialism as a profession, in the sense of being both an ideology and a licensed occupation or trade, and managers as a government-encouraged professionalising occupation, it is possible to make better sense of many of the recent changes imposed upon the public sector. It also underlines the difference between policy formulation and implementation, highlighting the different motivations of those who design the policies from those who are charged with executing them. As a profession, managers will be chary of a free market, preferring to establish control of their market. This is an aspect that the following chapters on privatisation tend to confirm. Furthermore, it would suggest that, whilst the driving political forces are ideologically motivated, there will be a pragmatic element who recognise the flaws of managerialism (contrasted to the liberal ideal), but in any case pursue it in order to secure control over the bureaucracies of the state, to cut costs and gain for themselves freedom to act, a freedom that the complex treaties of the Welfare State had increasingly denied the democratically elected part of government. It is ironic that in choosing managerialist solutions these politicians are creating a structure that claims the right to manage, due to special expertise, unfettered by arcane ministerial accountability. It is the age-old professional claim to autonomy, one that sits awry with the need to ensure political accountability as the foundation of liberty.

CONTROLLING BUREAUCRATS

Various glib lists and phrases have been coined to try and encapsulate the Conservative Party's reforms of the civil service. These include the 'three Es', Economy, Efficiency, Effectiveness (Elcock, 1991, pp. 34–7); to which is often added a fourth 'E', Entrepreneurship (Pollitt, op. cit., p.139). Another attempt identifies 'four key ideas: efficiency, management, accountability and culture' (Metcalfe and Richards, 1990, p.28). Only one word is needed, however; that word is 'control'. Used as part of a prefix to the words in the preceding list (control through, or control of) its descriptive efficacy is clear. The purpose of the reforms since the election of Mrs Thatcher's first government is control of the central bureaucracy; control over its numbers, its power, its ability to resist political control, its responsiveness to change, and its influence upon policy-making. The promotion of managerialism and its enshrining within a succession of reforms is simply a concerted attempt to impose the suzerainty of elected politicians upon the permanent bureaucracy.

The distrust of the civil service and momentum for its reform centred upon Mrs Thatcher herself. One gifted chronicler of Whitehall argued that:

> Though always ready to exempt those who have served her closely and personally, she nevertheless detests senior civil servants as a breed. Mrs Thatcher simply does not believe that people of flair and enterprise should sign up for a job in the civil service. (Hennessy, 1989, pp.633–44)

He argues that in its intensity Mrs Thatcher's regard for the civil service is almost Marxist in that 'she appears to treat them almost ... as a class with their own values', she is a believer in the 'guilty men' theory and senior civil servants responsible for the construction and maintenance of the consensual welfare state rank high in her 'demonology' (ibid., p. 592). To that end Mrs Thatcher made a 'clear commitment to reduce the size of the civil service and increase the efficiency of government' (Metcalfe and Richards, 1990, p.1). Informed by experience and their liberal/conservative ideology, Mrs Thatcher and many of her Party colleagues profoundly mistrusted the civil service upon their election and regarded it as a parasitical organisation. In this sense they became an anti-government government; they saw their accession to power as an opportunity to provide the civil service with its nemesis.

It is in describing the nature of this nemesis that the aforementioned lists prove useful. The promotion of managerialism involved a lauding of private sector management and the belief in generic principles of good management, principles, it was argued, which were found in the private sector, but which often proved all too absent from public administration. These principles included:

1. the pursuit of economy in administration;
2. the projection of efficiency into the implementation of policy and the routine functions of the public service;
3. the use of performance indicators to measure the effectiveness of officials in achieving their goals;
4. the promotion of a more entrepreneurial approach to management and administration, using incentives like bonuses and performance payments, attempts to end national pay scales and inject competition into the activities of public officials;
5. a desire to change the culture of Whitehall and;
6. a belief in the need to impose new kinds of accountability, not only to ministers and Parliament, but also to consumers/customers/citizens.

To this end a series of major reforms were implemented which, in chronological order, involved:

1. the creation of an efficiency unit by Lord Rayner, a businessman from outside of the civil service, but one nonetheless with extensive Whitehall experience;
2. the introduction of a Management Information System for Ministers (MINIS), by Michael Heseltine into the Department of the Environment, and later variations upon this theme as it was infused throughout the Whitehall machine;
3. the development and imposition of the Financial Management Initiative;
4. the enactment of the *Next Steps Initiative* and the creation of Executive Agencies.

Taken as a whole, these developments were an attack upon the service of Sir Charles Trevelyan that had inherited the commanding height of post-war British politics. After a brief examination of that service, each of the reforms will be studied in turn.

MRS THATCHER'S INHERITANCE

The civil service that the incoming Conservative Government of Mrs Thatcher acquired in 1979 was the Twentieth Century incarnation of the plan by the Nineteenth Century reformer, Sir Charles Trevelyan. Sir Charles himself did not live to see the service created in his image by Haldane, Hankey and Fisher, in the early decades of this century, but in the consensual society of the Welfare State Trevelyan's model found its raison d'être.

The origins of the civil service can be traced back to the Court of the Saxon Kings and William the Conqueror's 'Henry the Treasurer', in the Tenth and Eleventh Centuries (Hennessy, 1989, pp.17–19). It is more usual, however, to recognise that the modern civil service owes its existence to the developments of state, Empire and industrial economy when Britain was at the zenith of its power in the Nineteenth Century. The creation of new offices of state (the Home, Foreign and War Offices between 1782 and 1794), the expansion of the power of the East India Company and a growing awareness that corruption and patronage were inefficient methods of appointment began to coalesce into the realisation that there was a need for reform. Within parts of Whitehall and the Whig hierarchy of Gladstone's ministries, this realisation took on the momentum of a reform movement, led by Trevelyan. It culminated in his report (with Sir Stafford Northcote) of 1854, which was inaugurated by Gladstone, using the device of a Treasury Minute, in 1853 (ibid., p.37; Drewry and Butcher, 1988, pp.31–46). The Report, a mere twenty pages long, and its preceding enquiry were a model of conciseness and economy, an example future commissions and their publications on the service singularly failed to emulate until *Next Steps*. It was followed that year by Macauley's classic *Report on the Indian Civil Service*.

Northcote and Trevelyan's main recommendations and conclusions were:

1. The need to divide the service into superior and inferior categories, that is between intellectual and routine mechanical tasks.
2. Young men should be recruited at an early age into the service and provided with a lifetime career. The Report asked 'whether it is better to train young men for the discharge of the duties which they will afterwards have to perform, or to take men of mature age, who have already acquired experience in other walks of life.' Trevelyan plumped for the former.
3. The need to establish an independent central Board or commission in order to administer recruitment through open competitive examinations. That is, people were to be recruited on merit, not through patronage. Furthermore, the examinations were to be literary rather than professional or technical and, for the highest posts, to be of university standard.
4. Promotion must also reflect the merit principle, rather than favouritism and nepotism.
5. Trevelyan was concerned at the fragmentary nature of the service and wanted to allow greater career flexibility between departments (Hennessy, 1989; Drewry and Butcher, 1988).

The Report laid the basis for a service that had at its head:

> an efficient body of permanent officers, occupying a position duly subordinate to that of the Ministers who are directly responsible to the Crown and to Parliament, yet possessing sufficient independence, character, ability and experience to be able to advise, assist, and to some extent influence those who are from time to time set over them. (Quoted in Hennessy, 1989, p.38)

Despite initial difficulties, successive governments and service heads introduced the system by degrees. For example the MacDonnell Commission in 1912–15 recommended open competitions for professional posts and in 1918 there were the major Haldane reforms. Treasury control over the other departments was being established as a parallel reform. The Treasury gradually acquired the power to vet departmental estimates and all plans requiring expenditure (from 1866). It also successfully fought for the right to oversee civil service pay, personnel numbers and organisations (from 1919), a function it temporarily lost with the establishment of the Civil Service Department following the Fulton Report in 1968, but regained after Mrs Thatcher abolished the Department in 1981. The Treasury, therefore, is the most powerful department in Whitehall, enjoying what one of its members described to Hennessy as a form of 'delegated democracy' in that as 'Parliament is incapable of exercising its financial responsibilities ... (w)e must do it for them' (ibid., p.397).

Two World Wars, the Depression and the establishment of the Welfare State led to a massive expansion in civil service numbers. Between 1940 and 1945, Britain fought a total war with state direction of all economic resources, including industry, food and people. Absolute control over work and food rationing was relaxed slowly until finally repealed in the early 1950s, but the establishment from 1945 of the National Health Service, social security, unemployment and education policies, plus a series of massive nationalisations of major industries, led to the extension of the power of the civil service into the lives of the majority of the population. Britain acquired a largely directed economy where the activities of the market were severely curtailed. There was economic planning, demographic planning (for example in the form of New Towns) land-use planning and industrial planning and controls. Through the establishment of this corporatist edifice, the civil service dutifully implemented government policy, but it increasingly came to be seen by the New Right as also using its key position, as the repository of information and expertise, to maintain the structures of the corporate state and to make policy within them. Even those who did not see a conspiracy argued that the bureaucracy had acquired a (limited) power of veto over politicians (Smith, 1979, Middlemas, 1979). In 1975, the post-war civil service numbers peaked at 747,000 (Hennessy, 1989, p.261). Most of these people were employed in low level routine jobs, the mechanical workers, to use Trevelyan's definition.

The complexity of the service, the influence of its leaders and the efficacy of its actions were questioned by a growing number of people by the 1960s. The criticisms from the 1960s until Mrs Thatcher's reforms concerned:

1. managerial ability and efficiency;
2. competence in training and personnel matters;
3. background and representative exclusivity;
4. tenure and privilege;
5. accountability and secrecy.

The Fulton Report of 1968 found:

1. there was a dominant philosophy of amateurism;
2. too few civil servants were trained in management;
3. insufficient scope was given to technical experts, be they accountants, economists or scientists and engineers;
4. there was inadequate attention given to personnel matters and career training, promotion was too dependent on seniority and the Treasury ought to not combine management with its financial and economic functions;
5. there were too many classes and this led to 'rigid and prolific departmentalism';
6. there was not enough contact between the community and the civil service;
7. there was too much secrecy;
8. the service was socially and educationally exclusive.

Fulton and others were arguing that the reforms of the Nineteenth Century were insufficient for the late Twentieth Century. There was a need for technical experts in the policy-making positions, on-top and not just on-tap. The mores of a Whig aristocracy were out of place in the modern world and there needed to be greater social representativeness and career flexibility; people had to be able to move across departmental divides and the service as a whole had to recruit more personnel from industry. Most of all, the service needed to acquire some managerial expertise.

Fulton's recommendations included a call for more training, the recruitment of people with relevant degrees, the establishment of a civil service department (headed by the Prime Minister) and a civil service college.

The latter two proposals were successful (the Department later being abolished by Mrs Thatcher). Most other proposals designed to overcome the defects Fulton found were either thwarted or implemented with a half-hearted tardiness. There were various reasons for this which included trade union resistance and the unwillingness of the higher ranks to tinker with a system that they had benefited from and believed worked well, a notable exception here being William Ryrie, an Assistant Secretary at the Treasury, who submitted evidence to the Committee predicting government overload and calling for swingeing reforms in training, organisation and the nature of ministerial responsibility (Hennessy, 1989, pp.190–4). The final reason for the failure to reform was the lack of Prime Ministerial follow-through. Both Wilson and Heath sought to reform the civil service, but found their time taken up dealing with economic and industrial crises. Mrs Thatcher was to learn from this crucial mistake.

Added to the foregoing criticisms were those of business and right-wing politicians. The businessman who headed Mrs Thatcher's Downing Street Policy Unit in 1979, Sir John Hoskins, helped to draw up a paper for the Cabinet detailing priorities and strategy for the new Conservative administration. On his list were the words 'Deprivilege the Civil Service' (ibid., p.628). It is a phrase the then head of the civil service, Sir Ian Bancroft, found 'populist and silly' as it was a strange notion to 'come into office on the basis that you are going to try and worsen the conditions in which your senior staff work' (ibid., p.629). Silly or not, it reflected the Conservatives' concern to change what Rayner christened 'the culture of Whitehall' (Metcalfe and Richards, 1990, p.16).

The essence of this culture has been variously portrayed by Pliatzky, (1984), Heclo and Wildavsky's analysis of the Treasury (1974) and Kellner and Crowther-Hunt's wider review of the civil service as 'Britain's Ruling Class' (1980). These view Whitehall as a village, with a shared culture and norms of behaviour. There is an ethos of cultured intellectualism which owes much to the elite background many of the administrative class officials share, of private education and attendance at the older universities. The unspoken, indeed often unwritten rules of etiquette discovered by this analysis reflect the insulated world of Whitehall and prove virtually impenetrable to outsiders. To this careful academic work has been added a corpus of New Right folklore – life-long tenure with inflation-proofed pensions, good pay and agreeable working conditions, combined with power without accountability – to complete the picture of a pampered elite civil service ripe for 'deprivileging'. That few within the Whitehall village would recognise this as a true reflection of their own situation did not deflect the assault; it is a cardinal rule of warfare that we must first demonise the enemy before we feel able to kill him.

Far from being pampered, civil service salaries at most levels over the past thirty years made a poor contrast with the senior posts in the private sector to which they could be roughly compared. As to agreeable working conditions, anyone who has spent any period of time in Whitehall will know that outside of Ministers' private offices conditions are often cramped and always under-resourced. In at least one Department of State the corridors of power are covered in cracked green linoleum and flanked by flaking walls. Furthermore, it is a fundamental error to argue that there is a Whitehall culture. Certain traits may be identified across the senior civil service, but the traditions and beliefs of the various departments of state are as different as those across the regiments of the British army, or indeed, different European regiments. For those engaged in 'mechanical' work in the provinces conditions of service can be almost Dickensian in the poverty of their environment. A growing body of work identifies not a Whitehall culture, but Whitehall cultures (Pitt and Smith, 1981; Gray and Jenkins, 1985, 1991; Hennessy, 1989). Lee, for example, notes how little is known of the Cabinet Office compared to the Treasury, but identifies an ethos at variance with that which exists in other departments, (1990, pp.235–42). This is not to lapse into a functionalist explanation, but merely to record an observable trait. The Whitehall village can appear to be as federal as a collection of Swiss cantons.

If there can be said to have been an identifiable thread to the Whitehall cultures then it is in the ethics of the senior officials, at least until the managerialist onslaught. O'Toole has interpreted the influence of T.H. Green (the Victorian Idealist philosopher) as being fundamental here. The role of senior public officials is the almost Platonic one of the Guardian class, according to O'Toole's analysis of Green's philosophy:

> Although all people are called upon to lead a moral life, there is one group of people upon which it is particularly incumbent to act with these moral principles in mind: the governors, both politicians and officials. Government is, after all, called upon to create the conditions in which morality shall be possible. However ... (i)t may ... be argued that politicians, no matter what their political party, are quite incapable of acting in any other way than with Utilitarian principles in mind. This then leaves officials as being the keepers of the 'common good', or to use a phrase they might be more at home with, the 'public interest'. (O'Toole, 1990, p.340)

The dilemma here, as O'Toole points out, is that officials are the servants of ministers. It is ministers who derive legitimacy as the representatives of a popularly elected Party and also from the sanction of Parliament, hence the constitutional fiction of ministerial responsibility which argues that all the actions of officials are, in theory, the actions of the responsible minister; the convention being derived from the rule of law and the sovereignty of Parliament (O'Toole, 1990, pp.340–1). There is a further dilemma here for officials, however, in that where there is a conflict between Parliament and the government then a question arises as to where the civil servant's primary allegiance lies; it may be to ministers, to Parliament or to 'The Crown' (ibid.). Recent events in Britain have thrown this problem into stark relief (Ponting, 1985; Chapman, 1978).

The angst brought about by the charge of amateurism from Fulton onwards caused senior officials to declare their professionalism, in that they they professed an ethic regulating their work and a body of knowledge specific to that work; 'Our ethic is simply stated. We stand committed to neutrality of process', argued one member of the Home Office (quoted in O'Toole, 1990, p.345). Such neutrality is eloquently encapsulated in The Armstrong Memorandum, *Note of Guidance on the Duties and Responsibilities of Civil Servants*, issued by the Head of the Civil Service following a series of challenges to the usual position of anonymous obedience by civil servants, including the aquittal of a senior official, Clive Ponting, on a charge of breaching the Official Secrets Act by disclosing ministerial mendacity to Parliament. Armstrong reiterated the underlying ethic of the service of Trevelyan by stating:

> Civil Servants are servants of the Crown. For all practical purposes the Crown in this context means, and is represented by, the Government of the day ... the civil service serves the Government of the day as a whole, that is to say Her Majesty's Ministers collectively, and the Prime Minister is the Minister for the Civil Service. The duty of the individual civil servant is first and foremost to the minister of the Crown who is in charge of the Department in which he or she is serving. It is the minister who is responsible, and answerable in Parliament for the conduct of the Department's affairs and the management of its business. It is the duty of civil servants to serve their Ministers with integrity and to the best of their ability ... the British civil service is a non-political and disciplined career service. Civil servants are required to serve the duly elected Government of the day, of whatever political complexion. It is of the first importance that civil servants should conduct themselves in such a way as to deserve and retain the confidence of ministers ... That confidence is the indispensable foundation of a good relationship between Ministers and civil servants. (Ibid., p.348)

Hennessy regards Armstrong's note as 'a restatement of the timeless verities of the civil service' (1989, p.346).

The officials' own association (the First Division Association), in producing their code of ethics, adopted a position very similar to Armstrong's traditionalist stance, beginning with a statement about officials being politically neutral servants of the crown (ibid.). According to most interpretations of the Armstrong rules the only legal recourse open to an official faced with behaviour by a minister which he or she considers to be illegal or immoral is to complain to the Head of the Service, or resign. Armstrong's memorandum (and the FDA's code) are silent about the 'integrity' and constitutionally proper behaviour of ministers. Whilst Armstrong's view represents the traditional ethical code of the civil service it is a 'parody of political practice' (O'Toole, 1990, p.348) in that it conjures up a Weberian nightmare of a 'professional' civil service conniving with a dishonest Executive to mislead Parliament, to the extent that 'Bureaucracy naturally welcomes a poorly informed and hence a powerless Parliament' (Weber, quoted in Hennessy, 1989, p.347).

Viewed from this perspective, it would be a foolish government which would seek to overturn such a culture, since it contains as its central ethic a devotion to obedience which would not be out of place in an Augustinian order of monks. Yet things are rarely what they seem. The ethics of senior officials are certainly imbued with a sense of obedience and public service, but these are elemental supports used both for their individual defence and collective search for autonomy. Seen in the context of ministerial accountability and collective Cabinet responsibility they guarantee civil servants anonymity and immunity; if the minister is responsible for all decisions and civil servants are merely ciphers proffering advice and then meekly implementing decisions, they cannot be held accountable and may not be blamed when things go wrong. The goal of the Conservatives' reforms was to highlight the theme of obedience, therefore, and then to align it with managerial rectitude, that is, civil servants were not only going to do as they were told, but they would do so efficiently, effectively, economically, and be held accountable for those actions. Managerial competence was to be grafted onto their code of professional ethics. Just how that was achieved is the subject of the next chapter.

NOTES

1. See for example, Bartlett, 1973; Brittan, 1973; Hirschman, 1970; Niskanen, 1973.

3 Enforcing Bureaucratic Change

> I think we are looking at a different kind of Civil Service, certainly below about Grade 7 (Principal). We may no longer be looking at a career Civil Service in the future, we'll just be looking at employment ... with the lower grades being part of a flexible local job market, rather like local authorities. (Deputy Secretary, Grade 2, interviewed 1991)

> There was great slaughter in London, Quentavic and Rochester. (*The Anglo Saxon Chronicle*, AD 842; 1983 edition)

In the cultivated world beloved of Whitehall mandarins, the arrival of what is variously described as 'managerialism', or 'New Public Management', was viewed in some quarters as being akin to attacks by heathen Norsemen. The elegant cultural assemblage, painstakingly fashioned over generations, was rudely prodded from its serene self-confidence. This chapter continues the theme of the British Government's dissatisfaction with the machinery of the state, and explores the radical changes imposed by the Conservatives upon the civil service, before examining the impact of those changes upon the accountability of the public sector.

THE CALL FOR RAYNER

Sir Derek (now Lord) Rayner, had a distinguished career with the firm 'Marks and Spencer', before joining Mrs Thatcher in Downing Street after the 1979 General Election. He had been seconded to Whitehall once before, again under a Conservative Government, in 1970. He worked on procurement in the Ministry of Defence for Prime Minister Heath, and recalled:

> When I first arrived in a ministry in 1970 I was amazed that there were no kinds of financial management that I knew in business and that the head of finance was certainly not an accountant by training or experience ... and yet we were dealing with 10-year forecasts involving billions of pounds. (Quoted in Hennessy, 1989, p.593)

The experience was common to many of industry's secondees and they began to lobby for change. A management consultant (an experienced accountant) who was seconded to the Department of Trade and Industry in the early 1980s was even blunter than Rayner. He described how:

> One of the things I used to do as a consultant when I went to an organisation, in order to get a feel for what was going on, was to ask questions about the sheer size and shape of the organisation and its operations. I did that with a couple of Government Departments, you'd ask questions about the numbers of people or how much money was spent on a particular type of activity and so on. And someone would go away and produce a piece of information. Then you'd find that this part of the information was an accurate piece of information, that bit was this year's budget, this other bit was somebody's estimate, and this bit was something else. This was all aggregated and presented as the answer, there was no thought as to the quality of the information that was being presented, it was just an answer. (Interview)

In Rayner's opinion the job of senior civil servants in areas like defence procurement was 'to make sure the rule book was in force', an observation that Hennessy argues illustrated the 'classic 'umpire' function being pursued by a classic product of the Northcote-Trevelyan Report' (ibid., p.594).

Rayner, whilst seeking efficiencies, discovered that no one in Whitehall knew how much it cost to actually run the machinery of government (Fry, 1988, p.6). After considerable effort, it was found that in 1985–6 the gross running costs for the civil service were £12.3 billion, which was about 3.4 per cent of the Country's then GDP (ibid.). Fry laconically noted that:

> Given that, broadly, every £1 billion extra on the Civil Service pay bill adds another penny to basic rate of income tax ... a Conservative government committed to cuts in direct taxation was not as unreasonable as it was sometimes portrayed in wishing to cut Civil Service numbers and to limit its pay increases. The sheer scale of departmental running costs invited economies too. (Ibid.)

Chosen by Mrs Thatcher to be her Efficiency Adviser, Rayner used his business experience to launch a process of constant departmental reviews mainly using young officials ('Rayner's Raiders') to examine 'specific blocks of work ... [and] working to a strict timetable and reporting to him as well as to their permanent secretary', seek out waste and report on ways to ameliorate it (Hennessy, 1989, p.594). But the resources devoted to Rayner initially amounted to only two senior civil servants, two or three secretaries, himself on a part-time basis and middle-ranking officials released from departmental duties for strictly limited (usually ninety-day) periods. Rayner could not hope to provide a comprehensive management review of the service, but then that was never his purpose, indeed he specifically eschewed it. He talked about 'digging boreholes into areas of activity and applying lessons from the detritus across the whole of the civil service' (Hennessy, 1989, pp.595–6). His secret weapon against civil service recalcitrance was the 'ultimate deterrent' of Prime Ministerial intervention. With hindsight Rayner's activities appear as a trial-run for the Next Steps. Hennessy caught the essence of Rayner's approach, arguing that it:

> was in complete contrast with the Grace Commission, President Reagan's 1981 equivalent in Washington with its 161-strong executive committee and its 'wall-papering' of all departments of the Federal Governments [*sic*]. But, large or small, he and his outfit would have had minimal to nil influence from day one but for what Rayner called 'the unique political imperative' created by Mrs Thatcher, as 'support for the initiative was not extensive among other ministers or at the higher echelons of the Civil Service'. (Ibid., pp.594–5)

Both the Fulton and Rayner experiences showed how important the patronage of the Prime Minister is to the process of reform. When Wilson lost interest in the 1960s the momentum behind the Fulton Report was lost, whereas Mrs Thatcher maintained the impetus. The dissimilation with the American experience of Grace is marked and is returned to in the following chapter.

Rayner's strategy evolved with the establishment of the Efficiency Unit he headed within the Prime Minister's Private Office. He sought to achieve fast initial successes that could be presented to the political and administrative heads of departments, and therefore set up several small initiatives 'designed to produce discernible benefits in a relatively short time and to demonstrate that there were serious shortcomings in the management of the Civil Service' (Metcalfe and Richards, 1990, p.7). To this end:

1. Young middle ranking officials, usually high-flying principals, were taken out of departments and given ninety days to conduct and report upon their individual departments. They were to identify areas of waste, inefficiency, duplication and overlap. The scope of the scrutinies was wide-ranging and involved topics such as the organisation of

Ministry of Transport vehicle (MOT) tests and the forensic science service of the Home Office. One of the goals at this stage was to illustrate that action was both necessary and possible to overcome past poor performance. Mrs Thatcher took an active interest in the reports and several were made to a Cabinet team in her presence at No. 10 (Metcalfe and Richards, ibid.; Drewry and Butcher, 1988, p. 202).

2. 'The second part of the strategy was designed to consolidate and integrate the evidence from the scrutinies and build a case for reform that would be credible within the civil service as well as outside it ... A major assumption in Rayner's strategy was that, to a large extent, reform had to be an internal process.' (Metcalfe and Richards, 1990, pp.6–7)

In 1986 the national Audit Office reviewed Rayner's scrutinies and reported that between 1979 and 1983 (when he left Whitehall) there had been five programmes with a total of 155 scrutinies; savings of £421 million a year had been identified, although for political and electoral reasons not all were implemented by ministers (Fry, 1988, p.7). The scrutinies recommended savings via changes in administrative procedures, departmental activities, the mode of delivering services, purchasing practices and staffing levels. Some revealed official behaviour that was clearly ridiculous, such as the now infamous practice of a Ministry of Agriculture Laboratory in Reading which bred rats for in-house experimental purposes at a cost of £30 per rat, whilst a nearby private sector laboratory bred similar animals for a mere £2 each (Metcalfe and Richards, 1990, p.10).

Despite Prime Ministerial support, Rayner clearly felt that savings were more easily identified and changes in management better implemented by working with, rather than against, the departments of state. To this end the departments themselves provided the scrutineers, then participated in the choice of areas for scrutiny. Following the presentation of the report, ministers took the final decision on implementing the recommendations relating to their department (ibid., p.11). The Efficiency Unit increasingly sought to standardise elements of this process in order to facilitate a more universal application. That is, Rayner attempted to increase the way in which reports could be 'read across' the service.

To facilitate this the Unit produced a report for civil servants and ministers which contained sections on 'What happens to scrutiny reports' and 'What needs to be done'. There were also two pull-out booklets (pink for officials, blue for ministers and 'managers') which outlined the process of a scrutiny and guided the scrutineers through establishing an 'action plan' to writing their report, emphasising the need to ask questions relating to the scope of the departmental activity/procedure being reviewed and the issues, tasks, techniques and resources involved. The blue book contains the timely reminder for ministers that:

> The Prime Minister has a continuing interest in the use of scrutinies to improve value for money in departments. (Efficiency Unit, 1985)

Initially scrutineers were chosen for all-round ability rather than technical skill, an obvious example of civil service behaviour reflecting the cult of the generalist. Such people were open to pressure from their departments as they had to resume their careers within the organisation they were reviewing. In the early years there is evidence that some officials were victimised as a punishment for writing unfavourable reports, one person often cited as receiving such treatment is Clive Ponting. Both Thatcher and Rayner let it be known that they took a very dim view of such behaviour. In later years a greater use has been made of specialists and even small teams of experts (Metcalfe and Richards, 1990, p.12). The programme has followed Rayner's design for it and grown to incorporate inter-departmental scrutinies and scrutinies that have applicability across Whitehall. The close Prime Ministerial interest has ensured that ministers achieved political approbation for making savings within their departments, itself a marked change from previous generations of politicians.

This is at the heart of what Rayner and Thatcher were attempting to achieve, that is a change in what Metcalfe and Richards call the 'Whitehall culture' (ibid., p.15). They argue that:

> Relying on political clout underestimates the extent to which the obstacles to reform are specifically cultural. The administrative culture is embodied not so much in explicit statements of function as in an almost taken for granted amalgam of beliefs, assumptions and values about the roles and responsibilities of civil servants. (Ibid.)

Whilst this perspective comes dangerously close to reverting to the anachronistic view of Whitehall as a monolith, it does reflect the belief of the Conservative administration that it was battling not only with tradition and intransigence, but with a firmly entrenched body of people at the heart of the state whose vested interests were at odds with the democratically elected government. Such beliefs do not have to be true in order to motivate politicians into action, merely believed. Rayner and Thatcher had learned the lessons from the failure of Fulton and used the experience to experiment with reform. They used Lord Rayner's 'boreholes' into the layers of the bureaucracy to find out what was beneath the surface, and to discern whether it was possible to mould the existing structure or if more drastic action were necessary. The experience that this provided aided the formulation of a wider attack upon the alleged inefficiencies within the machinery of the state. The attack was to take the form of the managerialist assault of the Financial Management Initiative (FMI) and The Next Steps.

THE 'REVENGE' OF FULTON: FMI TO *NEXT STEPS*

The 1980s saw the introduction of a plethora of reforms aimed at gaining control over the civil service. One senior official argued that:

> FMI certainly helped, but one of the troubles is that there have been so many initiatives that have overlapped that people have lost track as to which has done what. (Interview with a Deputy Secretary, Grade 2)

As an addition to the Conservative Party's corpus of knowledge, the lesson of Rayner (after Fulton) was one that the Far Left had been taught by Trotsky and then Mao: the need for permanent change, or 'revolution', directed from the centre, in order to effect lasting transformations within society and its state bureaucracies. This experience was gained in parallel with that of other lessons on the wider political stage, for example trade union reform, fiscal change and attempts to reconstruct local government. Metcalfe and Richards argued the Financial Management Initiative showed that 'lasting reforms are a succession of temporary solutions' (1990, p.210) and:

> one of the main purposes of the FMI is to instigate a shift in the culture of Whitehall from standards based on static, business-as-usual performance levels to expectations of year-on-year improvements in performance. Achieving this will be a major cultural change, much more important than using a reform initiative as a shock to the system ... which hopefully produces a one-off improvement in performance. (Ibid., p.192)

The FMI was an incremental progression from the totality of Rayner scrutinies, within the ideologically inspired attempts at managerial reform, and an essential prerequisite to the Next Steps. Its purpose was to inject individual managerial accountability into the Whitehall bureaucracies and it contained many of the ingredients found in Michael Heseltine's Management Information System for Ministers (MINIS), introduced into the Department of the Environment in 1980 as the result of a Rayner scrutiny into management information systems.

The FMI, therefore, married the search by Rayner and Thatcher for efficiency, with the desire of a Secretary of State (Heseltine) to control the collective knowledge of his department. The purpose of MINIS was to identify which officials were responsible for the department's different activities, and to enable ministers to calculate the costs of service delivery and administration. MINIS (or the different acronyms used by other departments for similar activities) has been absorbed into the Whitehall year with:

> the broad pattern laid down at the beginning – preparation of statements for each directorate within the department by the responsible under-secretaries, review meetings to consider the statements, with ministers and top officials participating, and action flowing from the review meetings – has settled down into an annual cycle. (Metcalfe and Richards, 1990, p.57)

There were some trenchant critics of MINIS within government, one official attached to the National Audit Office argued his view of MINIS:

> is that it was too simply just the drawing together of what was available within departmental accounting approaches anyway. I think the MOD version was much better. But it really didn't start as it should have done as a sort of top-down initiative in its objectives, and the other thing is that it didn't recognise that there was a dearth of management information. The thing we often came to was that management information was simply by definition whatever information you used to manage. (Interview)

It would be more accurate, therefore, to speak of a MINIS approach, one which requires that each of the directorates in a department provide information on:

1. their activities and objectives;
2. the priorities attached to these objectives;
3. the cost associated with them;

4. an assessment of the directorates' performance on each activity;
5. a forward look to set standards for future performance (Metcalfe and Richards, 1990, p.62).

It clearly fits into the annual financial round, aiding ministers in preparing their bids with the Treasury by providing them with (somewhat flawed) detailed knowledge of their departments and equipping them with arguments about need, as well as identifying areas of waste. As such, MINIS represents a successful progression from the attempts at policy analysis introduced into Whitehall during the 1960s and 1970s. Most of them, like Programme Analysis and Review (PAR), were ultimately unsuccessful (Gray and Jenkins, 1985).

Having grown out of a Rayner scrutiny, MINIS and its associated activities across Whitehall paved the way for a more general managerial innovation in the form of the FMI. MINIS' contribution was to educate officials and ministers into thinking managerially about the constituent units of their departments, the tasks they performed and the interconnections therein: an essential element in private sector management, but novel to Whitehall. MINIS, like Rayner's scrutinies, was flexible, in that its implementation varied over time and within departments, as such it was a graft onto the official body that bore a smaller risk of rejection. Once again the lessons of Fulton were being linked to those of Rayner in the implementation of a new initiative. Once people had become attuned to this it was possible to proceed further with the reshaping of the machinery of government.

The FMI was launched in 1982 and introduced throughout the civil service in 1983 (Cmnd 9058). A series of government publications outlined official goals and subsequent progress toward them (Cmnd 8616, 1982; Cmnd 9058, 1983; Cmnd 9297, 1984). The most succinct expression of the FMI's aims came with the government's reply to the Third Report of the House of Commons Treasury and Civil Service Committee, that is, the FMI was to:

> promote in each department an organisation and system in which managers at all levels have:
> a. a clear view of their objectives and means to assess and, wherever possible, measure outputs or performance in relation to those objectives;
> b. well-defined responsibility for making the best use of their resources including a critical scrutiny of output and value for money; and

    c. the information (particularly about costs), the training and the access to expert advice that they need to exercise their responsibilities effectively. (Cmnd 8616, para 13; see also Fry, 1988, p.8; Drewry and Butcher, 1988, p. 205)

The implications were clear: private sector management techniques and individual accountability were to be introduced into the civil service.

Pollitt labels these techniques a 'litany of managerialism' and lists them as:

     (i)   A regime of tight cash limits and cash planning.
    (ii)   Staff cuts.
   (iii)   The introduction of a system of performance indicators which stress economy and efficiency.
    (iv)   The introduction of individual staff appraisal on a more formal and extensive basis than had existed before.
     (v)   The introduction of merit pay schemes, linked to appraisal.
    (vi)   Proposals for more devolved budgetary systems, giving greater budgetary responsibility to 'line managers'.
   (vii)   Proposals for more extensive management training.
  (viii)   The introduction of new planning systems which emphasize the achievement of concrete, short-term targets.
    (ix)   Rhetorical emphasis on responsiveness to the consumer. (1990, p.83)

Although Pollitt's list refers to managerialist changes generally, the establishment of the FMI led to these reforms either being introduced directly into the civil service, or indirectly in that it prepared the ground for their implementation.

Accountable management was the aim of the FMI from its outset, the convergence of obedience with individual rather than collective responsibility. In order to attain this goal, responsibility has been delegated down the line to middle and even junior managers, with the purported goal of freeing senior civil servants (the traditional 'mandarins') for policy advice work with ministers, the setting of overall targets, and a general oversight role. The delegation has been implemented in three ways:

1. Top management systems; whereby senior officials and ministers are provided 'with information on the scope and scale of departmental operations and the use of departmental resources', this is a clear continuation of the MINIS principle, although the acronyms vary and are, for example, MINIM for the Ministry of Agriculture and ARM for the Department of Trade and Industry (Gray *et al.*, 1991, p.47).

2. Decentralised budgetary control; which is concerned with operational management, assisting departmental managers' 'focus on their operational and financial responsibilities by providing a hierarchy of cost centres'; again this varies in nature and scope across departments (ibid.).

3. Performance appraisal; which assesses the efficiency and effectiveness of performance. There is an especial 'emphasis on a range of indicators of both operational achievements and their costs' with departments being required 'to publish these in annual public expenditure white papers as part of the process of increasing accountability. There has also been an intention to use the indicators to inform the allocation of resources' (ibid., pp.47–8).

The implementation stage of the FMI policy was imbued with the lessons of Fulton and Rayner. A small central unit was established, the Financial Management Unit, which comprised a mix of civil servants and private sector consultants. Its full-time staff rarely exceeded six people. Their purpose was to guide and oversee the strategy within the departments, a practice which ensured 'a heterogeneity of organizational and political contexts and a variety of conceptions (some limited) of public sector management,' as departments adjusted the policy to their own situations (ibid., p.48).

Under strong pressure from the Treasury, the Cabinet Office and the Prime Minister, departments were forced to accede to the principles of the FMI and show a willingness to implement them through publishing White Papers detailing their plans, a process some less managerially oriented ministers were as tardy as their officials in pursuing (ibid.). The FMU was succeeded by the Joint Management Unit, which was itself subsumed within the Treasury in 1987 as the Financial Management Group, leading some officials to view it as merely a Treasury cipher designed to further extend that department's control over the rest of Whitehall. One senior official in a small policy department argued that:

> The real problem is that the Treasury expects certain things to be done across-the-board and they are not flexible enough to accept that in certain instances it is not appropriate to be doing certain things, particularly in a small policy department. And the way they rabbit on about the need for performance measures for policy! They expect us to constantly produce more than we can and when we ask them for advice they turn round and say, 'Well it's up to you, but we do expect more in this area.' This, I think, has given the FMI a bit of a bad name when it could have been

avoided. It was taken over by the Treasury. They didn't use it within the philosophy within which it was originally introduced, they saw it less as a way of giving managers their head, but more as a way of instilling greater cost control. The central organs of the Treasury had developed their own theology and this was pushed down the departments' throats whether they liked it or not. They lost the spirit of the thing; it became a club to bash departments with. (Interview)

That rather defeated the original intention of the designers of the FMI's policy, although it did reflect the resurgence of Treasury power under Mrs Thatcher. One senior official in Whitehall with considerable private sector experience argued:

I think a major problem [with the FMI] was that they couldn't decide whether it was a financial initiative or a management initiative; in the end it just became an accounting initiative. A lot of accounting systems were developed; it was very necessary. (Interview)

In his view the FMI was a natural precursor to the *Next Steps*, but its own contribution was, therefore, limited to the implementation of essential financial and management accounting techniques, basic managerial tools which were astonishingly absent from public sector management in any relevant numbers until FMI. This is a perspective widely held by senior officials in Whitehall charged with implementing managerial reform. One has argued that:

I think there is a genuine willingness on everybodys' part now to take a rather more hard-nosed approach to management, and an appreciation that management is not actually something that you give to the elderly duds who can't analyse. I think there's far more resource awareness right through the system. (Interview)

In other words, there has been something of a cultural change brought about in that senior officials are now at least aware of resource implications and the need for management techniques to control the resources used to implement policies. Even the official from the policy department three quotes above argued that:

I think there is less fat around and a better sense of direction and I think that's occurred because of FMI ... I think there has been a genuine cultural change among many senior managers. They now feel that their main job is not to draft something very elegantly, but it is to actually manage and control people at work. By and large I think people like and accept having what they are supposed to do set down much more explicitly; they expect to have their performance monitored against what is set down and in due course to be rewarded on that basis. (Interview)

Gray *et al.* reflect that an important lesson from the FMI is that its:

varied development confirms the differentiated character and context of government activity must be accommodated in the design and implementation of financial and related reform (1991, p.57).

This is a conclusion shared by the analysis of Metcalfe and Richards (1990, pp.178–210), which emphasises the need to address the multiplicity of structures, roles, and services provided by the public sector in an imaginative, sophisticated and above all flexible way. To this end the FMI has been superseded by the *Next Steps*.

THE *NEXT STEPS*

The *Next Steps* is the most fundamental restructuring of the British Civil Service since the Northcote–Trevelyan reforms of the last century. It is the process whereby large numbers of civil servants are transferred into semi-autonomous executive agencies and is designed to effect a further cultural shift within Whitehall, combining a reassertion of ministerial ascendancey in policy making with civil service economy, efficiency, effectiveness and accountability in policy implementation. It represents the apotheosis of recent managerial change, but implicit within it is an official obligation to accountability different to that found in traditional interpretations of ministerial responsibility.

In hiving out many administrative activities (and civil servants) from departments into semi-autonomous agencies, where they are under the direction of chief executives, the *Next Steps* is implementing a policy of decentralisation that formed one of Fulton's major recommendations in 1968. Whilst the original location of these activities remain the sponsoring departments, an extra layer of accountability has been added with the insertion of the chief executives. The decision to classify the heads of these organisations using private sector labels is itself indicative of the government's priorities. Thus large sections of public administration are now responsible to Parliament through ministers via chief executives;

it is a more distant relationship to the legislature than hitherto in the UK, one reminiscent of the old public corporations.

Next Steps provides for the freeing-up of senior civil servants and ministers from the mundane activities of routine administration, whilst providing the flexibility necessary for economy, efficiency and effectiveness in service delivery. Davies and Willman have reiterated that one of the main problems leading to both poor management and policy making has been the traditional departmental structure: 'the Minister is invariably more concerned with policy than management which he is ill-equipped and too pressured to deal with adequately' (1991, p.3). To this end *Next Steps* frees managers in the new organisations to pursue their goals using private sector management techniques, whilst being assessed on performance indicators set by ministers and the sponsoring departments. To the extent that it promotes the cult of the 'professional' manager, *Next Steps* is in danger of de-politicising swathes of public administration, in a manner successfully pursued by (for example) the medical and legal professions or the nuclear industry (Wilding, 1982; Pollitt, 1990; Massey, 1988). It represents a move away from the structuring of public administration into departments according to their 'purpose' (such as defence) and into units that variously reflect 'process' (for example forensic science or statistical collation); 'people' (such as the new Child Support Agency and the RAF Training Agency); and 'place' (for example Cadw, the agency dealing with Welsh historic monuments). This is a re-emphasis of the organising philosophy behind the UK's national public administration for over a century.

A product of the Efficiency Unit's Kate Jenkins, Karen Caines and Andrew Jackson, *The Next Steps Initiative* was launched by the 1988 publication *Improving Management in Government: The Next Steps*, but thereafter known after the then Head of the Efficiency unit as the Ibbs Report. It was clearly seen by the Unit as a logical increment to Rayner scrutinies, MINIS and the FMI. The authors argued that:

> As a result of initiatives taken since 1979, the management of government business is much improved, especially in those parts of government where there are clear tasks to be performed and services to be delivered. But there is still a long way to go; in particular there is insufficient sense of urgency in the search for better value for money and steadily improving services. (1988, para 1)

The Report emphasised the need to bring about 'the changes needed in attitudes and behaviour' (ibid.) a clear warning to Whitehall that the government's advisers intended to maintain the pressure for cultural change, or Pollitt's 'ideological imperialism'.

The team's terms of reference were:

1. to assess progress in improving management;
2. to identify successful measures in changing attitudes and practices;
3. to identify obstacles to better management;
4. to report to the Prime Minister on what further measures should be taken. (Efficiency Unit, 1988, Annex B)

To this end the Report's main findings began with general approbation for the belief that 'civil servants are now more cost conscious' and that some good management systems were in place (ibid.). As a result there had been manpower cuts and budgeting systems which were the two measures 'most effective in changing attitudes' (ibid.). Yet obstacles to progress remained, the authors argued that:

1. there is insufficient focus on the delivery of government services (as opposed to policy and ministerial support), even though 95 per cent of civil servants work in service delivery or executive functions;
2. there is a shortage of management skills and of experience of working in service delivery functions among senior civil servants;
3. short-term political priorities tend to squeeze out long-term planning;
4. there is too much emphasis on spending money, and not enough on getting results;
5. the Civil Service is too big and too diverse to manage as a single organisation. (Ibid.)

There are loud echoes of Fulton in these findings, but the main thrust is the managerial one of devotion to efficiency, economy, effectiveness and competence. The report is the authentic voice of government frustration at Whitehall's inability to reform itself after nearly a decade of Conservative attempts at change. Henceforth more radical measures would be imposed.

Next Steps sought to shift the emphasis given to generalists within the 95 per cent of the civil service engaged in service provision and to reorient it in favour of experts and professionals. The authors identified three main priorities for the government:

1. The work of each department must be organised in a way which focuses on the job to be done; the systems and structures must enhance the effective delivery of policies and services.
2. The management of each department must ensure that their staff have the relevant experience and skills needed to do the tasks that are essential to government.
3. There must be a real and sustained pressure on and within each department for continuous improvement in the value for money obtained in the delivery of policies and services. (Ibid., para 15)

The team emphasised the need for a strong ministerial lead in order for the Report's recommendations to be implemented. The major recommendation was for the establishment of agencies to 'carry out the executive functions of government within a policy and resources framework set by a department' (ibid., para 19). The Report said an agency might not even reside within the government service if it were felt that the job could be done better elsewhere.

The Report was clear on how the agencies were to be run:

> These units, large or small, need to be given a well defined framework in which to operate, which sets out the policy, the budget, specific targets and the results to be achieved. It must also specify how politically sensitive issues are to be dealt with and the extent of the delegated authority of management. The management of the agency must be held rigorously to account by their department for the results they achieve. (Ibid., para 20)

The main control was to lie with the Minister and the Permanent Secretary, but once the policy and the framework were set 'the management of the agency should then have as much independence as possible in deciding how those objectives are to be met' (ibid., para 21). The obvious implications for ministerial responsibility were identified by the authors, who observed that:

> placing responsibility for performance squarely on the shoulders of the manager of an agency also has implications for the way in which Ministers answer to Parliament on operational issues. Clearly Ministers have to be wholly responsible for policy, but it is unrealistic to suppose that they can actually have knowledge in depth about every operational question. The convention that they do is in part the

cause of the overload we observed. We believe it is possible for Parliament, through Ministers, to regard managers as directly responsible for operational matters and that there are precedents for this. (Ibid., para 23)

This paragraph cut to the heart of ministerial responsibility and the accountability of the Executive to Parliament. Its subsequent acceptance in the implementation stage of the *Next Steps* has led to a questioning about the nature of accountability that is fundamental to the future of public administration in the UK. The problem is to identify the location of democratic accountability, as opposed to managerial accountability. Determined not to become ensnared with such fine constitutional points, the team urged rapid implementation and thought that two years should suffice for the implementation of their plans for the radical restructuring of public administration in the UK. In the event, that proved only slightly optimistic and marked a substantial improvement on the time it took to implement Northcote–Trevelyan.

THE PATH TO *NEXT STEPS*

Richard Luce, when Minister with day-to-day responsibility for the Civil Service, said that:

> there should be no underestimate of the importance the Government attaches to ... these *Next Steps*. (Cm 524)

The government therefore embraced much of the Report and sought to implement many of its recommendations, including the crucial call for the establishment of agencies under an accountable manager. Its reply to the Eighth Report of the Treasury and Civil Service Committee (which had concerned itself with *Next Steps*) carried the promise that;

> The Government believes that the Agency programme will bring about lasting improvement in the quality and efficiency of government services; and will maintain the pressure for rapid and extensive change to achieve this ... Within this, the priorities will be:
> * setting demanding targets for improvement and developing better performance measurement systems and techniques;
> * delegating more responsibility for operational matters to managers;
> * applying and adapting where necessary the best private and public sector management techniques;

- directing training and career development towards improving the management of services;
- introducing where appropriate more flexible pay and personnel arrangements;
- devising and introducing appropriate financial regimes for Agencies;
- monitoring Agencies' performance to ensure that it progressively improves. (Ibid., p.3)

The government had grasped the recommendations of *Next Steps* as the way forward, as indeed the next step in its goal of reforming the governance of the UK. Yet this was hardly surprising since the members of the Efficiency Unit who wrote the Report constructed it in the government's own image. *Next Steps* was not a plan for the future; the government already possessed that and had expounded it in numerous documents and political speeches. *Next Steps* was simply a guide to that plan; the authors were acting as interpreters of the creed and illustrating a way in which it might be realised; the Report represented a Jesuitical implementation, not a Pauline conversion. *Next Steps* therefore provided a vehicle for the further restructuring including greater attention to training, managerial efficiency, privatisation (where possible) of government functions and the use of non-party-political secondees from industry to provide greater managerial expertise. With these goals in its sights the government resolved to 'carry the iniative forward urgently and with determination' (ibid., p.11).

THE IMPLEMENTATION OF *NEXT STEPS*

The government was true to its word and there was a rapid pace of change. The implementation followed a familiar pattern with the government establishing a small but powerful 'Next Steps Project Team' in the Cabinet Office, led by Peter Kemp, an official of Permanent Secretary (Grade 1) rank, but closely monitored by the Head of the Civil Service, Sir Robin Butler and (of course) the Prime Minister. The first ten executive agencies were established during 1988 and 1989, with 8,000 civil servants working in them; a futher thirty-four had been set up by the end of 1990 (bringing the total number of officials in the hived off agencies to about 80,000). Years 1991–2 saw another thirty-two Next Steps agencies up and running, which (with the reorganisation of the Inland Revenue and Customs and Excise) brought over 285,000 officials into agencies or executive units out of a 1988 total of 570,000 civil servants (Price Waterhouse, 1991). The government aims to push about 450,000 civil servants into these agencies by the end of the 1990s (Dunleavy, 1989, p.266). Yet there seems to have been no real attempt to define what an agency should be. The Ibbs Report simply used it to define 'any executive unit that delivers a service for the Government'. As is usual in the UK, the practicalities were left deliberately vague in order that they may evolve.

For the first ten agencies, ministers appointed departmental civil servants to the post of Chief Executive, usually someone who was in effect head of the service or section that was being hived off. But for nearly all of the last forty appointments an open competition was held, with the successful candidate being paid at rates reflecting civil service Deputy Secretary or Under Secretary levels (Grade 2 or Grade 3). The agencies vary in size from fifty officials (the National Weights and Measures Laboratory) to over 68,000 employees (Social Security Benefits Agency). As befits the lessons of FMI, each agency has a slightly different relationship with its parent department, each has a different policy on recruiting outside experts, either as managers or into professional posts, and each agency has a different perception of its purpose and degree of autonomy. Davies and Willman note that:

> basic questions are whether activities can become discrete administrative units sufficient in size to justify any major structural changes that might be necessary; activities should be concerned with the delivery of services and should not require the day to day involvement of the Department or its Minister. (1991, p.19)

In short, there is no such thing as a typical agency, the whole system has been founded upon the perceived need for flexibility. Before establishing an agency, departments must first consider whether it is best to privatise the activity, abolish it altogether, or contract it out.

In keeping with the original recommendations for establishing executive agencies, the parent department, in consultation with the prospective agency's managers, design a framework document which seeks to ensure that 'responsibilities are defined and objectives made clear' (Efficiency Unit, 1991, para 2). An integral part of this is the establishment of service delivery guidelines, financial targets and key performance indicators. The latter are the main innovation for Whitehall. Examples include those of the Land Registry Executive Agency, established in July 1990, whose 10,500 staff must seek to ensure that:

92% of pre-completion applications to be handled in four days (compared with 91% at the start of the period) and the average handling time for post-completion applications to be reduced from 7 to 5 weeks;

99.7% of pre-completion applications to be handled free of error (compared with 99.5% at the start) and 99.75% of post-completion applications to be handled free of error (compared with 97.25% at the start). (Price Waterhouse, 1991, p.15)

This and other lists are somewhat longer, but as an example of performance indicators the extract serves to illustrate the nature and the obvious limitations to the process, an issue returned to later in this chapter.

ASSESSING *NEXT STEPS*

Whitehall's view of *Next Steps* is mixed, but essentially sanguine. Having been forced to learn the new managerial techniques senior officials have discovered their efficacy in controlling the unionised 'mechanical' workers, whilst freeing time for more exciting policy work. *Next Steps* has provided kudos via ministerial approbation, whilst not (as yet) significantly denting the power of the mandarins. It has allowed the appearance of momentous change, indeed the actuality of structural change, whilst preserving the Whitehall empire. It may even have enhanced the power of senior civil servants by insulating their administrative chattels from the prying eyes of the legislature, an issue returned to later.

The support for the agencies, however, is shared by a wider constituency than the mandarin class; a civil service union leader has argued that the main impact of *Next Steps* is the division between the delivery of services and the policy advising role of the higher echelons. Such a division is central to providing a better standard of service to the public and to the employees within the vast staffs of the bureaucracy. His view is that:

the difference this time is that somebody's actually grasped the nettle of separating the operational Civil Service from the administrative Civil Service, and that means, of course, separating management from policy making. And all the times in the past we've had these various reviews ... the Priestly Commission, the Fulton Committe, all the rest of it. Most of these pointed the way forward, but at the end of the day, all that happened was tinkering, and what's happening now is quite radical ... We can see on the one hand disadvantages – possibility of diffused management, lack of control in industrial relations matters and so on. On the other hand there is a crying need for improved management per se in the Civil Service, and I think we do feel that there is an opportunity here in the agency concept of improving management, giving better quality services to the public, and perhaps a better deal for the staff as well. (Jones, *Analysis*, BBC, 31/5/90)

It is unusual for the intended victims of a 'war on waste' to praise the very instrument intended to cause their demise, or to use a phrase quoted in the previous chapter, to 'de-privilege' them. For the senior officials the benefits are those outlined in this and the previous chapter, and by Dunleavy. For those more junior, pay flexibility is thought by their leaders to follow structural flexibility (Treasury permitting), and in a service where there is a fairly high turn-over of staff in the lowly clerical and support grades, a re-assessment of staffing levels may also lead to a higher value being put on those who remain. Thus, a leaner, more efficient service may also provide better pay in jobs notorious for their low remuneration, a factor which in the past has led to serious recruitment problems in some parts of the country. One senior official with considerable experience of setting up Executive Agencies commented that:

I think you can overestimate the extent to which there's a national career Civil Service. The typical civil servant is female, aged below twenty-five and doing a clerical job away from London. And basically interested in bringing home a wage packet each week, rather than actually pursuing a career. (Interview)

Be that as it may, *Next Steps*, if it continues to be implemented imaginatively, and loosens the potential death-grip of the Treasury, will be able to deliver 'a change in emphasis from managing people's careers to encouraging self-motivation' (ibid.).

The Efficiency Unit's own review of progress in 1991, *Making the Most of Next Steps: the Management of Ministers' Departments and their Executive Agencies*, was similarly optimistic, but with a note of caution:

We found that *Next Steps* has generated renewed enthusiasm and increased commitment to improving value for money and quality of service. This is most marked in Agencies and can also be seen to varying degrees within Departments. But there is a strong conviction that there are areas in which more progress can be achieved. These are:

getting the context right
empowering the chief executive
reappraising the role, organisation and size of Departments. (1991, para 2.2)

Getting the context right involves establishing clear guidelines within the framework document for what is required from the Agency in terms of service delivery and its relationship with the parent department. The onus here is primarily upon the department, particularly with regard to giving a high priority to setting targets (with performance indicators), and establishing sound financial and accounting systems within the Agency.

Empowering the Chief Executives involves enabling them to exercise 'responsibility and accountability for the efficient deployment of the resources in their charge' in order to allow them to deliver better value for money (ibid., para 2.6). Yet the authors realise the special nature of public sector management within their new creation in that:

> Moves towards greater delegation have to take account of areas where it may remain important to have the capacity to maintain standards across Government. The principles of fair and open competition in recruitment, the political impartiality of civil servants and certain aspects of pay and grading are examples of such areas. Nevertheless, there should be a progressive move towards the widest measure of delegated management. (Ibid.)

Viewed logically, the sentences in this paragraph almost equate to a non sequitur, particularly in the light of earlier discussions with regard to New Right theory and the ideological liberalism of its practitioners. These aims do reflect the government's belief, however, that it can retain the classic virtues of the civil service, whilst importing the managerial virtues of the private sector. But it is just such a limitation that can hamper reform when it is linked to old notions of ministerial accountability. Davies and Willman argue:

> The British approach ... has been characteristically equivocal ... carefully conforming to conventions of public accountability which anyone observing Parliament knows to be virtually defunct. The new approach to public management which Next Steps represents requires this nettle to be firmly grasped. If senior officials ... are unable to let go of Agencies it is because they cannot for as long as we persist with the sham of Ministerial responsibility which dictates the structure of the whole Government machine. (1991, pp.24–5)

Agencies' framework documents are themselves limited, therefore, by strictly circumscribing the areas of delegation. They make clear the parent department's and the Treasury's control over strategy and money supply:

> within the overall disciplines of cash limits and targets set, managers are free to make their own decisions on the management of staff and resources except for any specially reserved areas. (Efficiency Unit, 1991, para 2.7)

Clearly it is managerial freedom on the government's terms, or perhaps more accurately, a Treasury-guided and defined managerial emancipation.

Re-appraising the role, organisation and size of departments is one of the more troublesome elements of *Next Steps*. *Making the Most of Next Steps* argues that there has to be a distinction between a department's role in providing policy support for ministers and their need to support ministers 'in establishing Agency objectives and monitoring perfomance' (1991, para 2.10). There will be as yet unforeseen effects upon Permanent Secretaries, in their role as Accounting Officers, both for their departments and the agencies within the remit of their department. There will also be inevitable reorganisations of departmental size and structure; again a timetable for this will be largely finance driven and therefore Treasury controlled (para 2.14). At all times the key phrase to resonate through the reform is 'flexibility', with the authors identifying it as fundamental to the continued success of *Next Steps*. As such there is no 'typical' agency, rather four groups:

1. Agencies which are fundamental to the mainstream policy and operations of their departments: for instance the Employment Service or the Social Security Benefits Agency; Mainstream Agencies.
2. Agencies which execute, in a highly delegated way, statutory (usually regulatory) functions derived from the main aims of the department: for instance, the Vehicle Inspectorate, the Patent Office or Companies House; Statutory Agencies.
3. Agencies which provide services to departments (or other agencies) using particular skills: for instance, Government Research establishments or the Information Technology Services Agency in DSS; Service Agencies.
4. Agencies which are not linked to any of the main aims of a department but nonetheless report to its minister: for instance, HMSO or Historic Royal Palaces; Peripheral Agencies (1991, Annex A).

Within this typology the new agencies report a common set of preoccupations; working out their relations with the parent department is their single biggest concern after trying to improve service to their customers (Price Waterhouse, 1991, pp.5–9). Often, of course, their main customer is the agency's parent department. The main problems in the relationship with the parent department involve (in descending order of magnitude):

1. budget discussions;
2. personnel problems;
3. policy advice;
4. customer service;
5. relations with Parliament (ibid., p.9).

The question of accountability looms throughout these headings, and it is to this that the chapter now turns. The difficulty is in deciding precisely what is meant by 'accountability' in the context of people, Parliament and money.

PROBLEMS OF ACCOUNTABILITY

The Problem

Traditional public administration analysis, of the type criticised in chapter 1, cannot adequately cope with change on the scale outlined in this chapter and there is a danger that future debates about the nature of the public sector will take place in disciplines other than political science. Such neutered perspectives are, in any case, profoundly unhelpful in understanding political developments, which is why the analysis of this book has insisted upon viewing public administration within a broader theoretical framework, as the administration of political policy: Price's 'seamy side' of politics. This is not a unique quest; for example, Dunleavy has pursued a similar argument by evolving a bureau-shaping model of administrative politics which by focusing:

> on a central state defined in terms of effective ministerial control means that superficial changes in the nomenclature or status of component organisations within this apparatus do not materially alter the scope of [this] analysis. (1989, p.267)

In his view:

> the *Next Steps* reforms will just make possible a finer grain delineation of analytically defined agencies without any alteration of the fundamental basis for academic study. (Ibid.)

To this extent he claims that his model (originally formulated in 1983) was able to predict a re-organisation along the lines of *Next Steps* as 'policy-level officials will favour hiving off in terms of their demand-and-supply calculation for budgetary increases' and that it 'provides strong incentives for both senior officials and government ministers anxious to constrain government spending' (ibid., pp.268–9).

Such observations go some way towards claims of a partially predictive social science, indeed that is one of the purposes of constructing analytical theories. It would be foolish, of course, to claim these theories are anything other than tools of analysis; they serve the purpose of aiding understanding, not of divining the future: the latter is an activity that remains firmly within the realm of astrology and other show-business frippery. But in providing a clearer understanding of political activity analytical theories enable observers to predict the likely consequences of certain limited types of political activity. It is partly for this reason that in the last chapter it was more helpful to view Pollitt's comments about the changes in central government from the perspective of the ideology of professionalism, rather than his belief in an ideology of managerialism. The wealth of case study material available on professional behaviour suggests that to be the proper interpretation, and in any case allows a greater predictive element in the analysis. Such broader analyses are essential to understanding the effects of *Next Steps*, why they took place and why they are likely to be successful. The concatenation of central state reforms have followed a logical, if incremental pattern, driven by the liberal/conservative ideology of the government and partly shaped by those charged with implementing them. The effects may be assessed from a variety of perspectives. The rest of this section will first explore some of these.

Accountable to Whom?

Sir Douglas Wass, a former Joint Head of the Civil Service, argued that, whilst he was in favour of the Conservatives' quest for efficiency (whilst eschewing the charges of undue 'privilege' and 'parasitism'), the proper calls for public accountability meant that:

> the search for efficiency will sometimes bring us up against constraints which are imposed on the service by Parliament and the public – the expectation, for instance, that it will be able to account, ex post facto, fully and in detail, for all its expendi-

ture and indeed all its acts. Such constraints apply much less strongly in the private sector. Then there is the question of equity in the state's treatment of the citizen. Are we prepared, for example, to see a measure of inequality in the treatment of discretionary benefit claims if this will reduce the cost of administration? How far are we prepared to delegate decision making and the choice of resource expenditure to line managers, for example to the manager of a local office? Will ministers be prepared to say in reply to political criticism that, in order to streamline the administration, a junior official has been given discretion and must take and defend his own decisions? Parliament, through the Public Accounts Committee, pays close attention to the detail of how public money is spent; but the principles which underlie this approach may have to be modified if a combination of economy and delegation lead, as they might well do, to a measure of rough justice in administration. (1983, pp.9–10)

Given that these concerns were expressed some five years before *Next Steps* was mooted, the question of accountability they raise is one that has begun to vex those charged with ensuring its implementation; they go to the very heart of civil service notions of constitutional propriety and official responsibility, or lack of it. The different political parties have been nudged by interest groups to begin producing various charters extolling their commitment to the idea of accountability. But there are various types of accountability. That is, there is the accountability of service providers to the service consumers, the accountability of the public sector to the electorate via Parliament and ministers, and the accountability of individuals and organisations to society via the courts and (in the case of the public sector) their function of judicial review. The difficulty for observers and practitioners alike is in deciding which version of accountability takes precedence and the methods used to implement (or in some cases to 'measure') it.

In a particularly prescient section Wass foresaw the accountability problems that agencies were likely to engender:

> Although my generation of civil servants has been brought up to regard every act taken by an official as an act in the name of the minister, our successors may therefore have to be prepared to defend in public, and possibly without the shield of ministerial protection, the acts they take. (Ibid., p.12)

There would be a need, therefore, to establish 'a new relationship between the official and Parliament', as a result of which 'the unique responsibility of the minister will be altered' and the 'status and role of the official will take on an important new public dimension' (ibid.). In addressing these issues, Wass was careful to trace the constitutional thread of accountability which runs through our political system. The supreme authorities are the Crown, Parliament and the courts, and each has well-defined responsibilities and powers. So far as the Crown is concerned, and of course it is as a part of the Crown that public servants function, the responsibilities may be either prerogative or statutory. But whatever form that they take, the exercise of any of those responsibilities may be questioned by Parliament ... But the route of accountability is only an indirect one, for the interface between the Crown ... and Parliament ... has for the greater part of our modern history been the relatively narrow one of ministers – although lying behind ministers are the enormous departments of state over which they preside. These departments are daily performing functions, all the minutiae of which the relevant minister cannot possibly be aware of. It is, I think, the lack of opportunity for the tribunes of the people to call the servants of the Crown to account for their acts which has given rise to so much debate in recent years. (Ibid., p.11)

Instead of following the American example, instituted after the Revolution, of reorganising the structures and responsibilities of the different parts of the government system, to force the organisations of the state to comply with their constitutional duty to account for themselves, the British have formulated *Next Steps* and appointed a new layer of Chief Executives. Jessop has called the broader approach of the Conservative governments, of which this is part of the reform process, one of 'putting politics back in command' (1988, pp.37–40), whilst another left-wing critic has referred to the mix of strong centralised ministerial control combined with the liberal market ideology as 'the free economy and the strong state' in his book (Gamble, 1988).

Whereas in the US the constitutional forms of accountability are given substance by the power of the Congress, similar British constitutional precedents and practices are undermined by the power of the Executive, masquerading under the cloak of Crown prerogative. The strong party system and the lack of a constitutional umpire, along the lines of the US's Supreme Court, mean that in the UK Wass's 'Tribunes of the People' are in practice armed with paper darts or (on the government's side of the debating chamber) are in thrall to the ruling party. Even if the UK were to adopt a modern Bill of Rights, enforced via a Supreme Court, the supremacy of the Crown in Parliament is such that any subsequent law (perhaps passed in days or even hours like the emergency legislation of the Official Secrets Act) could suspend or override the Bill. It may even be that a Minister acting through an Order in Council could (as now under various statutes) order a temporary cessation of civil liberties (Hailsham, 1976).

Accountability, therefore, assumes many shapes. Campaigners for greater accountability within the British political system are better advised to concentrate upon reform of the electoral and party system, within a wider European legal system, than gadding after a fatuous Bill of Rights, or Citizens' Charter.

Parliamentary Accountability

Members of Parliament, quick to note curtailments of their powers, if often tardy in overcoming those challenges, have complained that the *Next Steps* executive agencies are in danger of slipping from parliamentary oversight. Rather than publishing written answers from the agencies to parliamentary questions, one of the cornerstones of parliamentary control, the answers have simply been placed in the Commons library (*The Independent*, 28/6/91). Even Conservative backbench MPs, normally supportive of *Next Steps,* were concerned; one argued that the Public Accounts Committee could lose effective control over the agencies, staffed as they are by civil servants and funded from public monies. Since the establishment of the agencies and similar reforms in the National Health Service, ministers have been tending to pass questions over to the public officials for answer; one MP argued that, 'It is not a far step from that to envisage questions not being answered at all' (ibid.). Indeed, seemingly straightforward questions for the new agencies such as, 'How many social security frauds have been detected?' or 'How many people are on youth training?' have been deemed 'operational matters for the agency, not policy matters for ministers' (*The Independent*, 20/6/91).

Some agencies, entirely funded by monies voted by Parliament, have simply refused to provide backbench opposition MPs with what they regard as commercially confidential information (ibid.). Were this to escalate, there would be a clear breach of the traditional powers and duties of Parliament to hold the Executive to account. No doubt as the agencies develop their new roles will not include the wilful evasion of Parliamentary accountability; even ministers with decades of experience have tended to baulk at flagrant mendacity in the House or abstaining from ministerial responsibility. If provoked long enough even backbench MPs have been known to exact retribution from authoritarian or recalcitrant members of the Executive.

The point to note is not that the agencies have been established without the thread of accountability being clearly delineated, but that it appears to have been wilfully tangled on occasion, with ministers claiming no knowledge of operational matters and pointing to the framework documents to illustrate the new 'arms' length' approach that departments have adopted to large parts of British public administration. The agencies themselves, however, have used the same documents to show that as far as they are concerned their accountability is through the department and therefore the minister to Parliament, and as such it is not proper for them to fuel 'party political' debates by providing answers to backbenchers' questions.

It may be, however, that concern as to new routes to secure accountability is simply part of the process of coming to terms with the new structures. Certainly there appears scant fear about parliamentary accountability in Whitehall, where the concern is for:

1. the accountability of agencies to departments and thereby to ministers;
2. the accountability of agencies to Parliament and the Public Accounts Committee;
3. general accountability of agencies to their customers.

There is a similarity between Whitehall's view and that of Davies and Willman, who scathingly write that:

> it is indicative of the impoverished role of Parliament that the Next Steps Initiative … was not introduced by legislation voted by Parliament after informed and constructive debate, but by an executive action announced by the Prime Minister. (1991, p.35)

Parliament gives the impression of having to struggle to keep up with the pace of change. A senior member of the National Audit Office argued that:

> There's a mixture of things there. There is this question about Parliamentary questions and the extent to which the answers appear in Hansard or up in the Library, and that's seen as a problem and it's something that Parliament could tackle if it really wanted to and maybe will. From the NAO's point of view, in terms of accountability I don't think there's any real negative sides to it [*Next Steps*], I think mostly it's positive. What we're getting in Agencies are areas of activity in a way being ring-fenced, being more readily identifiable from within the department: being required to set performance measures, targets, being required to produce an annual

report and accounts. So therefore some elements have become more readily visible and therefore something for which there is more straightforward potential for the NAO to review on a regular basis. When it comes to Parliamentary accountability, then it's really up to Parliament as to what to do with the annual reports ... but I don't expect that they will look at them in detail, all fifty of them a year. As you know they only look at Appropriation accounts when there's some major issue arising. But other Select Committees will now have an annual report, take perhaps the Social Security Department, where 90%, or thereabouts, of the department's activities will be reported in a formal way every year. There's nothing to stop the Select Committees calling for evidence on all of them as a regular event. Just the Treasury and Civil Service Committee now reviews progress on the Next Steps on a regular basis, but why shouldn't the Social Security Committee call in the Head of the Benefits Agency to discuss his performance? (Interview)

This official, like others of similar rank, holds the opinion that it is up to Parliament to set the agenda, MPs themselves must illustrate and insist upon the ways in which agencies will be held accountable. One senior official simply said that parliamentary accountability is 'effectively accountability to the Public Accounts Committee' and the PAC has called very few Agency Chief Executives before it (interview). The confused response of Parliament is a weak and distant cry when contrasted to its powerful American cousin.

Another senior official, directly involved in implementing *Next Steps* within a large department, argued that with regard to accountability:

things are not settling down too badly. Obviously the key document on settling the accountabilities to begin with is the framework document for an Agency, and we went to town quite a lot on our framework document, spelling out precisely who was accountable to whom for what and the relationship between the two accounting officers (the Permanent Secretary) and (the Chief Executive of the Agency) with his own vote and therefore accountable for that vote. So in strict Parliamentary accountability for money spent terms, we've not so far bumped up against any problems at all. (Interview)

It is ironic that it was this official's department that MPs have been amongst the most critical of, albeit in informal ways. Yet the official parried these complaints by saying:

On things like the handling of PQs [Parliamentary Questions from MPs], we got a certain amount of resistance to begin with from MPs saying they didn't like the idea of being fobbed off to Chief Executives. In practice I think we had eight queries out of a total of something like 550 handled and there's now a very ready acceptance that [the Chief Executive] should deal with these written answer PQs and should also deal with correspondence that comes in from MPs. They know that if they don't like the answer they can come back again via the Secretary of State and there are no quibbles about that. (Interview)

Yet to be truly accountable, Parliament must itself be involved in the process by which framework documents are established. Parliament needs to increase its activities in planning policy, scrutinising its implementation and representing interests (Davies and Willman, 1991, pp.37–41). For civil servants the lines of accountability to Parliament are clear. The problems, such as they are, are to be addressed by MPs, officials will respond to parliamentary pressure, exerted via ministerial directions. Ministers will issue such an order if placed under sufficient pressure by the House of Commons. The implementation of such pressure is dependent upon the effects of the electoral system and party discipline.

Officials see the implementation of *Next Steps* as leading to a modernisation of accountability as well as management practice. One senior civil servant said that:

There is a formal contract with a Chief Executive of a kind that normally no Civil Servant has with a Minister. So that there is something there, targets that somebody can be measured against, so people can be seen to be delivering or not delivering. This whole charade of Ministerial accountability, of the kind that [a Secretary of State] and others now very rightly reject, by saying well [a national scandal] isn't the Minister's fault. You get away from that because if somebody escapes from a job centre without a job the relevant chief executive is directly responsible, he can be held to account and it's accepted that he can be held to account and it's not something over which you then get ministerial dodging ...

At the local level the responsiveness, the accountability is vastly increased because you can get the local MP going to his local job centre or whatever it might be, and saying, 'Hey, you didn't do the right thing by my constituent', and getting a very direct answer without going up and down through all the filters. That again seems to me to be an increase in responsiveness and accountability, not to Parliament, but to the public, it's Citizens' Charter territory, which is a good thing. We tend to confuse accountability with looking after money as opposed to thinking about what's the policy of what we're doing to people ...

The traditional doctrine of accountability has been that civil servants are responsible first and foremost to their ministers, not to the Government, and not to the public, certainly not to the public because they might start being bloody-minded and individual and want to do things to help the public that ministers don't believe they should do. I think that setting up agencies to serve the public, coupled with a Citizens' Charter, actually gets behind that quite a lot and certainly people out in job centres will see their responsibility as being first and foremost towards the clients that they are serving and not towards ministers. (Interview)

These views are quoted at length to show the almost blase attitude to the breathtaking changes that are taking place in British public administration. The structure and operations of the public sector are in the process of being transformed, but the essential powers of the centre and of ministers are being retained, so in Whitehall terms it can viewed as a little tinkering round the edges. From the perspective of senior officials, Whitehall is implementing changes that will enhance accountability, any problems that MPs discover are routine matters it is within the power of Parliament to rectify itself: they are of little concern to the civil service, which sees traditional lines of accountability being maintained and augmented.

The introduction of various Citizens' Charters are designed to provide the citizen qua customer some redress over the services delivered by public officials, but this is a means of supplementing public accountability which bypasses Parliament. The Charters may be seen as an attempt by John Major to 'bolt on' a measure of accountability to the reforms initiated by Mrs Thatcher, but they treat citizens as pseudo-customers, it is the accountability of the market-place. They are a weak and colourless substitute for properly constituted legislative oversight.

AGENCIES, MINISTERS AND DEPARTMENTS

For officials the major changes come in the relationship of the parent department to the new agencies. Clearly the agencies are part of the departmental structure. An impervious division between policy-making and implementation cannot be made; indeed the Fraser report of the Efficiency Unit recognised this, and was in turn approvingly quoted by the Treasury and Civil Service Committee of the Commons, which warned against any artificial distinction between policy and execution (1991, para 36). The Frazer report argued that as *Next Steps* evolved departments needed to formulate a 'clear statement of their evolving role and the part their agencies play in the delivery of their policy objectives' and that this is allied to a consideration as to 'how best they can support Ministers in their roles in relation to Agencies' (paras 2.10–2.12). This is a goal that brought forth the retort from the TCSC that the Treasury and Cabinet Office should themselves work out the role of the centre of government regarding the burgeoning agencies (ibid.).

The Price Waterhouse survey of Executive Agencies showed that the relationship between new agencies and the parent department claimed much of the time of senior agency managers and that these contacts were 'dominated' by budget discussions (1991, p.9). This reflects the partly blurred lines of accountability in that both the agency's Chief Executive and the department's Permanent Secretary are the responsible accounting officers, answerable to both Parliament and the Minister. As civil servants all departmental and agency officials are subject to the Armstrong Memorandum and are therefore wholly accountable to the Minister for everything they do. Davies and Willman call it 'perverse' of the authors of *Next Steps* to say that agency managers must 'be prepared to show real qualities of leadership' when fettered by the old constraints of ministerial responsibility and that the report (and indeed subsequent official papers) have been 'wholly inadequate in dealing with this dilemma' (1991, p. 26). They argue that:

> The role of civil servants and of Ministers needs redefinition before responsibility for management can be devolved. Otherwise Agencies are trapped in a dilemma between independence, which is essential to the Next Steps interpretation of good management, and accountability. Their structure has been determined by a constitutional convention which no longer works. (Ibid., pp.27–8)

As such, they argue attention needs to be given to the four main roles that a department plays in relation to its agencies, namely those of 'the provision of a policy framework, target-setting, resource allocation, and monitoring' (ibid.).

These would be fair criticisms if it had been the government's goal to wholly set the officials free, or to liberate technical expertise within the civil service; that is, to allow an extension of professional power. For those who would benefit by such a move, the Davies and Willman interpretation is valid. As this and the previous chapter has sought to explain, whilst sections of the civil service have sought to promote themselves as professionals, and ministers have harnessed that dynamic, the Conservatives' primary goal has been to control the bureaucrats. To this end efficiency, effectiveness and managerial competence have been weapons in the campaign. The thought that agency chiefs should be free to pursue their own ends is as much anathema to ministers as it is to permanent secretaries. Agency freedom *per se* is in any case a chimera. The whole purpose of *Next Steps* was to recognise and promote flexibility; as such each department has to organise its relations with agencies to best suit its goals.

This means that a department like Employment, which has responsibility for statutory Non-departmental Public Bodies, like the Health and Safety Executive and the Advisory Conciliation and Arbitration Service, will have a more federal and decentralised tradition within which to set its agencies than, say, Social Security which has been more centralist and hierarchical. Agencies within departments that have a history of federal relationships have, therefore, tended to evolve a more decentralised relationship themselves. An official from a department with a decentralised tradition argued that this has been carried over into the management of that Department's Next Steps Agencies and that:

> We have certain Group policies, particularly relating to personnel and common standards on things like IT where we need to have compatible systems. But on things like purchasing it is all pushed out and done by individual [Agencies], even though we might get some economies of scale by pulling everybody in. It does militate against some efficiencies and it's a deliberate policy that comes under review and scrutiny from time to time, when we bump up against a particularly silly case. But on the whole we think the pay-off is in allowing management devolution and people to feel responsible for their own thing and to tailor things to their own needs ... We have set [an Agency] targets for the business and we are not going to stand in the way. I compare in particular what we are doing with what's happening in the [another Department] and its agencies. I sit on [their managing board] and I think they are very much more dirigiste, centralist; very much more managerial. The Permanent Secretary chairs the board on which the heads of their Agencies sit and he is giving them all orders of a kind which we have just not seen [another Grade One] giving to our Agency Chief Executives. (Interview)

Yet this official's department, whilst giving agencies a great deal of managerial freedom, set tough performance indicators and retained tight control over the central programme budget. It was this that was turned into a way of controlling the agencies as they had to bid for funds to carry out work. That is, they were converted from being departmental divisions into captive contractors with only limited power over resources other than that which the central department and ministers felt able to devolve.

Performance indicators have been chosen as one of the tools of measuring agency success. They have been integral to Whitehall's managerial reform since the inception of FMI and act as a surrogate for the private sector's profit motive. Performance indicators are usually enshrined within the framework document and are negotiated between the Treasury, the parent department and the agency. Whilst they may be restructured, performance and other payments are often triggered by them and re-negotiation is not encouraged as they are in any case periodically reviewed. Each agency has a set of indicators peculiar to it and these relate to general goals such as recovering costs (the National Engineering Laboratory) to placing a set number of the unemployed in work within the financial year (Employment Agency). Most agencies have about half a dozen indicators.

The ability to measure and report on things is the key element of performance indicators. There are major problems in persuading officials that what has been selected is the right thing to measure and also that the right target has been set. Chief Executives (and the Treasury) are conscious that the National Audit Office will comment upon the performance measurements in its annual report, as indeed will the agency itself. One official was candid about the problems encountered in one part of government with an oversight and commercial policing role:

> As a fascinating example, [a department] in the early days of FMI were looking at performance measures and they had a set of priorities for their inspectorate. The first priority was the discovery of major frauds and the sixth priority was the routine visits to [traders]. The measurement system showed that what got reported on a week in week out basis was the routine visits, so that was where all the effort went – that which was being measured, and it was easy to measure it, easy to record it, easy to report it and easy to show success.
>
> The other issue is the quality of the reporting. It's a set of ... statements, assuming it's a well-drawn-up set of statements, that has to be an accurate and truthful reporting of the state of that organisation. What it does not do is let you know whether the underlying financial management is good or bad. It doesn't let you measure in the absolute sense the reasons why you may have a good performance, it may be something fortuitous or it may be something due to very hard and solid work ... Well, you may report that you've achieved break-even, which was your target; that may be an accurate report. But if you go in and do a value for money study, you may say that break-even wasn't good enough, they could have done far better, or break-even was a magnificent thing to do in the circumstances. What concerns me is that by establishing targets and performance measures for agencies and publishing them on an annual basis, that will set our agenda for review. (Interview)

The fear that, by setting performance indicators, officials will skew their performance to meet those measures, rather than the needs of the agency, is one that was voiced by many officials throughout Whitehall. Although most also tended to agree with the argument of an official who had considerable experience in establishing Agencies, when he said that:

Next Steps has improved and sharpened up target setting generally throughout Whitehall immensely, but there is still a long way to go in getting it right. The Treasury has been developing guidance ... Most of the early targets have been financially driven because they are in many ways the easiest to come up with first. But even quality of service targets can often be made measurable, through things like turn round times. The more difficult ones are the ones where the quality of the Agency's performance is not measured in terms of the speed with which the decision is made, an example is the Planning Inspectorate. Speed is not necessarily the best guide here, how do you measure the quality of a Planning Inspector's judgement? It is an area where Whitehall will learn by experience. Ministers set the targets each year and we will learn through a series of trade-offs. It is better to have some targets rather than no targets at all. (Interview)

Thus speaks the authentic voice of a pragmatic Whitehall Mandarin, promising that, although there are some 'difficulties' in the policy departments and in terms of measuring quality, the civil service will 'muddle through'.

Dunsire, Hartley and Parker actually attempted to test the belief that privatisation or a move to agency status could improve performance, but, after examining performance indicators and attempting to measure actual performance, came to the conclusion that their results were 'as cloudy and perplexing' as those reported elsewhere and that 'life is rather more complicated than the prescriptive theories assume' (1991, p.38). Once again the truth that departments (or bureaus to use the Public Choice terminology) are complex organisations that vary over time and place has tended to complicate attempts to measure the rhetoric of reform. The complex motivations of those employed within the public sector, the inherent difficulties of their occupations and the public interest constraints they work under, severely limit attempts to introduce pseudo-markets using private sector management theory. On the whole this is recognised by the officials themselves, if not always by ministers, and there is an attempt to include quality measures in the framework documents. But here officials will find themselves pushed back onto questions of a utilitarian nature and the problem of measuring happiness, an enigma cost-benefit analysis once sought to address, the results of which were contemptuously dismissed by Self as 'nonsense on stilts' (1970).

Carter has noted that earlier attempts to introduce performance indicators met the criticism that they often ignored effectiveness, efficacy, equity, quality and consumer concerns (1991, p.90). Performance, therefore, 'is a complex and contestable concept ... whether or not an organisation has the benefit of a bottom-line' (ibid., p.99). For *Next Steps* agencies the questions of performance indicators will be centred on whether they can 'become recognised as instruments of democratic accountability' and come to be seen as ways of making governments answerable to Parliament (ibid., p.100). As such if *Next Steps* is to facilitate democratic, or rather parliamentary accountability then it must signal the end of the old form of ministerial responsibility and usher forth a greater role for the legislature. The most effective way in which this could take place would be for parliamentary committees to become involved in the setting of performance indicators and the restructuring of framework documents, leading to chief executives becoming the only accounting officers of their agencies, answerable to Parliament.

It is doubtful if this will occur. Agencies operate according to the rules of the Armstrong Memorandum, subject to the whim of ministerial control, Ministers are not anxious to tamper with this. In any case the purpose of *Next Steps* is not to diminish ministerial control of the executive and hand it over to the legislature. On the contrary, the agency concept is designed to strengthen the hand of the government in its dealings with the permanent members of the executive. Commentators who fail to appreciate this point miss the whole purpose of *Next Steps* from the perspective of the Conservative Government. It is in this evasion of parliamentary interference, contempt of the 'professionals' for constitutional practice and desire by ministers for strengthened control, that the essence of the UK's managerial reforms at the centre of government can be seen most clearly. Even the Citizens' Charter is designed to by-pass Parliament, reinforcing the individual citizen directly against executive malpractice. There are some obvious similarities with the US experience, but there are even more dissimilarities. The American tradition of checks and balances, underpinned by a written constitution policed by the courts and enforced by a powerful and independent legislature means that the executive-dominated British system, the very 'tyranny' the old colonies overturned, is carefully guarded against. As such, attempts to control American bureaucracy have followed a somewhat different path to that of the United Kingdom. It is to these issues that the next chapter turns.

4   Managing Federal Bureaucrats

> One highly respected career executive with experience in OMB and other agencies told of one of the Carter (political) appointees coming into a meeting early in the administration and saying, 'We hate you guys.' These Carter appointees came to do battle with the bureaucratic behemoth. (Pfiffner, 1988, p.93)

> In the last decade, we have seen Presidents Carter and Reagan successfully run anti-Washington, anti-government campaigns for the highest office in the land ... The public seems to forget that America's civil servants have been responsible for some of America's most important advances as a people, as a society and a civilization. It was a civil servant who stood her ground against the use of the drug thalidomide, and saved thousands of our kids from horrible deformities. It was a civil servant who discovered sonar and radar, which protect travelers and our very national defense. It was a civil servant who was instrumental in developing safe vaccines for polio, measles, rubella. It was a civil servant who invented the first modern computer. It was a civil servant who helped develop resistant strains of rice that now feed hungry children in emerging nations. They are the first to help in natural disasters here and around the world. And it was a civil servant who took the first step on the moon, and civil servants who gave their lives in the Challenger disaster. (Hon. Gerry Sikorsky (Chair), to the Subcommittee on Civil Service of the Committee on Post Office and Civil Service, June 28 1989, House of Representatives).

INTRODUCTION

For federal civil servants labouring under the 'anti-establishment' disdain of President Carter, the election of the anti-state President Reagan appeared merely a continuation of the old order. To those undergoing sustained attack one enemy can seem much like another. The motivation for the objurgation, however, had undergone an ideological transformation; whereas Carter was by nature a liberal-democratic managerialist who chided the federal bureaucrats for waste, sloth and inefficiency, Reagan was simply anti-state. In this respect President Reagan shared a New Right perspective on government with Mrs Thatcher, but unlike the UK, where this had led to a fundamental restructuring of the civil service's culture and organisation after 1980, in the US the elected politicians were content to control the federal bureaucracy with a combination of extensive politicisation and malign neglect. There is no American counterpart to *Next Steps*. In some ways the growth of the federal bureaucracy had predated and prophesied *Next Steps*. The multiplicity of executive and regulatory commissions and their close ties with private sector organisations was something that Grant McConnell (1966) dealt with more than twenty-five years ago; the introduction of innovatory 'sunset' laws was an attempt to prevent the perpetuation of such agencies. There are clear lessons here for the British.

Americans have always been ambivalent about the role of the federal bureaucracy. Even though the subject of the administration was addressed in *The Federalist Papers*, the Constitution is strangely silent about the structure and role of the federal service, referring only to 'executive departments' (O'Toole, Jr, 1987, p.17). Whereas those following Hamilton sought a strong federal executive able to give social and economic guidance to the US, others were more inclined to jealously protect the role of the states and curb the executive through the strength of the Congress. With few notable exceptions (which included the Civil War), the views of the latter group have generally prevailed (ibid.). Much of the development of the federal service has reflected the difficulty of maintaining the separation of powers inherent to the political system, in the light of the increase in the size and influence of the civil service (sometimes referred to as the rise of the administrative state). Yet sophisticated administrative systems are an adjunct to modern industrial nations. Americans have had to struggle with the need for such a structure, whilst reconciling its existence with their decentralised and predominantly ideologically liberal political system. At no stage in the development of the American polity have centralising challenges (from either Left or Right) come close to determining the political agenda. Though at various times strong or self-obsessed leaders like F.D. Roosevelt and Nixon have attempted to challenge the separation of powers. The development of the federal civil service, therefore, has to a large extent been predetermined by the prevailing ideological orthodoxy of the Republic (see for example, Hellinger and Judd, 1991).

Wilson's 1887 article, *The Study of Administration*, attempted to define the role and organisation of the bureaucracy. Its values were to be effectiveness, efficiency and economy, with the process of administration being sundered from the political (Conant, 1988, p.892). That is, policy-making ought to remain the proper preserve of democratically elected politicians and their appointees, whilst the implementation (or execution) of those policies was the duty of career bureaucrats. These issues have already been dealt with in an earlier chapter, but the result of the debate underlines that the approaches the British and Americans took were closer to each other than to those of continental European countries. There grew up a belief in the need to separate administration from politics, and politics from any absolutist tendencies. To this end the separation of powers, identified by Eighteenth Century English writers as essential to the preservation of liberty, assumed a preeminence in the US. Barry Karl has even argued that the framers of the Constitution had rebelled against George III because of his failure 'to become the hero of their Republican ideal' (1987, p.26)! Both the UK and the US 'came to believe in the most fundamental kind of separation of powers in their political systems', in that they instigated the separation of political power from institutions 'concerned with the search for truth', either religious or scientific (Price, 1983, p.150).

In Britain such a separation has been more honoured in the breach. In America it is the arena where the Presidency and Congress (and competing elites) often meet to haggle and sometimes duel over the governance of the Union.

The rest of this chapter will examine these issues. After first analysing the early developments in the federal civil service, briefly tracing the reforms of the Eighteenth and Nineteenth Centuries, there is a review of the modern attempts to expand Presidential control over the bureaucracy whilst also trying to improve its delivery of goods and services. There follows a discussion of the impact of recent Republican Presidents upon the system, especially Ronald Reagan, whose administration came to power explicitly committed to reducing the power, size and scope of the federal civil service. Unlike Mrs Thatcher's cultural revolution regarding the civil service, as continued by her successor Mr Major, Mr Reagan opted for an incremental approach to reform. His decision to politicise the federal service and hack away at the edges had more to do with the reality of congressional power than any lackadaisical approach to his New Right manifesto. Mr Bush, however, tended to be more conciliatory towards the federal civil service from the outset of his Presidency.

EARLY GROWTH

The estimated figure for all civilian executive branch personnel in 1992 was 2,887,150 employees (*Government Executive*, April 1991, pp.28–32). This included 1,169,645 people in civilian agency employment (the civil service 'proper' in Western European terms), plus 942,184 civilian personnel employed in defence work and 775,321 postal service employees (ibid.). Under Presidents Reagan and Bush the federal workforce had grown by 43,000 (1980–1990); the typical employee in 1990 was 42 and earned about $32,000 per year. It is a picture of a federal service that the Founding Fathers would have found difficult to comprehend. Yet this is only a tiny part of the public sector; most public sector employees in the US are to be found in the states, each of which replicates the federal separation of powers and staffs its own administration. In some of the larger states like California, Texas and New York, the public sector budget is considerably more than the GNP in many developing nations; this subject is returned to in chapter 6.

It is this extensive number of public sector employees that has given rise to the term 'the administrative state'. Yet for the first 150 years of the Republic the federal bureaucracy was very small, numbering only about 3,000 at the end of the Federalist period, marked by the election of Andrew Jackson and the Democrats (Wilson, 1986, p.125). By the time of the Pendleton Act (also known as the Civil Service Act of 1883), there were still only about 95,000 federal officials and most of them were postal workers (ibid.). The Founders left to Congress the matter of how the heads of the executive departments were to be appointed, held accountable and removed from office. In the event the only point of contention within Congress was the manner of removing the departmental heads. Eventually the President was given the sole right of removal by the slimmest of margins, the casting vote of Vice President John Adams (ibid., p.126). If the vote had gone the other way the civil service could have become a 'legal dependency' of the legislature and the development of the federal administration would have been very different (ibid.). Indeed, something akin to the British doctrine of 'ministerial accountability' may have evolved in order to efficiently implement the policies of Congress: Secretaries of State reporting directly to the legislature instead of to the President and Congress. As it is, the issue of the President's right to remove public officials is still periodically challenged and there is a long list of court cases testifying that this is a battle the Chief Executive continues to fight from time to time.

The original departments followed the laissez-faire example of their British counterparts and were small, with limited duties. The State Department, the first to be created, consisted of the Secretary of State and nine officials, whilst the War Department did not exceed eighty employees until 1801 (ibid.). It was the steady advance of the frontier, population and industrialisation which led the growth of the civil service, but the major periods of bureaucratic expansion were the two World Wars, the Depression and President Johnson's 'Great Society'. The enlargement of the civil service marked a shift away from a Congress-dominated political system to one where power was more equally shared with the Presidency. This allowed the growth of the administrative apparatus to be coordinated and kept accountable to Congress via the President. With the President being the country's chief executive, the Presidency became the major source of policy and legislative coordination, formulation and implementation; he became the Chief Clerk to Congress and the Union (Neustadt, 1980). The slow evolution of this process perfectly illustrates the flexibility of the American political system in coming to terms with the demands of providing both the administrative framework necessitated by nation-building during a period of industrialisation (and post-industrialisation), whilst maintaining the reality of the separation of powers and the accountability of the executive to the legislature. It should not be forgotten, however, that the maintenance of this liberal ideal also involved the use of coercion and repression against 'dissident' groups (Hellinger and Judd, 1991).

The growth of the civil service also led to the phenomenon known as 'clientelism' (sometimes referred to as 'iron triangles'), an aspect of the relationship between the private sector, Congress and bureaucracy that has remained embedded in the workings of the political system (ibid., pp.135–7; Smith, 1988, pp.173–8). Clientelism began with the rapid industrialisation of the country after about 1860, when the government:

> began to give formal, bureaucratic recognition to the emergence of distinctive interests in a diversifying economy. (Wilson, 1986, p.135)

The new departments created after 1860 included Agriculture, Labor and Commerce; they began to devote their resources to the interests of particular economic or producer groups. Interest groups such as the postal workers' unions, the Knights of Labor and the Agricultural Society formed themselves into powerful lobbyists. Not only did they 'capture' the departments responsible for their economic interests, departments which they had in any case often lobbied into existence, they also organised to capture powerful groups within Congress so that the legislature became representative of the dominant economic interests in the country. One should not overemphasise the 'iron triangle' notion of the relationship between Congress and agencies, especially with the rise of what Loomis refers to as 'entrepreneurial' politicians (1988). Whilst the current situation is therefore considerably more complex than a set of triangles, the notion is a useful introduction to a sophisticated subject.

Throughout the Nineteenth Century a pattern emerged which remains at the heart of the political system. It is mainly responsible for the failure of Presidents Reagan and Bush to substantially reduce the size of the public sector in those areas they sought to diminish. Following the example set by the agricultural, labour and postal lobbies, other groups sought similar preferential treatment through a symbiotic relationship with Congress and the federal service. For example, the Grand Army of the Republic laid the foundations for the remarkable levels of aid given to veterns of the armed forces. The organised interests appealed directly to the legislature, sometimes aided by the departments and agencies of the federal service:

> In 1879 Congressmen, noting the number of ex-servicemen living (and voting) in their states, made veterans eligible for pensions retroactively to the date of their discharge from the service ... in 1890 the law was changed to make it unnecessary to have been injured in the service – all that was necessary was to have served. (Ibid., p.136)

In this way the 'pattern of bureaucratic clientelism was set' and rapidly developed (ibid.). By the election of President Reagan there were myriad groups operating in iron triangles at state and federal levels. The major lobbies remained agriculture, commerce and labour (although Reagan was to weaken substantially their grip on the public purse), plus the military/industrial complex and the civil rights groups.

FROM SPOILS TO PENDLETON

The election of Andrew Jackson in 1828 was heralded by Democratic Senator William Marcy's slogan, 'To the victor belong the spoils of the enemy' (Nelson, 1986, p.173). General Jackson's victory was seen as bringing to an end the first era of the Republic, dominated by the aristocratic Founding Fathers and the Federalists. It brought forth the period of party politics and its supporters believed it democratised the political system. It had a profound effect upon the civil service in that all the top positions were opened up to the political appointees of Jackson's Democratic Party, the incumbents of the former regime being obliged to vacate office.

The early civil service was dominated by 'kinship and class' (ibid., p.172) with most members of the federal government and senior office holders being from upper class families and owing their appointment as much to social position as managerial skill. Even though Presidents Jefferson and Adams practised a limited form of political patronage, pointing out, not unreasonably, that they could not be expected to wait for everyone to die or resign before appointing their people to office, many of the senior federal servants asserted a property and inheritance right to their offices, a practice inherited from colonial days. Jackson swept all this away, claiming it was corrupt and perverse (ibid., pp.136–7). In eight years he removed 252 federal officers, more than the combined total over forty years of his six predecessors. Yet, whilst he removed nearly all of the advice and consent appointments, Jackson only succeeded in replacing about ten per cent of the total civil service by the end of his second term (Case, 1986, p.286). Along with the institution of the spoils system, however, came a potential for corruption that was to lead for further calls for dramatic reform. The corruption was blatant from the start, in that:

> After professional consultants laboured in Andy Jackson's 1828 campaign, they were rewarded with government jobs. When the next campaign rolled around, these government employees gave kickbacks to the party to keep their jobs. (Boyle, 1991, p.247)

Apart from the modern illegality of such kickbacks, the practice of rewarding loyal election and party workers with jobs in federal bureaucracy has become firmly entrenched. Although there is now a distinction between career and non-career officials, the increasing use of political appointees at ever lower levels in the bureacracy is a method adopted by recent presidents to control the civil service. The managerial, indeed political naivety of some appointees was a major cause of the problems experienced by both Carter and Reagan. President Bush, however, appeared to have learned the lessons of his predecessor, a subject returned to in a later section.

The nepotism and corrupt abuses of the spoils system became the object of reformers' zeal, reaching tragi-farce proportions when President Garfield was assassinated by a disgruntled office seeker (Charles Guiteau) in 1881. Reformers were now able to claim that the spoils system 'equalled murder' and in 1883 after renewed pressure Congress passed the Pendleton Act to bring a measure of control to the system of appointments (Case, 1986, p.287). The Act created a Civil Service Commission that designed and implemented a system of appointments based on merit and fitness for service for those who joined designated career grades. Henceforth applicants would be subject to a common system of competitive examinations. The agitation which led to the Act was influenced by the changes taking place in European bureaucracies, with the British Northcote-Trevelyan reforms being particularly influencial. Congress, however, specifically eschewed the British example and established the new merit system:

> in such a way as to make it impossible to imitate the key principles of the British system, which were designed to insure a tightly disciplined officer corps cutting across the upper levels of all the ministries and dedicated to lifetime careers. The new American merit system was designed to prevent the development of an elite corps and to make it possible for candidates to enter the service at any age. It forbade the creation of a separate category of officers for the higher grades and made it impossible to establish any educational requirements except ... in scientific of professional categories. (Price, 1983, pp. 76–7)

Although the pay and grading system which eventually emerged created a relatively unified service, America thus forsook a second opportunity to establish an integrated tightly organised civil service, this time in order to preserve each job as a separate entity. This had the effect of preventing a disciplined coordination of policy and made the role of the Presidency that much more important, although it was to be the acceptance of the Brownlow Report in 1937 which provided the impetus for the expanded Presidency.

The Pendleton Act, however, did establish a uniquely American framework which made way for merit as well as political placements within the framework of the separation of powers (O'Toole, Jr, 1987, p.19). In the period prior to Pendleton, the Congress and the Presidency had fought each other over appointments to the civil service; neither could afford to relax its grip for fear of the other filling the administration with its partisan supporters. As time went on and the public sector expanded, this process became overly time-consuming. Civil service reform relieved the pressure on both branches of government simultaneously over a period of some years, allowing Congress to concentrate on its oversight role and for the first time recognising the President as the 'active head' of the administration (ibid.). The Act also allowed an inchoate politics/administration interface to evolve and be in place for the next phase of reform, of which Wilson's plea for an explicit boundary between the two formed a part. Pendleton, therefore, provided for the pursuit of Presidential-executive leadership and neutral competence (ibid., p.20). The growing propensity towards political neutrality in the bureaucracy combined with the growth of the civil service (and therefore the President's role in heading it) to usher in the next period of managerial reform, which occurred during the inter-war years.

FROM NEW DEAL TO NEW RIGHT: BROWNLOW TO REAGAN

The period of most rapid growth in the size and power of the civil service began with World War One, accelerated through the Depression, F.D. Roosevelt's New Deal and World War Two, before expanding into the fully fledged Welfare State of President Johnson's Great Society programme. It ground almost to a halt, but did not tip over into decline, under Presidents Reagan and Bush. Throughout this period reformers attempting to impose a management structure and political control have tried various tacks. The first of these was the report by the Brownlow Commission in 1937, at the height of New Deal Democratic America.

Reporting during a period of unprecedented unemployment, at a time when much of Europe was being subjugated by totalitarian regimes, the authors of the Brownlow Report were conscious of the need for government in modern industrial nations to set an example, indeed to take steps to provide for the reasonable expectations of the citizenry. The civil service was the organisational means by which this could be done, yet in the US the President was unable to manoeuvre the executive to act decisively. The Committee fretted about the dominance of Congress and the 'inability of legislatively controlled governments to get things done', as, 'without results democracy means nothing and ceases to be alive in the minds and hearts of men' (quoted in Conant, 1988, p.893). The committee summarised the problems of the machinery of government by noting:

> the effectiveness of the chief executive is limited and restricted, in spite of the clear intent of the Constitution to the contrary;... the work of the executive branch is badly organised;... the managerial agencies are weak and out of date;... the public service does not include its share of men and women of outstanding capacity and character; and the fiscal and auditing systems are inadequate. (Ibid.)

The observation regarding personnel recruitment and retention was to be self-consciously echoed fifty years later by the Volker Commission, reporting under President Reagan.

By 1936 there were over 100 separate federal agencies reporting to the President. Brownlow found this intolerable and recommended re-structuring the civil service to modernise the organisation and implementation of government business (ibid.; Moe, 1987a, p.45). The Committee argued there were general managerial rules or principles which ought to be followed; one of these related to reducing the President's span of control by rationalising the structure of the civil service. Again there was an emphasis on efficiency, effectiveness and economy; indeed, Thomas argues there was something of an 'efficiency craze' in the US at the time (1978, p.198). Interestingly, much of the criticism levelled at the bureaucracy has been repeated by both the Thatcher and Reagan/Bush governments, although the prescriptions for change have, of course, been considerably different. Brownlow also sought a greater degree of centralisation in order to effect improvements in service delivery.

The main specific recommendation of the Committee was the establishment of the Executive Office of the President, and twelve departments 'into which the independent agencies, regulatory commissions, and government corporations would be assigned' (Moe, 1987a, p.45). A hierarchical structure would be created in order to allow staff and line functions to be effectively maintained and policy instructions efficiently and effectively implemented, via a clear system of executive accountability which flowed out and down from the President. An increase in the merit system was envisaged, along with more effective use of career officials, many of whom were to be promoted to higher line agency 'leadership positions' (ibid.). The general acceptance of the Report and its implementation by Congress and Roosevelt laid the foundations for the modern Presidency and the major expansion of the civil service up to the time of Reagan, an expansion made necessary by the demands of war and welfare. Yet many of Brownlow's lessons have either been forgotten, or else wilfully misconstrued, as Moe argues:

> there is little interest in and even less respect for the subject of organisational management. The prevailing view held by those of all political persuasions is that organisational management is old fashioned box-shuffling and that 'principles' of organisation and management are best left to public administration textbooks, not to be followed in the world of real politics. (1987, p.46)

In a sense Moe is only partly correct, in that within the recent New Right governments of America there is enormous respect accorded to the managerial views of the private sector. It is public sector management that has been derided as mere 'public administration', with its prescriptions being overruled by the impetus toward political appointees being directed down into the very bowels of the civil service in order to oversee the implementation of policy.

The movement that gave rise to the Brownlow Report and ensured its general acceptance also spawned the Hatch Act. Passed in 1939 by a coalition of Republicans and anti-New Deal Democrats, the Hatch Act 'tightened the prohibitions on the political activity of federal employees' (Boyle, 1991, p.252). In 1942 this was extended to state and local government employees. The Act was strictly enforced by the Civil Service Commission, which did not shirk its duty to dismiss (or insist subnational governments dismiss) any public sector employee found engaging in any partisan political activity whatsoever. Occasionally this reached absurd levels, as when a Mr Archie Cole, a rural mailcarrier, was dismissed on the grounds that his membership of the Jehova's Witnesses constituted political activity, as they were opposed to war and therefore criticised the government (ibid., p.274). Such fierceness, however, ought also to be viewed as part of the constant vigilance of the American elites to prevent the growth of ideological challenges to the political culture of the nation (Hellinger and Judd, 1991). The attempts of reformers to secure a politically neutral civil service, therefore, sought to stymie all partisan activities and appeared at times to threaten the free speech of federal employees.

In a sense it was also self-defeating as, lacking any solid evidence, presidents tended simply to assume that the bureaucracy they inherited from their predecessor, particularly if he represented the other major party, was politically hostile and acted accordingly (Pfiffner, 1988, pp.90–5). It was to answer this Presidential criticism that Congress created Schedule C positions near the top of the career bureaucracy for President Eisenhower, after his election ended two decades of Democratic rule. These were specifically allowed to be political appointees designed to supplement the more usual patronage positions at the top of departments and agencies. The need for them was felt to reflect Republican suspicions that the bureaucracy was riddled with New Deal Democrats, despite the workings of the Hatch Act, and that the level of political appointment would have to go below the traditional career level GS 16. It was envisaged that these appointments were to be of a confidential or policy-making kind, made at agency head discretion and not subjected to the usual merit requirements (ibid.). The governments of Reagan and Bush were to take the principle of Schedule C appointments and push it much further in order to more fully politicise the implementation of their policies. This is a point returned to in a later section of this chapter.

The evolution of the federal civil service entered something of a pattern, with Republican presidents seeking to control the system through greater political control which may (as in Nixon) or may not (as in Eisenhower) also mean attempts at major structural reform, whilst Democratic presidents nearly always sought to combine greater political control with managerial innovation. The common denominator for presidents of all persuasions was their desire to improve their ability to make the civil service politically accountable. Sometimes the Congress would collude in this, more often it would not, fearing that an over-mighty Presidency would emerge from successful attempts to harness the power of the administration to a single office. The lesson of the Nixon Presidency is that if the potential for abuse exists then individuals will be tempted to subvert the democratic process; this was underlined when it was revealed that ethically scrupulous civil servants refused to bow to an order to audit the tax returns of the President's Democratic opponents (ibid.).

For Nixon's staff this merely confirmed suspicions that the bureaucracy was riddled with their partisan opponents.

The direct result of Nixon's Presidency was the election of Jimmy Carter who, true to Democratic form sought to restructure the civil service. Despite the evidence that the civil service was an ethical check on the activities of the previous administration, Carter ran for office as an avowed outsider, critical of the 'Washington establishment'. He told a meeting of his party:

> Our government in Washington now is a horrible bureaucratic mess ... we must give top priority to a drastic and thorough reorganization of the federal bureaucracy. (Quoted in Pfiffner, ibid., p.93)

Mr Carter was using the word 'bureaucracy' in its pejorative rather than political science sense. His remedy for the evils of the 'horrible bureaucratic mess' was the Civil Service Reform Act (CSRA).

There were eight provisions in the original proposal, and although these were somewhat modified during the passage of the Bill, they give an indication of Carter's aims:

1. The abolition of the Civil Service Commission and the creation of the Office of Personnel Management, the Merit Systems Protection Board, and the Federal Labour Relations Authority.
2. New and stronger provisions for the protection of whistleblowers.
3. Limitations on veteran's preference for non-disabled veterans (this provision did not pass).
4. The creation of performance evaluation systems, the purpose being to increase productivity and to establish a link between performance pay and federal managers.
5. Creation of merit pay system for mid-level managers which, in conjunction with the new performance evaluation systems, would reward excellent performers with financial bonuses.
6. Creation of the Senior Executive Service. This component of the reform was intended to create a top level of elite generalist managers, on the model of the British higher civil service. Membership of the SES would become part of a rank-in-person system, would compete for financial rewards, would be eligible for training and development opportunities, and would participate more actively in policy formu-

lation and design activities. Ten per cent of the total SES positions government-wide was open to political appointees.
7. The creation of a new Research and Development Authority, which was intended to foster innovation and creativity in federal organisations and personnel.
8. The original package reaffirmed the government's commitment to affirmative action and equal opportunities, embracing the concept of a socially representative bureaucracy (all of the above eight points are taken from Ingraham and Rosenbloom, 1988, pp.311–12).

Much contained in points three to six would have found favour with those responsible for the British reforms begun two years later; indeed, there was much in Carter's approach that die-hard Republicans in the Congress found to their liking. As was noted at the start of this chapter, those civil servants who served under Nixon, Carter and Reagan, found little difference in the Presidential approach to career officials. One long-serving federal official argued:

> You should know a couple of things, we have now had several Presidents in a row who became President in part through what we, as civil servants, consider to be civil service or Washington bashing. Reagan was by no means the first. Jimmy Carter before him had been very much an outsider and proud of it. Carter had been laudatory with regard to the role of outsiders and the opposite with regard to the role of insiders, meaning in large part the role of the civil service. (Interview)

In seeking to enshrine political neutrality and managerial excellence within the bureaucracy, Carter's loathing of the Washington elite was transformed into as caustic a set of dealings with officials as any undertaken by the New Right Republicans who followed him.

The provisions of the Bill were a result of deliberations by the President's Reorganization Committee (PRC), established and chaired by Carter himself, although much of the detailed work was carried out by the President's Personnel Management Project (Ingraham and White, 1988, pp.317–19). The PRC quickly concluded that the federal service was unnecessarily complex, unrepresentative of society, inefficient and unaccountable, unable to reward merit and excellent performance, and unable to provide sound policy advice at its top levels for politicians (ibid.). The CSRA sought to remedy these dysfunctional elements of the bureaucracy, simultaneously providing politicians with better policy advice from the permanent officials, training and rewarding those officials according to performance or merit, and establishing a better line of command to implement policy decisions and hold the bureaucracy accountable. Integral to this was an attempt to improve managerial efficiency using the latest techniques (such as zero-based budgeting) transferred from the private sector and Mr Carter's period as Governor of the state of Georgia. Carter delighted in the minutiae of policy management, and through his detailed planning on the CSRA hoped to work the same root and branch reforms on the nation that he believed he had implemented in Georgia.

The establishment of the Senior Executive Service (SES) held the greatest promise of effective reform. It was to :

> provide each new administration with a broad set of managerial tools that it can use to control the bureaucracy and achieve its policy goals. (Pfiffner, 1988, p.104)

In part the reform addressed the likelihood that the supergrades, that is the most senior officials at GS level 16–18, would have their greatest loyalty to their own programmes and agencies, rather than the goals of democratically elected politicians; a peculiarly Public Choice viewpoint for members of the Democratic Party. The CSRA sought to give greater personnel control to political executives, providing them with the authority to appoint their own top officials without having to get political appointees at the GS 16–18 level reviewed by the Civil Service Commission, or its successor the Merit Systems Protection Board. Political executives were given the flexibility to assign either career or non-career officials to most SES positions and to reassign SES members within an agency, a feat made more straightforward now that grade was vested in the person and not the post. Furthermore, the instigation of performance indicators and annual review made it easier for top managers to discipline poorly performing officials, even to remove them from the SES altogether, whilst rewarding excellence with merit payments or promotions. The safeguard against politically inspired vindictiveness was the proviso that 'career executives cannot be reassigned against their wishes or evaluated within 120 days of a new President taking office or a new agency head being appointed' (Pfiffner, 1988, pp.104–6). A new administration is permitted to fill up to ten per cent of the SES positions with its own non-career appointees upon assuming office.

The provisions of the CSRA have been mainly operated by Republican Presidents. The nature of the ideological transformation in the White House with the election of Ronald Reagan made 'tinkering' with the structures of the civil service appear irrelevant; hence the belief that the SES could function in a policy advisory role has not been realised. Other goals have also been deemed to be irrelevant, especially those that involve affirmative action, or any weakening of the grip the elected politicians have sought to exert on the apparatus of government. Yet there has not been the wholesale reform of the civil service under Reagan and Bush that Britain saw under its New Right governments led by Thatcher and Major. It was not a hurricane that blew through the corridors of Washington DC, transforming all it touched and blowing away the detritus of New Deal/New Society welfarism, but more a chill wind that froze the system and allowed politicians to chip away at the edges.

PRESIDENTS REAGAN AND BUSH; THE NEW RIGHT MEN FOR THE JOB

With the election of Mr Reagan on an avowedly liberal/conservative manifesto many on the New Right looked forward to what David Stockman, in his political memoir, called *The Triumph of Politics* (1986). That is, they sought the implementation of the manifesto regardless of the views of the permanent officials and Congress. The Reagan Administration assumed office with a clear set of goals:

1. to reduce the size, scope, and influence of the federal government in American life;
2. strengthen defence;
3. reduce inflation;
4. balance the budget;
5. stimulate economic growth;
6. reaffirm certain traditional moral values (Carroll, 1987, p.107).

In order to achieve these aims, both Reagan and later Bush instigated a series of policies. These have included:

1. budgetary and personnel reductions in the civil service;
2. increases in defence and related agencies, since subjected to cuts with the end of the old Soviet Union;
3. reduction in marginal tax rates as incentives to work, save and invest;

4. tax reform to make the tax code fairer and to reduce tax expenditures as instruments of social and economic policy;
5. regulatory reform through budgetary and personnel reductions in regulatory agencies and increases in powers of the OMB;
6. shifting of responsibility for welfare and other programmes to the states and local governments;
7. shifting regulatory responsibility to sub-national government;
8. the appointment of judges committed to judicial restraint (ibid.).

Cutting across many of these policies was the need to ensure the effective control of the civil service and enforce its compliance to political direction.

Reagan's preparations for taking over the civil service began in earnest before the election. In April 1980 the meticulous planning was initiated by Richard Allen, who headed a team of 132 people divided into twenty-five working groups and 329 people divided into twenty-three issue-area groups (Pfiffner, 1988, p.16). Alongside these policy planners, William Casey, Anne Armstrong, Paul Laxalt, Casper Weinberger and Edwin Meese formed an executive committee, supported by seven deputy directors and an operations group of 100 transition teams that spread across the government after the election but before the official transfer of power (ibid., pp.16–18). The teams were given full access to files and they reported back on the status of agency operations, preparing detailed policy options and briefings for political appointees (ibid.). Pfiffner compared them to 'performing the symbolic function in the bureaucracy of an occupying army', although they also served to reward campaign workers without committing the administration to appointing them to office (ibid.). Hellinger and Judd saw the teams as part of an assault on the bureaucracy:

> composed not of policy experts but of ideological campaign workers, many of them seeking jobs ... they were charged with finding ways of linking various agencies together into a common effort to achieve the conservative agenda ... They gave the Reagan administration briefing books stuffed with recommendations for cutbacks, elimination of programmes, and plans for privatization and deregulation. (1991, p.192)

The teams were of mixed use; some were dismissed as soon as Reagan officially took office, others were appointed to post.

As well as the Cabinet and sub-cabinet appointments (of assistant secretary and above) there were also 700 non-career SES posts and 1,800 Scedule C positions that the Reagan team sought to fill. When he became President, Bush left most of the junior appointments to his agency heads, but the Reagan White House believed that only by carefully vetting the ideological credentials of even junior officials could it be sure of implementing its programme (Pfiffner, 1988). This close scrutiny was an essential ingredient in many of Reagan's early political successes. In some departments Schedule C appointments went down to very low levels in the hierarchy in order to enforce the loyalty of the organisation to the goals of the President. Aberbach has argued that:

> Political appointees in the Reagan administration were both much more Republican and much more conservative than those in the early Nixon administration. The Reagan administration made a concerted effort to recruit and select individuals 'loyal' to the President and his program, especially at the sub-cabinet level. In fact, it filled many sub-cabinet posts before cabinet members were even appointed. (1991, p.407)

This had severe repurcussions within the civil service, with senior career officials being denied any policy-making role during Reagan's first term; indeed, some high ranking career officials, used to giving policy advice, were forbidden to offer policy options and excluded from all but the implementation phase of the policy process. Consequently, they felt that they had 'suffered a sizable loss of influence over policy' (ibid., p.409). In some agencies, such as those with military functions, politicisation was very shallow, but in others it went so deep that one member of Congress observed 'you really can't get a promotion beyond the age of 35' (Schroeder, quoted in *Government Operations*, 1988, p.3406). Even allowing for a politician's hyperbole, the depth of politicisation in 'suspect' and targeted agencies was deliberately extended by the New Right as being the most effective way of controlling the civil service. Furthermore, like Thatcher in Britain, Reagan had learned from the failures of his conservative predecessors in government and was determined not to repeat their mistakes.

CONTROLLING BUREAUCRATS: IMPLEMENTING THE STRATEGY

The abandonment of the Professional and Administrative Careers Examination (PACE) in 1982, as a result of court challenges which showed it to be discriminatory in practice, allowed the federal government to return to a non-competitive and decentralised hiring of many civil servants (Ban and Redd, 1990, p.69; Ban, 1988, pp. 708–16). This was a judicial weakening of the concept of a unified career service based on merit as it allowed people to be appointed on what Ban has termed 'the buddy principle' (ibid., 1990). That is, managers appoint friends to positions of authority. It also further strengthened the position of the Reagan Administration in its purpose of controlling the bureaucracy, by adding to the process of undermining the CSRA's principles and thereby furthered the maintenance of the federal service as a decentralised, polyglot collection of agencies lacking a collective identity.

On assumption of office the Reagan team imposed a freeze on all new appointments to the career service; this was combined with reductions in force and lower personnel ceilings (Pfiffner, 1988, p.94). The 92,000 jobs cut between 1981 and 1983 as a result of this action, however, were offset by increases in the Department of Defense and intelligence agencies. A long-serving senior official in the Department of Health and Human Resources (HHR) remarked that during the entire two terms of President Reagan and the first term of President Bush:

> in areas of policy-making or in activities that are directed toward the implemen-
> tation of new initiaties, new policy goals of an administration (such as for example,
> the bulk of this department) there has been no new hiring. (Interview)

The result was a perceptible ageing of the bureaucracy. When this was combined with the banishment of senior officials from the policy-making process it led to a fall in morale, an issue addressed by the Volker Report.

The staff cuts were ruthlessly implemented, partly using privatisation, a subject returned to in more detail in the next chapter. A senior civil servant observed that the process had continued under three presidents, beginning with Carter, mostly as a cost-cutting exercise, and pursued by Reagan and Bush as an economy measure, but also a means of reducing the size of the government and facilitating managerial control:

> because the long-run costs of the civil service, the retirement programmes, the build-
> up of benefits, are very high. Some of the activities can be achieved at less cost by
> hiring-in firms who are either protected because of their lower benefit system or
> don't charge because of the nature of their contractural relationship with the
> government. This means you can achieve the same functions, quite often, by
> hiring-in private providers. Hence what used to be a blue-collar component of the
> civil service is in a remarkable degree shrivelled and withered. The guards on this
> building are all private contractors, the janitorial service is private sector hourly

waged folk, without any of the perks associated with the bureaucracy. The budget driven component of privatisation is high and to the extent that it can go on in parallel with the appearance of meeting promises to reduce the federal bureaucracy, that is to substitute private for civil service coverage, the Carter, Reagan and Bush Administrations have found this all to the good. (Interview)

The general thrust towards reducing government expenditure included cutting programmes, whole segments of government activities and pushing them away from the federal level and down to the states. Mr Reagan's first budget called for cuts in excess of $48.5 billion (Pfiffner, 1988, p.131). Yet one senior official countered the belief that the federal government's activities have simply been returned to the sub-national level by pointing out that:

> it's not clear to me, even as an analyst, never mind as a knee-jerk liberal democrat, at what level the states want responsibility independent of the cost. They have been pleased to get block grants which had revenue for them under their control; one doesn't have to be Machiavellian to wonder about why that might be the case. One could believe in patronage, one could believe in the power of the purse, all sorts of other things. But states have, by and large, not sought to exercise much of their residual powers under the constitution since the 1930s. (Interview)

As a result of this the public sector *per se* has been reduced in the US, at least with regard to its welfare functions. This important subject is returned to for a more detailed discussion in succeeding chapters.

The Reagan Administration took additional steps to stamp its authority on the federal service. All of the Inspectors General were dismissed, although some were later reappointed following judicial and congressional challenges. The Community Services Administration was wound up, an action that was planned and implemented by its own officials loyally serving the elected politicians. Finally, the Administration sacked all of the air traffic controllers who had voted to strike in 1981, an action that sent a clear message to the civil service unions that the President would brook no opposition (Pfiffner, 1988, p. 94). That these actions were taken early during Reagan's first term reflects the pattern of declining Presidential power analysed by recent observers (Neustadt, 1980; Pfiffner, op. cit.). The longer a President remains in office, the less inclined Congress is to grant him full implementation of his policies. The eighteen month period closest to his election is when he is at his most influential, Congress, in the case of Reagan at that time, being in disarray and inclined to honour the mandate provided by the General Election. Furthermore, the careful preparations by Reagan's team extended to identifying friendly (or amenable) Southern Democrats with whom it was possible to construct bi-partisan coalitions. As time progressed, these advantages began to slip away and something of a familiar American political stalemate developed, with Congress refusing to implement any more welfare cuts (due to constituency pressure) and the President refusing to remove his demands for them.

The contrast to the British New Right reform of the civil service is striking. There was no attempt to change the culture of Washington; Reagan had campaigned (like Carter) as an outsider and simply accepted that he would remain one. There was no attempt at root and branch structural reform. Nixon and then Carter had attempted this and Reagan's team viewed the results of these administrations as wasteful of time and energy, inefficiently using precious political resources, doomed to failure at the outset, unacceptably mutated by Congress and financially costly. Reagan relied upon deep level politicisation and an imposition of private sector management techniques where possible. The latter at least was similar to the Thatcher approach, but then there was nothing new in American presidents seeking to utilise these procedures. Eisenhower, Kennedy, Johnson, Nixon and Carter had all brought people into the government who sought to transplant these techniques to the public sector, for example MacNamara at the Department of Defense, and Carter's own effort to introduce zero based budgeting. The most obvious attempt made by Reagan in this area was the establishment of the Grace Commission, and that was not a noticeable success.

GRACE AND GRACELESSNESS: HOW TO LOSE FRIENDS IN WASHINGTON

The President's Private Sector Survey on Cost Control (known after its Chairman as the Grace Commission) handed its 47 reports to the White House in January 1984. Staffed by private sector secondees, the Commission produced 2,478 recommendations on cost-cutting and management changes to improve the management of the federal executive. The report is dealt with in more detail in the next chapter, but the manner of its preparation and presentation illustrated the contempt for the bureaucracy felt by many in the Reagan Administration. Few civil servants were actively involved in the preparation of the survey and little heed was paid to programmes of reductions already in place.

The White House assigned each of the recommendations to the agencies for implementation, although Grace himself recognised that over seventy per cent of the recommendations would require action by Congress. He accordingly began to lobby on behalf of his report (Bingman, 1986, pp.43–4; Hellinger and Judd, 1991, p.186). In the event only two significant pieces of legislation were actually enacted as a result of the report: the Department of Defense Authorization Act, 1986, and the Congressional First Concurrent Resolution of the Budget Fiscal Year, 1986. The Congressional Caucus established to lobby for the implementation of the recommendations was singularly unsuccessful (Bingman, ibid.). The reasons were fairly obvious. Grace failed to take into account the intensely political nature of many of his recommendations, those which appeared to abrogate previous commitments to civil rights and minority groups were destined to provoke the strongest possible opposition at the outset (Baber, 1987, pp.153–63). The contempt shown for Congress (Mr Grace had some particularly scathing things to say about the legislative process) and the bureaucracy combined with the attacks on welfare programmes to isolate the Grace Commission and condemn its recommendations to limbo. Many of the suggestions were in the process of being implemented by the civil service in any case. The Office of Management and Budget was particularly quick to note the apparent plagiarism of some of its efficiency ideas (various interviews). The lesson here, as in Britain, is that such large-scale and public attempts at reform are unlikely to achieve success. Stealth and incrementalism are often more effective.

THE IMPACT OF THE NEW RIGHT ON THE CIVIL SERVICE

The Volker Commission (National Commission on the Public Service, a private non-profit corporation made up of thirty-seven prominent citizens from across the American political spectrum) was established in 1987 to investigate what Mr Volker called the 'Quiet Crisis'; that is, the low morale of the career officials and a perception that it was becoming difficult to recruit and retain people of a sufficiently high calibre in the federal service, falling real salary levels and decades of political opprobrium being cited as contributory factors. Upon his appointment, Volker said the government:

> in general, and the federal government in particular, is increasingly unable to attract, retain and motivate the kinds of people it will need to do the essential work of the Republic in the years and decades ahead. (*Government Operations*, p.3404)

Congresswoman Schroeder put it more bluntly:

> How can you be surprised about the Pentagon procurement scandal when the guys overseeing those contracts aren't making enough to be able to live in Washington, and the guys receiving the contracts are driving those hotsy-totsy cars with telephones and expense accounts? (Ibid.)

The commission identified five major problems afflicting the federal bureaucracy: public perceptions; compensation; recruitment and retention; political and career service relationships; and education and training (ibid.).

Such was the concern raised by Volker's report that the Merit Systems Protection Board began investigating the views of former federal executives, especially those who had left the SES other than for retirement purposes. It found various reasons as to why executives left the federal service, but the most frequently cited reason was poor pay due to the expenditure restraints imposed by the President (1989, p.1). Yet non-monetary issues also accounted for a great deal of dissatisfaction, with forty-six per cent saying they left because they no longer enjoyed the work and forty-two per cent because they felt their skills had been used inappropriately (ibid.). Seventy per cent of former SES officials believed that the government had failed to establish a mechanism for attracting and retaining highly competent executives, and forty per cent complained of undue political interference amounting to capricious behaviour (ibid.). These former officials held the non-political skills and abilities of political appointees to the SES and Schedule C positions in particularly low regard (ibid.). One member of the SES diplomatically argued that:

> I have worked for at least a dozen political appointees of different shapes and sizes. If I had to take a stab at generalising about that environment, I'd say that we in the United States have trouble recruiting the best that the private sector has to offer. (Interview)

A later survey found similar complaints; in particular officials were concerned that the implementation of merit pay had been inadequately applied and other aspects of their job, such as the quality of training, were falling below acceptable standards (1990, p.37). One very senior member of the SES who had served at the politcal/career grade nexus for twenty years argued that there has been a need to recruit young high flyers and:

nurture the growth of these individuals in a way that prepares them for positions of responsibility at the top of government in a way that transcends the parochialism that is characteristic of various kinds of departments. (Interview)

Such a plea, in effect the emulation of the British or French system for an elite core, has very little chance of ever being passed by Congress, having been repeatedly vetoed in the past. Other problems related to the degree and level of privatisation. The official quoted in an earlier section of this chapter had expressed regret at the demise of the blue-collar civil service, but he was also concerned at the degree of policy and executive work being hived out to the private sector.

Other public servants expressed similar misgivings before the Congressional Committee charged with overseeing these matters. Senator Pryor complained that:

Earlier this month I held a hearing on this very issue [the use of consultants in government] and heard conflicting testimony about what these consultants are really doing for the EPA [Environmental Protection Agency]. If you believe the contract files, consultants are doing the following: researching FOIA requests; drafting memos for top EPA officials; preparing Congressional testimony; drafting internal agreements on behalf of the EPA; writing regulations. However, when you ask EPA officials, they say that the consultants aren't really doing the actual work, they are just 'assisting'. That leaves me with one unanswered question, if the consultants aren't really doing this work, then why are they being paid millions of dollars? (Evidence before the US House Committee on Post Office Civil Service; hearings on contracting at EPA and its effect on federal employees, Feb. 23 1989)

Yet no one should express surprise at the privatisation of large tracts of government work, for that is precisely what the New Right intended. The appointment of private sector (and presumably, ideologically committed) consultants was a feature of both the British and American administrations. Events in both countries have led to questions about the quality of these advisers, especially when they clearly lacked the public service ethic of civil servants. Privatisation of numbers of civil service posts in the US, through pay and hiring restrictions and Executive Orders forcing the contracting out of work, allowed a greater flexibility for senior managers in personnel matters. It also led to a greater degree of budgetary freedom and control, in that private contractors were not eligible for civil service benefits regarding tenure, pay rises, pensions, health and safety regulations and other considerations. Many, including quite senior people, were even employed on short-term contracts or hourly rates. They could be removed from the federal budget at very short notice. Finally, they were not members of one of the powerful public sector unions and therefore this privatisation of the federal government was also a method of disciplining the workforce. The changes made by the New Right, then, allowed the process begun by Carter and his CSRA to continue. It reduced the rigidities of the system and made for greater decentralisation of management through privatisation, whilst strengthening political control and this has led to some abuse of the merit system, particularly in hiring practices (Ban and Redd, 1990).

Recent work by Aberbach, however, does seem to refute some of the more alarmist claims of those who have taken up the banner raised by Volker. Whilst finding some evidence of low morale due to 'bureaucrat bashing' his survey also found that many of those who have left the service have been replaced by people with long service records and high levels of attainment. Indeed, many of the top civil servants in 1987, although younger than those they replaced (compared to the age at which their predecessors were appointed), displayed a high level of education, training, experience and commitment. Aberbach succinctly argued that 'contrary to the conclusion of the Volker Commission' it might be prudent to describe the 'very top of the civil service as revitalized' (1991, p.407).

Aberbach also notes another important change for the bureaucracy; that is, the replacement of Reagan by Bush meant that, although the New Right order was preserved, an anti-civil service President was replaced by someone dedicated to the public service. Indeed, even though Bush retained much of the New Right rhetoric, those who campaign vigorously for Reagan (for example, Buchanan) have detected in Bush something akin to traditional conservatism. Certainly he came to the White House 'an experienced Washington Hand' (ibid., p.414) and he displayed a liking for practical solutions rather than ideological crusades, emphasising the positive virtues of public service. Polsby has gone so far as to call him an American Tory (ibid.). Perhaps it would be more accurate to label him a 'High Tory'. His first term was marked by a genuine desire to tap the expertise of the civil servants and they have been allowed back to advise on policy; he even allowed agency chiefs to choose their own subordinates, a practice banished under the stern New right gaze of Reagan's Chiefs of staff (ibid., pp.414–16).

It is possible to tentatively suggest that the New Right onslaught on the civil service has been checked and may soon be reversed. Certainly more members of Congress appear to share Sikorski's view that America needs its civil servants and it may be time to adequately reward them again, at least if the government is going to be able to take an active role in dealing with the problems confronting the nation. Even the theoretical mainstays of the New Right appear to be under pressure; for example, a survey by Johnson and Libecap on agency growth and civil service salaries challenged the Public Choice explanations for bureaucratic motivation, arguing:

> the analysis reveals support for the ... hypothesis that federal employees have little incentive to support the expansion of their agency in order to increase their salaries. (1989, p.433)

Certainly explanations other than personal aggrandisement appear important to the officials themselves. One senior career official who joined the service in 1969 argued:

> Coming to government paid more than did academia in that era and on top of all that a knee-jerk liberal democratic enthusiasm led me to think that government per se was not only more financially rewarding, but emotionally and morally rewarding as well. (Interview)

The differential between academic and civil service pay remains. But, for a large number of officials, so does the reason for remaining in government, despite the managerial changes which they as professional civil servants have loyally implemented and on occasion have not only admired, but advocated. The next chapter explores the most dramatic of those changes, privatisation, in more detail.

5   The Resurgent Market: Privatisation in the US

> We have a government which alternates between being a halfwit bully and a philanthropist, only for its philanthropy it uses other people's money. The well is running dry. Besides, philanthropy belongs in the private sector. The government ought to get out of the business. (Schmidt, 'Dialogues on Government', *The Bureaucrat*, Summer, 1986)

INTRODUCTION

Whilst the previous two chapters have explored the impetus to new forms of public sector management, it is now time to turn to one of the major activities utilised by governments in their attack upon the centralising state; that is, privatisation. As part of a process of deconstructing the monolithic bureaucracies of the post-war Welfare State, privatisation has been employed on a global scale by administrations which are either anxious to benefit from the putative gains of a market economy, or merely to fulfil the stringent conditions required for financial support from the International Monetary Fund (Letwin, 1988). Whatever the reasons for its adoption, privatisation is an activity that often has a sudden and profound impact upon those directly affected, on the wider economy and also the voting (or non-voting) public.

This chapter, therefore, examines the definitions of privatisation, the motivations for its use and some examples of the implementation of it at the federal level of the US. The examples are chosen to provide an awareness of the scope of privatisation and should not be seen as an attempt at a comprehensive guide. The next chapter continues the theme with an analysis of the British experience, whilst chapter 7 examines the impact on the sub-national level.

There are, however, strong grounds for believing that the main liberalising phenomenon within the US has been de-regulation and that privatisation is an accompanying subsidiary activity (see, for example, Swann, 1988). This reflects the leading role of the private sector in the American political system, which has encouraged it to assume the management of goods and services nominally within the public domain, since before the first election of Ronald Reagan. As an integral part of 'New Right' government this has combined with a desire to oblige sub-national governments to accept a greater resposibility for their own affairs and re-emphasised individual responsibility. Privatisation, then, must be seen within the context of a perspective which sees 'government' as something that has grown too big and is in need of curtailing.

To this end the section dealing with the definition of privatisation is followed by a discussion of de-regulation, a process that has greater significance in the US than many European countries because American governments have traditionally been more chary than their European counterparts about taking private sector organisations into direct state ownership, preferring instead to curtail their activities with statutorily enforced regulations. Privatisation is important, though, because of the novel problems for management that it engenders for those in the process of relinquishing their direct control of a variety of state-provided products. In that sense its popularity throws up attendant problems that 'are every bit as difficult as those of direct government programmes, and perhaps even more so' (Salamon, 1989, p.x).

Some Definitions of Privatisation

Veljanovski argues that privatisation is simply to 'render private or to bring into the private sector' (1987, p.1). It is, therefore, 'the withdrawal of the state from the production of goods and services' (ibid.). It is a definition that embodies a degree of understated sophistication when compared to some of the more tortuous attempts at explaining the phenomenon. There is a general agreement amongst academics and practitioners about what this entails, and although Ascher identifies a plethora of different types of privatisation (1987) these can be reduced to the three broad categories of outright sales of the whole or parts of public organizations; contracting-out services previously provided by the public sector; and a miscellaneous heading under which can be found the use of state-provided vouchers to individuals, user-fees, franchises, loan guarantees, and government-sponsored enterprises.

The Salamon Report, of a panel of the National Academy of Public Administration, identified two distinct definitions. The first they categorised as a narrow definition, contending that:

> the term 'privatization' was coined essentially as a political slogan to describe the movement to reduce the role of modern government and transfer back to private hands responsibilities that governments had assumed in the modern welfare state. At its core, therefore, privatization essentially means 'load-shedding', the surrender by government of certain of its functions and their assumption by private for-profit and non-profit institutions. (1989, p.7)

The second definition Salamon refers to as the 'broad' approach, pointing out that, whilst the narrow definition has a certain precision to it, it is nonetheless rather restrictive in its application. The second approach, therefore, embraces:

> not only load-shedding by government, but also a variety of other forms of government action that involve reliance on the private sector. (Ibid., p.8)

A reliance that includes activities falling within the three aforementioned categories. The broad definition is the one that they opted to adopt, saying that it encompassed a

> fundamental distinction between government as a *financier, authorizer* or *overseer* of services, and government as a *producer* or *provider* of services. The broad definition extends the term privatization to the wide set of arrangements under which government remains involved as the financier or authorizer of services but relies on the private sector or the market for the actual provision and delivery. (Ibid.)

These distinctions are generic to the process of privatisation and have an equal application on both sides of the Atlantic. Indeed, they have a particular applicability for British local government as it reforms itself to comply with the competition policy provisions of the 1988 Local Government Act, an issue returned to in a later chapter. The role of government at all levels is changing from that of being a direct provider in many instances to that of being a facilitator, an enabler; it uses what the Salamon Report called its function as a 'financier, authorizer or overseer' (ibid.).

Privatisation, then, should be viewed as a tool used by governments to overhaul not only the structures of the public sector, but also to reform the culture of those organisations: the way in which they view their own functions, their relationship to the consumers of their activities, and the manner of their accountability. The analysis of this perspective is continued in a later section of this chapter, but first it is necessary to review de-regulation in the US, in order that privatisation might be set within its proper context.

DE-REGULATING THE US

The works of Swann (1988) and Gerston (1988) provide valuable guides to the process of de-regulation in the US, a subject to which American academics have devoted a large corpus of literature. Furthermore, there are valuable case studies of regulatory reform written by House and Shull (1986) (on environmental legislation), Eades and Fix (1984), Noll and Owen's book on interest group influence upon regulatory reform (1983), and Wood's analysis of nuclear safety regulation (1983), amongst a host of others. Useful though these are in illuminating the atmosphere of regulatory activity and reform within the American context, they are not specifically addressing changes in the management of the *public* sector. The earlier proviso remains, that is the process of privatisation performs an auxiliary role within the broader phenomenon of liberalisation. As an example of the narrower policy of changing the nature of control over government, however, it is itself of secondary importance to this study. Regulatory reform is about changing the nature of the control that the state exercises over the private sector, not about the way in which the government holds itself accountable.

Swann argues that although the share of the public sector in the US never neared the level of GDP found in Britain, there has been a sizable governmental involvement in regulating the economy. He points out that:

> In the US public opinion has not been especially favourable to concepts such as nationalisation. Thus where there have been conditions of natural monopoly – where, for example, economies of scale have indicated that for efficient production only one producer was required – rather than take the enterprise into public ownership the frequent though not universal reaction has been to leave it in private hands and to subject it to some form of regulatory surveillance and control. (1988, p.8)

It is this oversight that directly threatened the profits of some industries (such as natural gas), leading to a dearth of investment for modernisation, whilst in other sectors of the economy cosy and profitable relationships emerged between the industry and those charged with enforcing consumer protection legislation, a symbiosis endemic within the American political system due to the need to construct complex political/economic coalitions (Grant, 1989; Robinson, 1989).

A review of the the number of federal regulatory pages in the Federal Register illustrates the growth of regulatory legislation in America; 2,599 pages in 1936 grew to over 742,000 by 1977 (Swann, 1988, p.21). When this is compounded with the regulatory instincts of state legislators and the resulting deluge of Acts, Orders and Regulations which has flowed from the capitols of innovative states like New York and California, the burden of control was deemed to be a considerable hindrance upon the economy. From the late 1970s Congress and Presidents opted to reduce the panoply of restrictions successive Acts had placed upon industry. Important decisions included the Air Passenger Deregulation Act (1978), National Gas Policy Act (1978), and decontrol or increased competition within electricity (1978), communications (1979, 1981, 1982, 1983, 1984), and the money markets (1980, 1982, 1985) (ibid., pp.34–5). The wisdom of some of these momentous changes is often debated by air travellers, truck drivers and savings and loan investors.

Whilst the bulk of de-regulating activity took place during the tenure of Presidents Carter and Ford, President Reagan stiffened the regulatory procedure by insisting that before a new regulation was enacted a net benefit must be demonstrated (ibid., p.38). In addition to this his more ideologically committed appointees took the process to within the administration itself and to the field of antitrust, arguing that excessive government and regulation is a burden that needs to be lifted from the back of industry (ibid.). It is at this ideological juncture that de-regulation and privatisation begin to fuse. The impact of that fusion upon the federal and state civil servants is dealt with in more detail later. Whilst the activities of privatisation and de-regulation are, therefore, different, many of their aims remain the same, the two processes are merely different routes to the same goal. These aims include the search for greater efficiency in market and administrative terms, curbs on trade union activity and control over public sector costs whilst stimulating private sector growth. It is to these goals that we now turn.

BACKGROUND TO AMERICAN PRIVATISATION

Privatisation generated a growing corpus of literature, attaining a mention in 3,838 news articles alone in 1988 (Reason Foundation, 1989, p.5) and the Office of Privatisation in the OMB provides an updated bibliography for the subject which by 1990 was 105 pages long. There is not the space to review the mountain of literature and little can be gained, in any case, by attempting such a task here. The more modest purpose of this section is to examine the background to the American propensity towards privatisation.

A recent report by Touche Ross tends to view privatisation in the city and county governments of the US as a managerial, not a political tool to allow the implementation of programmes mandated by the federal government or voter initiative, but for which insufficient resources have been allocated. The report highlights a belief that the tension caused by the compulsion to provide collective services, combined with a perennial tardiness to vote the necessary money to cover the full cost of those services, has led to local governments 'turning to alternative methods to deliver public services', of which engaging 'the private sector to provide services or facilities that are usually regarded as public-sector responsibilities' is a favoured option (1987, p.1). It is this dynamic which has provided the greatest spur to the privatisation activities of most American governments, a dynamic created by New Right policies to be sure, but shaped by managerial imperatives and guided in its implementation by those who, like their managerialist predecessors of the 1960s and 1970s, view the art of governance from a very different perspective to that of the recent conservative political leadership in Washington DC.

At the national level the Reagan Administration established an Office of Privatization (OP) within the Office of Management and Budget (OMB) and in 1987 issued Executive Order (EO) 12615, *Performance of Commercial Activities*, which has been translated every year since then into a series of goals given to federal agencies. Often a part of the annual budget, EO 12615 goals encourage agencies to 'study a certain number of commercial jobs currently performed by Government employees to determine if they should be contracted out'. In the 1990 budget, these goals involved a review of over 54,000 full-time-equivalent (FTEs)) jobs (OP, 1989, p.40). At the sub-national level conservative administrations often share the federal perspective, yet even where there is not a common ideological commitment privatisation often remains the only option that allows the state and local governments to provide goods and services demanded by their citizenry or mandated by federal law.

Clearly, despite its ancillary role to de-regulation any analysis of the recent innovations in public administration in the US cannot ignore the impact of privatisation both as a policy *per se* and its importance for the implementation of public policies. As in the UK, privatisation has been integral to a swathe of manifestoes upon which politicians have been elected; elected, moreover, at federal, state, county and city level as members of either of the two main parties. A problem, however, is deciding the extent to which this activity represents a new element in decision-making, implying a novel method of managing the public sector, perhaps even a clear break with the incremental changes that can be identified within the American public sector. These can be said (somewhat) arbitrarily to start with the period of F.D. Roosevelt and to have developed with interventionist government, involving such approaches as corporate management, zero-based budgeting, planning-programming and budgeting, and 'consumerism'.

Some common threads run through many of the changes attempted by administrations as far back as Eisenhower and still preoccupy American policy-makers. These include 'value for money' in terms of efficiency; accountability and control of the bureaucracy; and a concern to inject private sector practices into the public sector. What distinguishes later changes from the earlier ones, however, is the expatiation by successive administrations since Nixon on the 'need' to significantly reduce the role of government, indeed, to discredit the nature of modern government itself and its tendency to intervene in order to provide collective goods and services in lieu of private provision (Bennett and Johnson, 1981). These components lend weight to the belief that there has been an acceleration of the changes which first appeared in the early 1970s and their aggregation from about 1980 into something approximating a new public management, as defined by Hood, although his warning that it has 'a slightly different emphasis' from those trends he identifies elsewhere is one that reflects the complex and private sector orientation of the American polity (1990, p.9).

It would be a mistake to attribute this entirely to conservative politicians; the Carter administration, at least initially, had an outsider's loathing of Washington (Pfiffner, 1988, p.93) and, as was argued in the previous chapter, much of the attack on bureaucracy and the de-regulation of American business that has occurred began under his leadership (Eades and Fix, 1984; House and Shull, 1986; Williams, 1988). It can be argued, therefore, that the easily identified elements of managerial incrementalism within the post World War Two developments of American public administration have combined with an ideological shift upon the election of Richard Nixon, a change accentuated and dispersed throughout the different levels of government with the election of the first Reagan/Bush administration. In its essence the ideological change meant that responsibility for seeking to correct inadequacies in the provision of basic 'rights', 'wants' and 'needs', as they were identified by the various reformers of the expansionist period of government, were deemed to be the responsibility of sub-national government, private organisations and individuals themselves. The era of federal 'big-government' intervention was at an end.

E.S. Savas, who served as an Assistant Secretary of Housing and Urban Development (HUD) under Reagan, argues that there were four pressures for privatisation in the US; pragmatic, ideological, commercial, and populist (1987, p.5). He claims those with a pragmatic urge to extend privatisation had as their goal the simple aim of 'better' more cost-effective public services. Ideological pressure came, he says, from a particular political philosophy identified with the advocates of liberal political and economic structures, their goal being less government as a safeguard to democracy and a boon to individual liberties and rational market-led decisions about resource allocation. Commercial pressure sought more business for the private sector, reducing the share of gross domestic product directed by the state in order that state-owned assets could be put to more productive use by the private sector. Populist goals were for 'a better society' in which people would have more choice in public services and establish a 'sense of community by relying more on family, neighbourhood, church, and ethnic and voluntary associations and less on distant bureaucratic structures' (ibid., pp.4–11). There is a clear overlap within these categories. Savas concludes that privatisation is 'both a means and an end' and that:

> privatization is the key to both limited and better government: limited in its size, scope, and power relative to society's other institutions; and better in that society's needs are satisfied more efficiently, effectively, and equitably. (Ibid., p.288)

In short, he believes the successes of privatisation are 'too evident' and that it cannot possibly be a transient phenomenon that will fade away when 'prominent proponents have left the scene' (ibid., p.291) as it is an idea which commands a considerable constituency of support, an important prerequisite also stipulated by Letwin, another advocate of the process (1988, pp.74–106).

Much of what Savas has to say would be familiar to most observers of the British privatisation programmes and the similarities are confirmed by Hanke, whose list of objectives for privatisation ring strikingly similar to those identified by Veljanovski (1987) and Letwin (1988, p.28). Hanke cites six major goals for privatisation:

1. the improvement of economic performance of the assets or service functions concerned;
2. the de-politicisation of economic decisions;
3. the generation of public-budget revenues through sale receipts;
4. the reduction in public outlays, taxes and borrowing requirements;
5. the reduction in the power of public sector unions; and
6. the promotion of popular capitalism through the wider ownership of assets (1987, p.2).

In the US, then, privatisation is seen as a method of controlling government, controlling the growth of government and also freeing resources in order to facilitate economic growth and efficiency.

Rarely are the advocates of new public management so blunt as Bennett and Johnson (or so lacking in the provision of evidence for their bold pronouncements) as when they state:

> As every taxpayer knows, government is wasteful and inefficient; it always has been and always will be. (1981, p.19)

It is difficult to measure the practical results of privatisation, they are usually of a political nature and even its most ardent yet thoughtful advocates accept that the process has results that are hard to quantify (Veljanovski, 1987, p.206). In the early years of the Reagan Administration, however, the views of Bennett and Johnson were representative of a large number of political appointees, particularly when they argued:

Our conclusion is inescapable. All the evidence, without exception, proves that the people of the United States can have better government – federal, state, and local – at much lower cost by contracting out the production of goods and services to private firms by competitive bidding. (Ibid., 109)

Unfortunately, the evidence was not as conclusive as the authors would have their audience believe. It is not possible to know what would happen if certain events were enacted differently; policy-makers do not have the ability to exercise that degree of control. The best that can be said is that the evidence marshalled by the proponents suggested that savings could be made. As in the United Kingdom, however, the greatest perceived benefits were political and fiscal in the sense of reducing taxation and borrowing requirements, they were not economic in the narrower micro sense.

That this distinction is accepted by the New Right is clearly recognised by Stuart Butler, an ardent supporter of liberalisation. Whilst accepting that there is a tendency to view privatisation as cutting the cost of government, he argues that in his opinion a deeper feature that is 'of far greater importance' is that:

by changing the pattern of demand for services, privatisation may prove to be a potent *political* strategy to reverse the momentum toward ever-larger government in the United States. (1987, p.4)

He proceeds to identify the constituency for interventionist federal government and points out that this intervention usually begins as a response to a perceived crisis or threat to society or as a scion of an existing government programme, 'usually a traditional all-American pork-barrel project' incrementally developed to aid a politically sensitive region. These events elicit an intervention from government that commands a constituency consisting of beneficiaries and near-beneficiaries, administrators/bureaucrats, service providers, and political activists (ibid., pp.5–7). As a result liberal politicians find that:

trying to overcome these spending dynamics by constitutional innovations or through a legislative war of attrition ... is like engaging in political sumo wrestling, in which each superheavyweight wrestler uses bulk and muscle to force his opponent out of the circle. The problem is that the would-be budget-cutters are perpetually at a weight disadvantage. (Ibid., p.8)

There is also a further source of public sector provision, that he has failed to identify, that results from the government creation of a market in certain products for which there is a perceived need and in which the private sector was (at least originally) unwilling to invest; uranium enrichment is an American example (see OP, *Privatisation in the FY 1990 Budget*).

Butler's solution to the liberaliser's problem is to develop an alternative constituency which creates a 'private-sector ratchet', that is, 'private-sector coalitions that are mirror images of the coalitions currently pressing for public-sector spending' (1987, p.9). These new coalitions create a momentum for lower taxation and the private provision of services. He cites the privatisation of public housing in Britain, the selling of profitable state-owned companies, and the use of tax benefits for the purchase of the private services, as examples of his private sector coalitions of interest (ibid., pp.9–13).

The urge to privatise then has two main sources, ideological and pragmatic; it is possible when dealing with general motivations to subsume Savas's other two categories within these two broad perspectives. The pragmatists, however, have been obliged to seek privatisation because of the success of the ideological liberals in shifting the balance of government away from intervention. It is the shrinking of federal and state monies for grand projects and the implementation of mundane (and often arcane) federally mandated programmes, such as welfare, housing and energy provision, which has pushed the pragmatists into the camp of the ideologues. In this sense the assault of the New Right upon the 'old' public administration using their 'new' public management has been successful, although Butler himself bemoans the limited success (in liberal terms) of Reagan's first term (ibid.).

Privatisation should be seen, therefore, as part of a broad spectrum of changes which include de-regulation, consumerism in the public sector (Hambleton, 1988, p.126), 'new' federalism which returns responsibility for raising money for the implementation of programmes to the states and then on down to the counties and cities, and an approach to the federal and sub-national bureaucracies which emphasises political control, staff reductions, hiving-out, and the infusion of private sector management styles (see also, Stockman, 1986).

ADMINISTRATION, MANAGERS AND PRIVATISATION

The Salamon Report identified several areas in which privatisation remains poorly understood, much of the debate becoming locked into 'philosophical terms' rather than addressing the 'nuts and bolts of actual operations' (1989, p.vii). This is a somewhat unfair argument since, as is made clear both elsewhere in this book and by others, the whole thrust of privatisation was fuelled by the dynamic of the New Right critique of the Welfare State, a critique which by its very nature was and remains iconoclastic, relying upon the force of reasoned debate rooted in *a priori* statements about the nature of government, rather than proceeding from a logical series of empirically tested observations. Salamon does provide the valuable service, however, of identifying the management challenges.

The Report concentrates upon three features which, it claims, have not been accorded sufficient attention by those involved in the different parts of the implementation of privatisation. These are that privatisation takes a variety of forms; it is not a new phenomenon; and that it involves serious management challenges (ibid., pp.vii–xi; 1–7; 25–43). Of these features the first has already been dealt with in this chapter; that is, that privatisation can be anything from the sale of a state industry to the provision of food stamps. The second feature notes the fact that private sector influence has always been powerful within the American governmental system, indeed contracting out 'for mail delivery predated the Constitution' and:

> The original secret service organization during the Civil War, an organization generally referred to as the 'spy agency', was in reality a contracting operation between the Department of the Treasury and several private firms. (Ibid., p.9)

Cohabitation between swashbuckling private sector merchants and the more entrepreneurial members of the clandestine sectors of government has appeared to continue, albeit not always with the knowledge or tacit agreement of Congress.

It is Salamon's third feature which concentrates upon the management challenges provided by privatisation. These are situated under four headings:

1. the changed nature of public management;
2. maintaining competition;
3. new skill requirements;
4. excessive regulation.

The changed nature of public management is a problem also identified by Flynn, who has argued that the 'traditional organizations of the welfare state are breaking up' (1990, p.152). Public sector organisations must learn to 'recognise the difference between control and support functions' as the changes lead to front-line managers both assuming greater autonomy and having it thrust upon them, a process which provides opportunities for them to evade central control and thereby also circumventing accountability (ibid., pp.164–8). The role of the public manager has been changed by privatisation from that of an implementer, as Salamon has argued, to that of a supervisor (1989, p.x).

The danger here is the loss of accountability due to the destruction of intricate chains of command. The gains in flexibility and productivity are bought through loss of control. Clearly there are techniques around this; indeed, in some cases this is not even a problem but one of the sought after benefits of privatisation. The difficulties arise, however, when

> the government manager is still held accountable for the expenditure of public funds, the exercise of public authority, and the ultimate results of public action. At the same time the government manager is required to share a considerable portion of the discretion involved in the operation of the public program with one or more private agents over whom he/she has only limited, indirect control. (Ibid., 26)

Examples include much defence-related work and loan guarantee programmes. Obviously the private sector organisations frequently have different goals to those of the public official who, although in nominal charge of them when implementing a government policy, lacks sanctions to enforce the necessary detail of control essential to the proper functioning of many programmes.

It is the reverse of the harlot's traditional prerogative, in that civil servants are now finding themselves saddled with the responsibility, but not the power of their official duties. In response to these contradictions, the US Navy has recently reversed some of the private sector gains within the Department of Defense, beginning with the implementatiomn of a fifty-two per cent reduction over five years in the budget for service contractors in the Naval Sea Systems Command and providing for their replacement by service personnel in order to enhance the service's in-house expertise and capacity (ibid.).

In the need to maintain competition the Salamon Report noted severe management difficulties. The whole purpose of increased competition is to reduce or even obviate the need for public servants to monitor the costs and quality of goods and services provided by private sector contractors fulfilling government funded or supported programmes. Yet the study carried out for the NAPA panel found that there are often significant barriers to companies intent on providing a service, barriers which, therefore, hamper competition. In addition cartel and monopoly arrangements evolve which reduce 'the effective scope of the market forces' (ibid., p.28). Results like these were found in several states and cities in activities as diverse as sanitation, refuse collection, housing and Department of Defense contracts. The report concluded that:

> Using market competition to increase efficiency is clearly an important impetus behind the privatization movement. The existence of sufficient competition is, however, far from automatic. Problems associated with public and private monopolies, oligopolies, and with government and citizens as captive consumers, will continue to arise if competition is lacking or distorted while privatization initiatives are pushed forward. Without fair and open competition, government will be less able to induce the private sector to act in a manner consistent with public objectives. (Ibid., p.32)

There is, of course, the potential for government organisations to seek recourse in competition law, which in the US provides for substantial (often treble) damages where it can be proved by the plaintive that they have suffered as the result of an unfair restraint of trade (Veljanovski,1987, pp.174–6). It is a valuable recourse not so widely available within Europe, and certainly not in Britain where individuals have to depend upon the crimminal law or the common law. The impact of EC legislation is promising to rectify some of the more blatant anomolies in this area (ibid.).

As to the question of new skill requirements, it encompasses a set of problems common to much of the Western World (Flynn, 1990). As new technology provides options for novel methods of social and workplace organization and as those options are pusued, then managerial practices will need to evolve to recognise these developments. Public sector managers will obviously require skills different to those they learned in the past. The Salamon Report noted that in America the need for the public sector to aquire those skills was not being adequately met. This can lead to serious problems of competency when important contracts are being enforced:

> Experienced procurement officials note that most problems with vendors occur because of ambiguous, ill-defined and poorly written contracts that did not include important details, parameters, and specifications. Indeed, federal prosecutors have sometimes been forced to drop charges against defence contractors suspected of fraud because procurement officials were unable to decipher the meaning of the contracts they had originally written. (1989, p.34)

Excessive regulation is a problem that the US has dealt with by attempting a comprehensive process of de-regulation. It is something that has not yet been attempted on a similar scale in Europe; indeed, the logic of privatisation within most West European countries has led to a considerable increase in regulation. Yet despite determined efforts to root out the worst excesses, there is still a substantial amount of regulation within the American economy. In the mid-1980s there were 60,000 pages of procurement regulation, a figure only recently reduced to the hardly modest sum of 34,000 pages (Salamon, 1989, p.35). The Federal Aquisition Regulation (FAR) encompasses almost 400 separate regulatory requirements whilst there are about 4,000 laws with some application to the procurement process alone, most of them relating to defence, the Department of Energy or NASA (ibid.). It appears, therefore, that:

> Regulation becomes, in a sense, the substitute in the world of privatization for what internal agency management accomplishes in direct government service delivery. (Ibid.)

Because the American political process emphasises the leading role accorded to the legislature in securing fiscal accountability and through that the general accountability of the executive and the expenditure of tax dollars, Congress has been tardy in its acceptance of de-regulation. Even New Right politicians anxious to eradicate unnecessary bureaucracy have been loath to relax tight congressional control over expenditure and the activities of private sector organisations which intrude upon the sensibilities of their constituents. The reasons are found with the high incidence of spectacular corruption scandals and the traditional propensity of American politicians to cultivate their voters. As a result of these pressures, Congress has added to the regulatory burden with a series of recent Acts which seek to control the privatised arena; they include the Competition in Contracting Act (1984); Small Business and Federal Procurement Competition Enhancement Act (1984); Defense Procurement Reform Act (1984); Defense Procurement Improvement Act (1986); Federal Civilian Employee and Contractor Travel Expense Act (1985); the Anti-Kickback Enforcement Act (1986); the False Claims Amendments Act (1986); and the Programme Fraud Civil Remedies Act (1986), amongst others.

It is also something of an irony, argues Salamon, that privatisation in America is hailed as a success because it frees former public organisations from the artificial restrictions imposed upon their freedom of action by government itself (1989, p.37) – activities such as equal opportunity policies properly enforced, staffing freezes, salary limitations, budget restrictions, personnel policies requiring strict procedures for staff dismissals and so on. There is a similar gain applauded for efficiency within European privatisation activities, a subject returned to in the next chapter. The implications for these claims are examined both there and later in this chapter.

In response to these percived problems, the Salamon Report constructed five guidelines for 'responding to the challenges of privatisation' (ibid., pp.xii, 43–9). They are:

1. Government reliance on the private sector to deliver public services is a legitimate and valuable feature of American government, and has been for decades.
2. There are significant differences between the public and private sectors that make certain forms of privatization, or certain areas of privatization inappropriate.
3. Privatization does not eliminate the need for public management; it only changes its character. As long as public funds or authority are involved, public accountability and control are essential.
4. Privatization puts special demands on private managers that the public sector must recognize and accept in their dealing with government.
5. Just as the private sector must respect the legitimate responsibilities of government, so also must government respect the legitimate needs of its private partners. (Ibid.)

These guidelines bring the subject back to the debate as to the nature of the relationship between the public and the private sectors, the role of the state with regard to individuals and the location of the border between the rights of citizens and their duties, which was rehearsed in the previous chapters. There is an echo in the guidelines of the Salamon Report of

Baber's points of difference between the public and the private sectors (referred to in chapter 1). These issues (and Baber's ten points) are returned to in the following sections of this chapter, but it is important to keep in mind the lessons of this and previous discussions: it is the government, acting as the responsible arm of the state, that alone can exercise sovereignty. All private activity is either condoned and encouraged or explicitly licensed by the state, a point that is emphasised by Moe (1987, p.458) and his expressed belief that economic considerations alone should not be the criteria by which government activity is assessed; that is, the state is the sovereign and has some special powers reserved to it. Clearly if this is true it is absurd to attempt to measure state activities as if they were mere changelings arrogantly substituted from the private sector. The difficulty for the advocates of privatisation is to explain whether it aids or hinders the process of calling the exercise of that sovereignty to account: whether, in fact, it is an essential adjunct to the process of defending and advancing the liberty of the citizenry. The next section examines the implementation of privatisation in the US in order to try and further illuminate the issues of this debate.

PRIVATISATION IN PRACTICE.

When discussing the American political/economic system it is important to recall its sheer size, relative to the rest of the world. The economy of the US is by far the largest on the planet, and even the second and third largest (those of Japan and Germany) are dependent upon external trade; the US could conceivably operate in isolation, albeit at a much reduced standard of living for its citizens and those of the rest of the world. The figures that apply to privatisation in the US are accordingly large. If the forms of privatisation are divided into contracting out, loan guarantees, government-sponsored enterprises, and vouchers, the scale of federal and state operations is seen to dwarf that of the entire domestic economies of many medium sized developed countries.

In 1988 the federal government spent over $200 billion on contracting out, most of this with the Department of Defense, which in 1987 spent over $155 billion on goods and services (Salamon, 1989, p.12). Simply purchasing the plethora of items required by the US military in 1987 involved over 15 million separate contract actions (ibid.). Federal loan guarantees, whereby the government advances its objectives by assuming 'all or a portion of the risk associated with loans made by private financial institutions, businesses, or state, local' or even foreign governments, stood at over $500 billion in 1987 and are set to rise by another several hundred billion dollars by the middle of the 1990s (ibid., pp.14–17). In addition to this, government-sponsored enterprises had a combined debt in excess of $665 billion by the end of 1988, a figure that the failed savings and loan institutions could increase by a factor of several hundred per cent, and the voucher schemes appeared to be using tax dollars at an exponential rate; in 1987 federal outlay was $11.5 billion for food stamps, $27.4 billion for Medicaid and over $75 billion for Medicare (ibid., pp.17–19). With a massive budget deficit worrying policy-makers, steps which promise the possibility of aiding the control of public expenditure are going to be given serious consideration to the extent that they will be acted upon.

The Federal Level

For many years it has been fashionable to caricature Ronald Reagan as a bumbling ham, unable to perform coherently if edged away from an autocue. Yet the work of Stockman (1986) and of Pfiffner (1988), among others, shows this to be an untrue representation:

> Ronald Reagan came to office with a remarkably coherent agenda and set of policy priorities. His first priorities to increase defense spending significantly and cut spending on virtually all domestic policy areas lent themselves to a narrow focus and simple set of values for his administration. This set of priorities was a litmus test in recruiting personnel for the administration. Personal and ideological loyalty were the primary criteria for appointees. (Pfiffner, 1988, p.58)

Pfiffner rehearses the degree of ideological and managerial cohesion which infused the Reagan administration. In this period of government:

> the tight Reagan White House control of administration policy and its legislative agenda was a far cry from previous attempts at cabinet government, whether Eisenhower's, Nixon's (first term), or Carter's. (Ibid., p.59)

The effect of this combination of ideological coherence and commitment when linked with a strong, collective-management style of government was to provide an impetus to the new public management of which privatisation was one of the key parts. It was aided initially by conservative control of the Congress, a benefit held for only a short time before a Democratic majority, less inclined to non-intervention, re-asserted itself. The administration set about ensuring that its policies were transported to each level and every organisation of the federal bureaucracy, using a combination of committed political appointees, structural changes (with the creation of the OP in the OMB), far-reaching investigations such as the President's Commission on Privatization (which reported in 1988), and Executive Orders (such as 12615) issued regularly as guidance for the day-to-day workings of the administration and which sought to infuse the bureaucracy with its ethos.

Those familiar with the nature of American politics, its checks and balances, of the separation of powers, untidy frequently ill-disciplined political parties, powerful Congress and well-informed, unfettered, indeed often contrary, legislators (see for example, H. Smith, 1988; Loomis, 1988), will be aware of the difficulties any regime would have in implementing the goals of the Reagan Administration; this did indeed prove to be the case. Much of the time of the Office of Privatisation was taken up with coalition-building amongst the legislators in order to implement the Administration's policies. A senior official in the OP argued, in terms that Butler would recognise, that, when opposing privatisation,

> Congressmen are doing more than 'simply going through the motions', it is more deeply felt than that. I think as a general rule members of Congress value federal activities and functions in their districts, not only in terms of the votes it provides, but it also provides a steady employment base, a steady economic base for their district. Even understanding that a private sector company is going to come in and do the same thing, the preference is for a governmental organisation there because it's more consistent and dependable and more predictable. (Interview)

As this official pointed out, the federal authorities became involved in certain activities because there 'really wasn't a market and the government made the market'. As already noted, uranium enrichment is an example of that kind of activity 'which we've just never gotten rid of completely because once they exist they develop constituencies of their own' and it presents a considerable problem to 'disassemble them'. Another reason is that identified by Butler and includes, for example, the Tennessee Valley Authority which was created in response to the economic depression of the 1920s and 1930s. The question of the TVA illustrates the difficulties of the privatisers as it has always had a formidable constituency of support which includes the legislative caucuses of several states, large private sector businesses, state bureaucracies, and power utilities. Efforts to put it onto the privatisation agenda had to move extremely cautiously, yet liberal think-tanks were pushing for this to occur. The privatisation proposals for the 1990 budget, however, did not mention the TVA, confining the administration to selling off the Alaska and Southeastern Power Marketing Administrations. These and hints that the other PMAs (Western area, Southwestern, and Bonnerville) were to be sold led both insiders and outside observers to expect a sustained effort to dismantle and sell the TVA in the near future.

Privatisation in the 1990 budget reflected Reagan's belief that:

> As the federal government grew, it took on improper responsibilities, and managed its programmes inefficiently. We undertook to return the Federal Government to its proper role. ... The Government and the private sector should each do what it does best. The federal government should not be involved in providing goods and services where private enterprise can do the job cheaper and better. (Budget message)

The list of operations that the administration successfully privatised includes the Great Plains Coal Gasification Plant, sold to the Basin Electric Power Corporation in 1988 for about $600 million and numerous similar relatively small-scale activities (ibid.). Proposals for future privatisations included things like the helium processing and storage operations and the naval petroleum reserves at Elk Hills in California and Teapot Dome, Wyoming (ibid.). These operations are themselves easily privatised, but the opposition is an illustration of the nature of American political debate about the subject. It is well summed up by the account of one of the officers responsible for attempting to negotiate a coalition in Congress for the necessary approval:

> Back in Teddy Roosevelt's era there was a sense that the navy was going to need vast storehouses of petroleum to run its fleet and they created the petroleum reserves in Wyoming and California. Essentially they are oil drilling operations and reservoirs, that kind of thing. Well, we no longer need that, we can get all of our oil and be satisfied very well from the private sector, so we've been trying to sell those as well. Again we've run into some Congressional opposition on those. This has been for a variety of reasons; it typically has to do with the state delegations, for example the California one which has the more active oil wells, these have a number of peculiarities that make certain interests want to keep them in Government hands. ... The local refiners are somehow concerned that they would be eliminated from the market if it was sold to another large oil company. Strangely enough we've got a teachers' association that says that their retirement pension funds

are somehow tied to it and they've got a lawsuit going with the Department of Energy. There's one powerful member of Congress who, when he first came in, there was talk of selling Teapot Dome and that was a scandal back in the early 1900s and by God he's not going to let that happen again and he's going to protect our natural heritage, and it's got nothing to do with the issue, but he's got an emotional reaction ... those are the kinds of forces we've got to deal with. (Interview)

Clearly these are forces that are the meat and drink of democratic political activity, but beyond the ken of an 'economically rational' approach to policy-making.

Federal Employees

Activities like the Naval Petroleum Reserve, the TVA and PMAs are examples of corporations, or even regional industries, that resemble private sector activities and can be sold-off as whole entities. A different approach is adopted with the traditional activities of the federal bureaucracy. Officials in the OP point to the more than three million personnel employed by the federal government in the civilian, military, and postal service sectors. Of these about 900,000 are still believed to be in jobs or positions that could conceivably go to the private sector in some fashion (source: various interviews). As a result there is an Executive Order that requires the OP to look at three per cent of the civilian employees a year and ensure that their jobs could not be better situated in the private sector.

The basic managerial method employed in seeking to hive-off these positions is straightforward. The agency is ordered to write a functional requirement of what they want; they then restructure their organisation in a way designed to make it competitive before pitching it against the private sector via a call for tenders. The agency must then pick the best private sector proposal, compare it against the costs of the government organisation and if the private sector are ten per cent or more less expensive then they are awarded the contract. An official in the OMB argued that:

we add a 10% cost differential so that we don't make transfers for minor savings, because we don't want flopping back and forth and it's a very traumatic kind of process so we don't want to have to go through it just for minor improvements. What we see when we do that is an average of about 30% savings whether or not it goes out to contract because just forcing them into the competitive process makes the in-house people look at their jobs differently ... because they had been essentially monopolists. It increases productivity and the statistics suggest that when the in-house bid wins it is by a margin of about 17%–20% cheaper than what they were doing it for before. When the contractor wins it's around 30%–35%. So just forcing them through the competitive process we think is worthwhile. (Interview)

These figures suggest that the greatest boost to savings and increases in productivity comes, therefore, for the upheaval of preparing to tender and the constructive activity of actually seeking to compete against the private sector; not the activity of privatisation, but the process of preparing for it. In short, shaking out the dead wood often appears to be as profitable as selling off the forest. The earlier caveat remains; actually measuring the benefits of privatisation is an elusive activity fraught with method-ological difficulties. One former Reagan Bureau Chief summed it up by saying:

Evaluation? Well that's a tough one. There are a lot of studies out there, a lot of private contracting firms do evaluation studies for the Government; go in and do surveys to see what's happening out there. But a lot of times you just don't have the data you want to go and evaluate something, you just don't have the output data well-defined to allow you to say, 'Well if this programme was a success what would you expect to find out there?' (Interview)

He also identified several activities that caused him a great deal of frus-tration during his period of office, notably the phenomenon that great effort had to be expended to get the legislature to agree to some minor changes that would bring about modest savings, only to find that the savings were a chimera. He said that it

turns out to be difficult to get real savings that you can notice in the short run, because if you really substitute something for the private sector you've got certain phase-out costs with what it costs under the civil service rules to lay some people off. That's a short term cost that you have to counter against expected gains down the road. Then of course, if you contract, you also have to pay some overhead and that kind of thing, and so you hear a lot of people say it is really more effective for the Government to do certain things. (Interview)

The benefit for him and other bureau chiefs was not the short-term economies, or indeed even the putative long-term savings, but the flex-ibility they were given as managers to respond to changing political and administrative circumstances. That is, the demand for many government services changes over time and the big advantage for bureau heads was that contracting out provided them with the ability to close one thing down and instruct another contractor to do something else 'more efficiently and more rapidly'. Unfettered by civil service rules, the public sector union resistance and the requirement to pay superannuation and other benefits, senior managers were able to respond to the challenges of their jobs within a budget that was shrinking in real terms (except for the military). Thus for this political appointee, and several like him, their experience of government fused an ideological commitment to the concept of privatisation with a managerial experience which taught them that, even if there were no large-scale financial savings, a successful fight with the Congress was worth it for the freedom of manoeuvre it gave them to do their jobs. This reason also won some converts amongst the top echelons of the permanent civil service.

One of the more spectacular attempts by the Reagan Administration to inject private sector techniques and attitudes into the public sector was, of course, the President's Private Sector Survey on Cost Control (known as the Grace Commission after its Chairman Peter Grace). Delivered in January 1984, the Report contained 2,478 recommendations with a stated potential saving of more than $424 billion. The Report, augmented later by Mr Grace's book recommended contracting out and hiving off as among the more effective ways of saving money. The General Accounting office joined with the Congressional Budget Office to plough through the forty-seven volumes spread over 1,300 pages. Ironically, the GAO and the OMB found that many of the reputed claims were repetitious (Bingman, 1985) and that a large proportion of the recommendations 'stem from problems and solutions already pointed out and analysed by the career civil service' (Bingman, Summer 1985, p.47). Indeed the GAO argued that in a large number of cases serving officials had made similar recommendations for savings.

The Grace Report received some predictable criticisms, one of the most informed is that of Baber (1987, pp.153–63) who built up an index of published criticisms and found that they can be filed under several headings. Three of the more damning are:

1. Personalities and procedures, some of which are of a purely personal nature and reflect on the integrity of Grace himself, who allegedly claimed that food stamps are a Puerto Rican programme: as Baber writes, 'at best such remarks can be interpreted as evidence of a

failure to recognise the uniquely public role of those acting in the name of the Government'; at worst they are racist. More penetrating methodological criticism is the charge that the Commission used too much unsubstantiated anecdotal material.

2. Programmes and politics; many of the criticisms here suggest that 'there is something unique about the tasks facing public managers' (Baber, ibid.). The recommendations on military procedure showed a marked ignorance of the need to maintain combat-ready forces properly equipped to meet hostile threats. The Commission also overlooked the effect that their recommendations 'might have on the performance and retention of government employees' (ibid.).

3. Law, fairness and feasibility; some Commission recommendations appeared to abrogate previous commitments to ethnic minorities, and to civil rights. When these are combined with some doubts about fairness then the chances of the Congress allowing the more controversial recommendations to proceed are slim. They are not, therefore, politically feasible.

Baber goes on to list (as reproduced in chapter 1) what he sees as the major distinctions between the public and private sectors. It is worth repeating them here because they aid an understanding of why legislators at both federal and state level have been tardy in their response to calls for the transmogrification of public administration into private sector management. Baber argues that:

As compared with the private sector, government:

1.   Faces more complex and ambiguous tasks.
2.   Has more difficulty implementing decisions.
3.   Employs more people with different motivations.
4.   Is more concerned with securing opportunities or capacities.
5.   Is more concerned with compensating for market failures.
6.   Engages in activities with greater symbolic significance.
7.   Is held to stricter standards of previous commitment and legality.
8.   Has a greater opportunity to respond to issues of fairness.
9.   Must operate or appear to operate in the public interest.
10. Must maintain minimal levels of public support above that required in private industry. (Ibid., pp.159–60)

Clearly, the differences between the private and public sectors are such that a naive attempt to effect a simple transference of private sector management techniques into government is doomed to fail. That is something clearly recognised at the OP, but was not self-evident in the Grace Report. At the end of the day, the freedom enjoyed by the private sector, indeed the private sector itself, is contingent upon a strong state enforcing the preconditions necessary for a free market. The best defence for that is a constituency based upon legitimacy, not malversation. The latter is encouraged when the proper boundaries between the public and private domains are thrown into the penumbra created by a constant denigration of the public bureaucracy and an often thoughtless parroting of the benefits of the private sector.

To this end Congress reflects the complex biases and concerns of the electorate which, like electorates elsewhere, seeks both to have government aid and programmes, but without having to pay for them. Yet Congress in the early 1990s laboured under unprecedentedly low public esteem, with the highest ever turnover in congressional candidates. The privatisation movement in the US has as its dynamic some affinity with the UK's *Next Steps*, in that it by-passes the legislative oversight process, devolving power directly to the 'consumers' of government services. As part of their attempts to encourage privatisation, the OP identified legislative impediments to the process. The impediments run to over twelve pages when just their titles and a brief outline are listed and include (under the 'As') 'Agriculture is precluded from selling loans made by the Agricultural Credit Insurance Fund', to (under 'Vs') legislation compelling the Veterans Administration to 'maintain medical care employment at an average of 194,140 FTE. These floors prohibit full consideration of privatisation or contracting-out alternatives.' Yet another large OP document (constantly updated) lists 'Proposed Congressional Prohibitions' on privatisation.

These congressional impediments are competing with Executive Circulars like No. A-76, 1983 (further revised in September 1988) which state:

> In the process of governing, the Government should not compete with its citizens. The competitive enterprise system, characterized by individual freedom and initiative, is the primary source of natural economic strength. In recognition of this principle, it has been and continues to be the general policy of the Government to rely on commercial sources to supply the products and services the Government needs. ... This national policy was promulgated through Bureau of the Budget Bulletins issued in 1955, 1957 and 1960. OMB Circular No. A-76 was issued in 1966 ... revised in 1967 and again in 1979.

The potential for conflict between the executive and the legislature and within the executive is here made obvious, indeed, it has provided much sound and fury in American politics. The dating illustrates, moreover, these are not, after all, new fights. They are also fights that are mirrored at the sub-national levels of government. It is to this that chapter 7 turns. Before that, however, it is instructive to contrast the American federal experience with the British central government's attempts to reconstruct the public sector in its New Right image.

6 The Parvenus' Market: Liberalisation in the UK

> The justification for privatisation does not derive from its economic attractiveness. It simply interprets the policy as a radical change in the institutional structure which shifts the locus of decision-making back to individuals and private organisations because that provides a more democratic basis for society and is necessary for a society based on individual autonomy. ... The link between private property, markets and liberty is a strong one and is the primary defence of privatisation. (Veljanovski, 1987, p.206)

> What is remarkable about this public choice is that its political character is rarely acknowledged or openly examined; it is disguised by rationalizations which themselves reflect the cultural tradition of privatism ... Yet, commitment to the cultural tradition of privatism remains a cardinal political choice and its political character is not erased by government decisions to exercise diminished public responsibility for urban areas and their residents. British and American governments, both national and local, should be held accountable for the consequences of this political choice. Such is the power of the tradition of privatism, however, that it acts to persistently erode any sense of public responsibility or accountability. (Barnekov, Boyle and Rich, 1989, p.232)

> For where your treasure is, there will your heart be also. (Luke 12.34)

For the British public sector, since 1979, the new economic liberalism of the Conservatives represented both an attempt to create (or re-create) a market in publicly provided goods and services, and a means to drag public officials from the obscurity of their calling, thrusting them into a massively expanded private sector. In some cases (such as telecommunications and gas) these upstart executives were to transcend the market entirely and move from their public sector monopolies to become some of the most powerful monopolists in the European private sector.

The last five chapters have described and analysed the implementation of New Right theory and its impact upon the British and American national bureaucracies. The extension of private sector remedies to the perceived ills of the state has provided an extended illustration of what

Pollitt calls the ideology of 'managerialism' and Barnekov, Boyle and Rich refer to as the 'cultural tradition' of 'privatism'. However one chooses to describe the manifestation of these phenomena, it has been a central argument of this book that the stated aims of the political reformers, whilst being shaped by New Right theory, have often been linked to wider goals that lacked a certain clarity of expression. Indeed, the bureaucrats themselves were sometimes to be found advancing varieties of privatisation in order to further 'professional' aims at odds with (or even opposed to) those of the politicians.

Whilst chapters 2 and 3 examined the unleashing of managerialism upon the British civil service, this chapter will explore the liberalisation of the wider public sector in the UK; that is, the theory and practice of privatisation in Britain. After noting the links to the American examples, I proceed to outline the recent history of privatisation in Britain. This is followed by a section analysing the attendant questions of accountability that are raised by this process, especially those pertaining to the nature of regulation (whether by Parliamentary oversight or statutory regulators), and the role and rights of consumers/citizens. Finally the privatisation of the electricity supply industry provides a short case study.

PRIVATISING BRITAIN: THEORY AND PRACTICE

The dynamics of the de-regulation and privatisation drive in the US, as identified in chapter 5, apply with equal vigour to Britain. There is little to be gained by reiterating the earlier analysis, but one or two points do bear repeating and expanding. Privatisation is a technique, not an ideology. It is a tool, a means to an end, not the end in itself, despite the fervour of its advocates, and it has been used by governments of different persuasions to achieve a variety of aims (Letwin, 1988; Graham and Prosser, 1991). It is primarily used, however, by liberal/conservative governments the world over to implement a set of changes within their economies and political structures enshrining the values of the New Right. Like Marxists, they recognise that social and political institutions tend to reinforce the dominant economic structures of a society. They have sought, therefore, to reconstruct the economic foundations of society, underpinning the market system to which they subscribe.

In order to implement these market reinforcements, the New Right governments of Britain and America have used their control of the institutions of government to reform both those institutions themselves and the wider economy. That is, by capturing control of the state (however that may be defined) the New Right have sought to reform the economy in such a way that the political system is itself also reinforced in their own image. This has variously been described as 'ideological imperialism' (Pollitt, 1990), the end of the post-war consensus or the 'death' of socialism.[1] Ironically, it could almost be viewed as a perverse reversal of Gramsci's theory of the war of praxis, in which he believed socialist parties needed to capture the ramparts and trenches of the state (to borrow his metaphor of trench warfare) in order to implement a democratic socialist reform of the economy along communist lines (1971).

Whilst such an analysis is similar to the views of the 'new institutionalists' (March and Olsen, 1984; Hall, 1986), it does not deny the position that '"the state" is a wider concept than that of government' (Graham and Prosser, 1991, p.3). The Conservative Party in Britain used their control of the institutions of the Welfare State to attempt to transform that state and society into something reflecting their (newly dominant) liberal market beliefs. This ideological impetus also illustrated something of a transformation for the normally pragmatic Conservative Party, a phenomenon that appeared to have largely run its course with the demise of the Thatcher leadership.[2]

In privatisation, the Conservatives found the perfect tool for imposing the changes in both structure and culture that they desired. At its simplest, privatisation is merely to 'render private or to bring into the private sector. In general terms it is the withdrawal of the state from the production of goods and services' (Veljanovski, 1987, p.1). The Party hoped that, when linked to the reform of Whitehall, privatisation would begin a process of cultural transformation, alienating the citizenry from state intervention and welfare dependency. In Britain its major objectives have been similar to those outlined for the US and can be chronicled as:

1. to reduce government involvement in the decision-making of industry;
2. to permit industry to raise funds from the capital market on commercial terms and without government guarantee;
3. to raise revenue and reduce the public sector borrowing requirement;
4. to promote wide share ownership;
5. to create an enterprise culture;

6. to encourage workers' share ownership in their companies;
7. to increase competition and efficiency;
8. to replace ownership and financial controls with a more effective system of economic regulation designed to ensure that benefits of greater efficiency are passed on to consumers (ibid., p.7).

Veljanovski argues that the order of his list reflects the chronological emphasis each of them has been given by the government. Yet two British objectives he neglected to include are of immense importance and can be found in the list Hanke provides as the goals for privatisation in the US. They are:

1. the depoliticisation of economic decisions;
2. the reduction in the power of the public sector unions (1987, p.2).

Despite Veljanovski's plea that in the early days the objectives of privatisation were 'purely financial and managerial' (1987, p.7), this has never been the case and illustrates his ideological position as much as that of the government. To seek to reduce government intervention in industry, to give nationalised industries access to the capital markets and reduce the public sector borrowing requirements, may well be merely financial and managerial, but they are also deeply ideological, reflecting the market and monetarist propensities of the Tory leadership.

Another criticism is that these British goals are inconsistent in both theory and practice. The desire to promote wide share ownership has often clashed with the goal of maximising revenue from the sales, as in order to encourage the public to purchase shares and prevent the political embarrassment of having the offer undersubscribed, the government resorted to a technique of low offer prices. When British Aerospace was sold the Government had a shortfall of £135.4 million in the receipts it gained compared to the public funds invested in the company after its nationalisation in 1977 (Graham and Prosser, 1991, p.91). In the case of Rolls-Royce a 'cash injection' of £283 million was made, whilst the water authorities were able to write off £6.5 billion of public debts and investments, only recouping £5.2 billion in the sale (ibid.). Furthermore, in selling off most monopolies as a whole, instead of splitting them up, the government was ensuring their future profitablity and underlining its own commitment to a politically successful privatisation in terms of wide share ownership and state withdrawal from industrial intervention, rather than the promotion of free competition. That is, the goal of privatisation won out over the goal of liberalisation (Marsh, 1991, pp.459–80; Graham and Prosser, 1991, pp.71–6). This point is further underlined when it is realised that, between 1979 and 1990, forty-three enterprises were sold off by private treaty. In some cases, such as Appledore shipbuilders and Leyland Trucks, the prices were not publicly disclosed. The government did not even bother with the process of auctioning most of these companies, but simply split them off from the public sector and negotiated their transfer with their own management (as in the case of the National Freight Consortium) or with large private sector organisations, some of which were foreign-owned. For the most part (excluding steel) the companies sold were small organisations, realising only about £2,647 million in total.

Hanke's view of the process is nearer the Conservative's own, but from a different perspective, when he re-states privatisation as a desire 'to reduce government involvement in the decision-making of industry', and as 'the depoliticisation of economic decisions' (1987). Privatisation provides for the insulation of industry from the explicit political process; it shields executives from the accountability of ministerial and parliamentary control, as such it contributes to the culture of managerialism and aids the power of those who claim to be 'professional' managers. These executives may have been taken from the anonymity of the public service and made visibly accountable to the new shareholders of the privatised organisations, but this is a limited accountability, one curtailed by the loss of explicit ministerial control over industry, a control for which they were ultimately answerable to Parliament. As such privatisation reflects the anti-state ideology of the New Right, an ethos that pervades much of British politics and has its echoes in the lack of a codified constitution (Graham and Prosser, 1991). Once privatisation began to gain its own momentum it became clear that the goal of competition and liberalisation was going to be secondary to the other more explicitly political aims.

With economic de-politicisation came an implicit desire to curb the power of public sector unions. The experience of the Conservative Party throughout the 1970s and 1980s led them to believe that the power of the Labour movement, rooted in the post-war consensus and the structures of the Welfare State, required substantial reform (Marquand, 1988, pp.52–83; Bulpitt, 1983). Privatisation was to aid the re-discovery of harsher managerial practices aligned to an often intransigent government industrial relations policy. The performance indicator for industry was to be profit, not social welfare functions. As such, staffing levels and productivity were subjected to rigorous scrutiny; indeed, management teams themselves had this applied to them by private sector management consultants both before and after privatisation.

Now that the verities of the Welfare State had been cut from under them, the power of the public sector industrial unions melted away. The re-introduction of a reserve pool of labour through policies of high unemployment, aligned with often massive job losses in the re-structured industries, such as the steel industry, served to successfully curtail the influence of labour on the economic decision-making process. As will be shown in the next chapter, for those unions representing members not in industry but the bureaucracies of local government, other novel forms of privatisation were introduced, sometimes mirroring the American examples, sometimes building upon the experience of central government at national level. These included (following various Acts of Parliament): compulsory contracting out for services, compulsory asset sales (for example council houses), deregulation of services; repealing monopolies, the right to private substitution and encouraging people to exit from state provision (Ascher, 1987). As a practical tool privatisation has developed a keen edge through use. In Britain, as in America, it has meant the abdication by government as a producer or provider of many goods and services, where it remains involved at all it is often as a financier, authoriser or overseer (Salamon, 1989, p.8).

As was the case in the US, privatisation in the UK has often been lauded for freeing former public organisations from the interventions and restrictions of government. It is ironic that this should be seen as a victory for markets when it would not require a change of ownership to simply relax health and safety regulations, free up restrictions on borrowing and investment, break up large conglomerations, or liberalise personnel and remuneration practices. Yet it is the pursuit of these very freedoms that has led some public sector executives to seek to transfer the assets of their organisations to the market-place (Dunleavy, 1986, 1990). The guidelines advocated by the Salamon Report for the United States (previously referred to in chapter 5) are also of value for the UK. It is certainly the case that privatisation in the UK began from a different position from that of the US; the advances of the Welfare State and the re-structuring of industrial policy via nationalisation were never accorded the same degree of success in the US as they enjoyed in Britain. Yet the transformation of the public sector wrought by privatisation has led to a somewhat shared experience for the two countries, including the establishing of constituencies of interest which have directly benefited from the process (Graham and Prosser, 1991, pp.19–28), albeit embarked upon from different perspectives and with different outcomes.

THE SCALE OF PRIVATISATION

In addition to being a process of de-politicisation, privatisation is the devolution of policy-making. As with many types of devolution, this does not necessarily mean a reduction in central government power, merely a re-emphasis away from day-to-day interventionism. There is nothing inherently new in the process of re-defining the relationship of the private to the public; the boundaries of private ownership have been debated in the UK since before the medieval period, usually in the form of a struggle between factions of the ruling elite. It was a goal of the post-1979 Conservative Government to significantly expand the private ownership of property, indeed to 'democratise' it by devolving ownership down from the state and a small elite to the majority of the citizenry. This devolution, through privatisation, was closely aligned to an industrial policy which sought to distance the government from intervening in the affairs of business. Indeed, the government disliked the very term 'industrial policy' and wherever possible it restricted itself to 'climate-setting' measures aimed at promoting an 'enterprise strategy' within the immutable rules of a market economy (Grant, 1989, pp.85–112). Both individuals and business were to lose some of the protections of the Welfare State and its corporatist tendencies, a culture which had done much to dispel uncertainty from the consensual post-war world of British industry and society (Middlemas, 1979).

For the majority of British subjects the concept of property ownership, whether in the form of shares or real estate, is a novel experience. Similarly, for a majority of British industrialists a post-war government explicitly eschewing an interventionist industrial policy (and meaning it) is unprecedented. The growth of public ownership of industry had begun uncontentiously with the establishment of organisations such as the Port of London Authority and the British Broadcasting Corporation in the first half of this century. The Conservative Party participated in these early expansions of state ownership and whilst in coalition with the Labour Pary during World War Two greatly expanded the controls over industry. With the implementation of Labour's plans for a Welfare State following its 1945 election victory, there followed a massive expansion of industrial control via nationalisation and detailed directives (ibid.). The Fabian belief in rational management and public intervention, in order to construct socialism, lay behind much of this expansion, as did an eclectic melange of High Tory paternalism and Liberal fraternalism (Smith, 1979; Middlemas, 1979). Despite electoral sound and fury, the general consensus of government intervention and a restricted private sector received wide approbation and formed the basis of a new status quo. Indeed, until 1979 successive Conservative administrations were content to accept the nationalised sector, de-nationalising only road haulage, some parts of steel, a brewery and two travel agents, in the period 1952–79.

Party politics were conducted within a diminishing sphere of manoeuvre as corporatist bargains struck by one government constrained the actions of the next (Smith, 1979; Marquand, 1988.) A crisis of government overload appeared set to paralyse effective administration, whilst elected governments were reduced to haggling on apparently equal terms with business and union leaders. The Conservative administration of Mrs Thatcher sought to change this by removing the Government from the day-to-day sphere of industrial policy, de-politicising many economic/industrial decisions and reducing the amount of the national income spent by government. It was an attempt to strengthen government by devolving, or delegating, some of its powers. Privatisation was to prove one of the government's most effective weapons in achieving these goals. It was used, as in the US, at both national and sub-national levels.

When the extent of the transformation wrought upon the public sector is reviewed from the perspective of the early 1990s it is surprising to recall that the 1979 manifesto, with which the Conservatives came to power, lacked a coherent commitment to privatisation; indeed the word was not mentioned at all. The new government was explicitly monetarist and its 'emphasis then was upon controlling the money supply, reducing public expenditure and cutting income tax' (Marsh, 1991, p.460). From 1979 the government built up the privatisation momentum gradually, exercising caution at every stage. The partial sale of British Telecommunications in

1984 was the point at which a slow trickle of small sell-offs was transformed into successive waves of major privatisations; it was probably the first time that the process could be said to resemble a coherent programme. Initially it involved only a partial sale of assets with the government retaining some portion of the whole, usually under fifty per cent. The privatisation of the larger organisations (but not BP) necessitated passing legislation which transformed their status, making them public limited companies which could then be sold off via a share offer on the stock markets. The Conservatives passed separate Acts of Parliament for each large privatisation, a procedure that was not followed in either the US or France. In the case of the latter 'all the privatization programme is covered by one piece of empowering legislation and one statute which deals with implementation' (Graham and Prosser, 1991, p.84).

During the period of the first Thatcher administration (1979–83), twenty-five public enterprises were involved, with Amersham International (radio chemicals), Ferranti, International Computers Limited and Fairey Holdings being outright sales (Veljanovski, 1987, pp.3–5). About £1,440m was raised in this first tranche of activity. Mrs Thatcher's second term in office (1983–7) saw the process gather pace and culminate in the sale of British Telecom (a partial sale of just over fifty per cent, with the remainder being made available in the financial year 1991–2) and British Gas. The latter has become one of the largest private sector companies in Europe and exercises a monopoly within the United Kingdom. The scale of the privatisation programme by the end of the second Tory term had grown such that:

> By the beginning of 1987, twelve major companies and a larger number of smaller ones [had] been privatised. This has transferred 20 per cent of the state sector and over 400,000 jobs to the private sector, more than doubled the number of shareholders in Britain and raised over £12 billion. In addition, over three-quarters of a million council houses have been sold, raising £8 billion for the government. (Ibid., p.4)

The third Conservative term of office quickened the pace and saw the privatisation of the water companies, the electricity supply industry, British Airways, the British Airports Authority, British Steel, the National Bus company, Unipart and Rolls Royce, and the Royal Ordnance Factories; bringing into the Treasury a total of about £26 billion (ibid., p.5). For the financial year 1990–1, proceeds from privatisation were about £5.5 billion and the Autumn statement by the Chancellor of the Exchequer in 1991 predicted that this would rise to about £8 billion for 1991–2 and remain at that level for two years (Autumn Statement/*The Independent*, 7/11/91). The Chancellor argued that the income would come from the second tranche of British Telecom shares to be issued and second and third payments from electricity and water shares, as well as second and third payments for BT shares in 1992–3; finally, the Treasury planned to privatise British Coal and British Rail (ibid.). By any standard

> the scale of privatisation is immense. In fact by early 1991: over 50 per cent of the public sector had been transfered to the private sector; 650,000 workers had changed sectors, of whom 90 per cent had become shareholders; 9 million people were shareholders, which represented 20 per cent of the population, as compared with 7 per cent in 1979; about 1,250,000 council houses had been sold, most to sitting tenants under the 'right to buy' provisions; and contracting out was well established in the NHS and the local authority sector. (Marsh, 1991, p.464)

An irony contained within the Chancellor's 1991 Autumn statement, however, was that:

> the Government was for the fourth year running forced to abandon the once dearly held political tenet that [its] spending as a proportion of national income should shrink. (*Independent*, 7/11/91)

Indeed the proportion of GDP spent by the public sector was to rise to over 42 per cent, creeping back up towards its high point of 47.5 per cent under the Conservatives in 1982–3 (ibid.) considerably more than the 40.5 per cent they inherited from the previous government, and which they strongly criticised. In both instances the reason for the increase was falling national income allied with a rise in unemployment which necessitated statutory expenditure on unemployment and social security benefits, as well as the close proximity of a General Election, when governments traditionally increase public expenditure to attempt to purchase voter approbation. The Public Sector Borrowing Requirement was also set to rise. Once virtually eliminated by the Conservatives, the PSBR is seen by many of them as an indicator as to how well they are managing the economy. Their goal is to have a balanced budget and squeeze out the PSBR. Again privatisation is a boon to those who hold to this position as receipts from asset sales count as negative expenditure (thereby reducing the need for borrowing) not as income. One of the original intentions of privatisation, indeed the thrust of the Conservative's policy making from 1979, was to reduce the amount of national income disposed of by the government. Such a policy is central to much New Right thinking (Bacon and Eltis, 1976) and its apparent abandonment in the Conservative's third period of office either marked a change in their approach or a realisation that the interventionist role of the modern state is a recalcitrant inheritance beyond the ability of even the most committed administration to reform.

If it is the latter reason then it tends to support the argument of Public Choice theorists like Butler (1987) who argue that the coalitions of interests manufactured by the Welfare State act as a ratchet to crank up public expenditure and prevent its reduction. Despite the difficulty of the struggle to control public expenditure, Conservative administrations from 1979 were at pains to emphasise the superiority of the private over the public, a reversal of the Welfare State's traditional perspective. But 'ideology was not enough; it had to be accompanied by the building up and maintenance of constituencies of political support' (Graham and Prosser, 1991, p.23); there had to be a shift of political and cultural emphasis in Britain. The shift of emphasis had become such that 'the question became increasingly not one of what should be privatised, but of when particular corporations, companies, trading funds and departmental activities should be sold off' (Swann, 1988, p. 258). Every organisation located within the public sector was forced to explain the reason for its call upon the public purse, those unable to convince a sceptical government were to prepare for a transfer to the private sector.

Privatisation, then, was to represent a monumental transfer of wealth, plant and employment out of the public sector and into private ownership. The levels at which this occurred were both national and local and the techniques ranged from small management buy-outs (the National Freight Corporation) through to outright sales (council houses, Jaguar, Rover) and massive share offers (telecommunications, gas, water and electricity). Certainly the sale of more than a million council houses and the expansion of share ownership greatly increased the coalition of people directly benefiting from privatisation (Graham and Prosser, 1991, pp.10-28).

Of the goals identified by Veljanovski as those of the government, however, the idealism of New Right theory had to give way to the realities of late Twentieth Century industrial economics. That is, several of the industries and all of the utilities are natural monopolies and therefore attempts at increasing competition within a newly constructed market can only be nominal. The political realities meant that a system of regulation had to be introduced to prevent the exploitation of consumers via the abuse of monopoly power and this necessitated a continuation of government involvement in the decision-making of industry, albeit at 'arms' length' with the establishment of non-ministerial departments in the form of offices of regulation. Furthermore, although there was clearly an increase in share ownership, many of those who invested in the privatised companies quickly 'stagged' their stake by selling at the earliest opportunity, their shares usually being bought by large institutional investors. The aforementioned underpricing, or discounting, of the shares can be measured by the difference between the price paid by the original investor and the new price the shares commanded on the stock market. Observers noted that the discounts have been far higher than those normally associated with private sales in Britain, about fifteen per cent (ibid., p.95). Prior to the sale of the electricity supply industry the underpricing of shares probably accounted for a loss of a further £1.9 billion in revenue to the Treasury (ibid.).

As to the issue of efficiency, the New Right are bullish, arguing that:

> the crucial question is not whether private property is more efficient than public property, because … that is a fairly meaningless dichotomy, but whether privatised but regulated firms are more efficient than nationalised industries in practice. (Veljanovski, 1987, p.92)

The efficacy or otherwise of privatisation with regard to achieving efficiency cannot be tested because we are not comparing like with like. The very act of privatising allows the companies involved to restructure their personnel, financing and marketing policies in a way that had not been countenanced within the public sector. In short, their goals were changed and so were the means by which they could attain those goals. Social responsibility was no longer to be a part of the ethics of the privatised companies, questions of this nature were to be left to the concern of the new regulatory bodies.

REGULATING INDUSTRY; ACCOUNTABILITY BY DESIGN

Regulation can take many forms. In the context of British privatisation policy it has tended to be used to control the operation of monopoly dominated markets in order to further the Conservatives' aims of enfranchising consumers, promoting competition (although this has not tended to dominate policy), and preventing the abuse of their power by the new monopolies or oligopolies. For many of the privatised companies, close links remained with the government in the form of government ownership of 'golden shares' and detailed regulation. The Electricity Act alone contains 67 distinct areas where the Secretary of State for Energy retains regulatory control over the industry, a similar oversight for the Secretary of State for the Environment was also written into the Bill which privatised water (Graham and Prosser, 1991, p.140). For smaller companies a golden share was instituted, whereby:

> the share capital of the company will contain one special-rights redeemable preference share of £1 held by the government or its nominee. Certain matters are then specified in the company's articles of association as being deemed to be a variation of the rights of the special share amd therefore can only be effective with the consent in writing of the special shareholder. The most common provisions specified are those which, if altered, would undermine the powers of the special share ... even a substantial restructuring of the company will depend on negotiations between it and the government, rather than the free play of market forces.
>
> Furthermore, although the impression is sometimes given that golden shares are a temporary device, there is generally no fixed time limit for their expiry ... sometimes a date is specified in the articles before which the government will not redeem the share; in other cases, the share may be redeemed on request. Even in the former case, this does not mean that the special share scheme will automatically be brought to an end at the first available date. (Ibid., p.141)

The government has used its golden share to prevent the take-over of newly privatised companies by foreign competitors; this was an issue of particular concern in the case of the water companies. There have been occasions, however, when Conservative backbench MPs have been more concerned at foreign take-overs than the government, their outrage preventing the loss of Land Rover to a continental competitor. In recent years the government has tended not to invest companies with a golden share, or not to use it where there is an opportunity. In the case of the sale of Jaguar to Ford, the government appeared to actually revoke its use of the golden share in order to thwart a bid by the rival General Motors, whilst with regard to the purchase of the privatised Britoil by the privatised BP, the golden share's existence and the government's attempt to use it provoked general confusion and proved ultimately pointless (ibid., pp.141–51). Golden shares apart, new regulatory bodies and statutory duties upon the government to intervene (or at least to be consulted) render privatisation in practice a long way from being the ideal implementation of the liberal abstraction. Despite its attempts to extricate itself from industry and its clear renunciation of an explicit industrial policy, the government was obliged to avoid abrogating all control over industry to the free market. The main reason for this is that in the case of many companies there was no free market and, even if there were, questions of national security and electoral strategy were interposed between the liberal ideal and the political reality. This quandary was at its most acute with the utilities.

Because utilities are natural monopolies there was no competitive framework, or market, into which they could be launched. This:

> clearly troubled the Conservative government in its early days in office. Sir Geoffrey Howe, for example, was far from clear as to what ought to be done about natural monopolies even if they were making a profit. It would, he argued, be wrong to entrust private owners with monopoly powers ... In due course however the government came to the conclusion that the absence of competition or substantial competition should not stand in the way of privatisation. The solution was regulation – a system upon which ... the US has been turning its back. (Swann, 1988, p.259)

By 1985, with the successful privatisation of BT under its belt, the government came to the conclusion that the evils of private sector monopoly were outweighed by those of public ownership. John Moore, the Financial Secretary to the Treasury declared that even for those organisations where competition was impractical the government would develop regulatory frameworks to control them, on the ideological grounds that the 'regulated private ownership of natural monopolies is preferable to nationalisation' (ibid.).

Given its wider commitment to liberalisation, it would have been natural for the Conservative Government to fully debate the implementation of a system of regulatory controls at the time the US was coming to the end of a period of de-regulation. This would have been especially apposite as one of the primary functions of privatisation had been as an aid liberalisation, albeit an end that at times has appeared to become subordinated to its means. The example of both regulation and de-regulation in the US provides evidence of the difficult, often fraught economic and political problems attending these activities. Yet in Britain there has been a surprising dearth of informed political debate surrounding the establishing of a complex regulatory system, replete with the panoplay of Crown powers vested in non-ministerial departments of state. When BT was privatised:

> a brief White paper emerged, but this simply repeated a ministerial statement about the future of the industry with less than a paragraph on the proposed regulatory arrangements (Cmnd.8610). As regards gas, no White Paper or considered consultative document was published ... Similarly, the White Paper on Electricity Privatisation (Cmnd. [*sic*]322) dealt with the issue in only five paragraphs. (Graham and Prosser, 1991, p.185)

In fact this was a slight exaggeration with regard to electricity, as *Cm*322 referred to regulation in other paragraphs such as those relating to standards of service, but the general point about a lack of public debate or apparent official concern is well made. The only detailed analysis can be found in the Littlechild reports (1983, 1986) on regulating BT's profitability and the economic regulation of the water industry (Graham and Prosser, 1991, pp.186–7; Swann, 1988, pp. 270–1).

Littlechild's New Right credentials were widely known and applauded in government circles; indeed, he was to become the first Director General of the Office of Electricity Regulation. In his papers he was anxious to stress that regulation ought to protect the consumer from the effects of monopoly power and the best way to do this was to foster competition, or to mimic market pressures. He was keen to avoid many of the pitfalls he identified in the American system of regulation, most noticeably the problem of agency capture, where the regulator 'goes native' and begins to lobby on behalf of the industry being regulated. The best way to avoid this was to reduce the contact between the regulator and the industry to a minimum and therefore to rely on a mechanism which would simulate a market and protect consumers whilst stimulating productivity. A member of OFFER's senior management team argued that:

> the prime relationship is that between the companies and the customers, and it is not our view that regulations should get in the way of that, and for the most part we are aiming to put in place a framework that maximises the chances of that relationship developing successfully. (Interview)

He arrived at the widely used RPI-x formula, where RPI is the retail price index and x is a figure set by the regulator (ibid.). The difficulties here are that some of the regulatory duties relate to social, not economic constraints. An example is the requirement placed on BT to provide services to rural areas and emergency services (Graham and Prosser, 1991). Furthermore, the setting of x is a highly political process open to prolonged negotiation between the industry, the regulator and the government, as well as consumer groups. Finally, if the regulator relies for technical and commercial information primarily from the industry then clearly the office is still open to utility capture. American experience tends to confirm that a more active and continuing interest by the government is the best way to prevent agency capture, especially when it is allied to providing adequate independent expertise for the regulator.

The various Acts which paved the way for privatising the utilities also allowed for the creation of the new non-ministerial departments which were to regulate the industries. These are:

1. for telecommunications the Office of Telecommunications, or OFTEL;
2. for the water industry two bodies were created, the Office of Water Supply, or OFWAT, which is concerned with regulating the industry and consumer protection, and the National Rivers Authority which has a mainly environmental role;
3. for gas the Office of Gas Supply, or OFGAS;
4. for the electricity supply industry the Office of Electricity Regulation, or OFFER.

Each of these offices is headed by a Director General who is appointed by the relevant Secretaries of State. But these are not political appointees in the American sense, rather the government has gone to some length to stress the independence of the new agencies and their heads, hence the decision to make them non-ministerial. In a sense it is a harking back to the old Morrisonion ideal for the nationalised industries in that the government wants them to be seen as at 'arms' length' from the government of the day, performing their regulatory functions independent of both ministers and industry. That said, however, the Directors General do have some functions that require them to act in an advisory capacity to the relevant Secretaries of State. For example, 'they must be consulted before the granting of licences; they are also under a general duty to give information, advice and assistance to the Secretary of State … either on request or on their own initiative' (Graham and Prosser, 1991, p.191). Furthermore, just as in the days of the nationalised industries, informal meetings, perhaps over lunch, between senior civil servants or even the Minister and the Director General can result in some firm 'steers' being given to the latter. To refuse to be steered often meant that a person failed to be re-appointed to a second term of office (Massey, 1988, pp.52–107). There is no reason to believe that in a governmental structure, unreformed in the sense that it is still permeated with informal networks and private decision-making, anything will have changed with respect to such pressures. Other commentators have likened this to the lack of constitutionality within the British political system, contrasting it to the concern shown in the US to maintain the separation of powers at all levels of government (Graham and Prosser, 1991, p.209).

The major function of the regulators is to enforce the enabling licences and their conditions, issued to the operators. For example, under the 1989 Electricity Act, the Director General of OFFER is charged with protecting customers and promoting competition in the industry, controlling certain prices, settling disputes between producers and consumers and between producers, issuing licences for the generating, transmitting and supplying of electricity, investigating complaints and fixing the highest price for which electricity can be resold. OFFER has also approved Codes of Practice by the various generating and distribution companies which attempt to set out the service the Electricity Supply Industry (ESI) will provide. Similar functions are performed by all the regulators, whose role has been modelled on that of the Director General of the Office of Fair Trading (OFFER, 1991; Electricity Act, 1989). All the regulators are expected to review the activities 'their' industries are engaged in and to publish information and advice regarding them. Clearly there are also specific duties relating to their industries that are unique to each regulator; in the case of gas this tends to reflect the monopoly position of British Gas.

This company's position also illustrates the weakness of the regulator with regard to promoting competition and controlling prices. Competition policy, and therefore to a large if often indirect extent also prices, is policed by the Monopolies and Mergers Commission, the Department of Trade and Industry, the Office of Fair Trading, the European Commission and also the regulator. A barrage of complaints since privatisation to these bodies by consumers and others about the alleged abuse of its power by British Gas has led to a series of investigations of the company's behaviour (Graham and Prosser, 1991, pp.199–207; Swann, 1988, pp. 260–72). Little had changed by 1992, other than some feeble tinkering with the company's ability to extort money from its captive customers quite so blatantly, particularly the industrial users who had been subjected to the discriminatory pricing policy criticised by the Monopolies and Mergers Commission (ibid.; also Gas Consumers' Council, 1989). The privatisation of electricity had as one of its unstated goals the intention that the new structures would not repeat the government's mistakes over gas and telecommunications.

Both companies were sold without major structural reform, transforming public sector monopolies into private sector ones: monopolies, moreover, powerful enough to defy the attempts of regulators to curb their more outrageous abuses. After the first investigation into its activities, British Gas was censored by OFGAS for refusing to supply the Director General of Gas Supply with the information he needed to implement new tariff schedules (Graham and Prosser, 1991, p.206). One senior member of OFFER's management team recalled the incident with wry amusement:

> Some of the earlier regulators found they didn't have information-getting powers that were strong enough. I think McKinnon found that with British Gas. He first of all asked for information to sort of check that the price control was being complied with, and he found they said, 'Go away! We have given you the minimum and we are not going to give you any more.' In the end he did get what he wanted, but he had a big fight with them. (Interview)

British Telecom's painful adjustment to the private sector earned it the sobriquet, 'the most hated institution in the land', as it fought the threat of competition, whilst extracting huge profits that did not appear to be warranted in terms of improved service to the community (*The Independent*, 20/11/90). The nature of the privatisations of these utilities reflected the government's greater attachment to making the process of privatisation a success and of widening share ownership. Creating a market where there had never been one and thereby engendering a degree of competiton was lower down on the political agenda. Consequently this was to hinder the new arrangements put into place to enforce control and accountability.

These arrangements have generally been loose and ad hoc, despite following the pattern established by the procedures applying to the Office of Fair Trading. For example the duties imposed upon the Secretary of State for the granting of the initial licences for operators under the Water Act are minimal (although impressive duties to intervene, and enabling powers to do so, are explicit in other areas of concern). For water and telecommunications the setting of the x figure in the equation RPI-x have been enveloped in secrecy and 'commercial confidentiality', as have the negotiations over generating contracts in the electricity industry (Graham and Prosser, 1991, pp.211–13), whilst the setting of the non-fossil fuel element that electricity suppliers are obliged to include requires only that the Secretary of State consult the Director General of OFFER (ibid.). If the regulator wishes to vary the terms of a utilitiy's licence without the agreement of the operator then the Director General must refer the matter to the MMC, only when the Commission's consent has been given may the regulator enforce a change. This procedure has only been invoked once, against telephone chatlines; mostly the regulators have tended to seek to negotiate with the operators (ibid.). Parliamentary scrutiny of the privatised companies is at best minimal and both ministers and the executives of the new companies routinely deny information to Parliamentary Select Committees on the grounds of commercial confidentiality (various interviews). Thus privatisation of the utilities appears to have further pushed decision making into the shadows and out of public scrutiny. The links between the regulators and the new companies, and between ministers and the regulators are marked by informality and secrecy. As such there appears to have been a move away from explicit accountability and public involvement in the policy process.

There is a clear contrast between the flexible, ad hoc, often cryptic new British regulatory agencies and the older American version. In the US the mode of regulation reflects the constitutionalist nature of American politics with its emphasis on checks and balances, federalism and separation of powers. Furthermore, the belief that sovereignty is vested in the people and not in institutions led to the introduction of the Administrative Procedure Act, which as early as 1946 established that agencies:

- were required to keep the public informed of their organisation, procedures and rules;
- had to provide for public participation in the rule-making process;
- must provide uniform standards for the conduct of formal rule-making and adjudicatory proceedings;
- were to restate the law of judicial review. (Graham and Prosser, 1991, p.220)

Even today such an Act would be considered revolutionary within the UK's public sector. Its implementation throughout the American regulatory sector certainly did not prevent some agencies being prone to 'capture' by their clients, but the relationship between them, major consumer and other interest groups, the government and the legislature has consistently been more open than in Britain. Furthermore, the emphasis on judicial review has allowed the American courts a wider role than the British courts, to the extent that they have 'played a central role in the development of administrative procedure' in open court (ibid., p.222), whilst the British judiciary have been restricted to a narrow interpretation of procedural propriety and *ultra vires*, that is deciding whether ministers and officials have kept to their own often arcane rules. Moreover, since 1946 the Americans have also passed (and judicially refined) the Freedom of Information Act, the Government in the Sunshine Act and the Federal Advisory Committees Act, all of which have underscored public accountability functions. British courts have been almost wholly excluded from the British privatisation process, certainly the judiciary were not a consideration within the formulation period and their impact upon implementation has been minimal even where it has been exercised, as over the sale of the Trustees Savings Bank.

The experience of privatisation in Britain has provided a lesson on the relationship of the government to the governed that illuminates much of the argument in chapter 1. The British penchant for pragmatic flexibility and a government unfettered by irrevocable statutes (in the form of a codified constitution) or administrative codes (as in the rest of the European Community) has been seen at its most unrestrained over the period 1979 to 1991. The law has been 'overwhelmingly an expression of governmental will' and:

> scrutiny and legitimation has been the business of extrajudicial bodies, in particular parliamentary debate and the *ex post facto* scrutiny of the Public Accounts Committee. (Graham and Prosser, 1991, p.244)

The nature of the British political process, with its emphasis on party discipline, executive dominance, Crown prerogative and legislative compliance, means that such scrutiny and legitimation is considerably less than in the US or other EC countries. As Graham and Prosser have argued:

> In Britain, the role of the law has been almost wholly instrumental; it has been a means by which the government can implement effectively its chosen goals ... The role of the courts has been purely technical in the few cases where they have been called upon; they have had no clearly constitutional role in assessing the compatibility of public actions with constitutional principle. Moreover, important areas of practice have been outside the scope of any judicial control. (Ibid.)

Privatisation has illustrated the secretive, informal nature of the British political process and in part also its lack of accountability. But it has also shown how attempts to extend the role of the courts in the area of official accountability and judicial review are likely to fail unless there is a reform of the political system itself. There is one area, however, where privatisation has been a major success in terms other than those of the Conservative Government: as a method of evaluating past policies. It is to this and the other issues we now turn in the form of the case study of electricity privatisation.

PRIVATISING ELECTRICITY

The privatisation of the British Electricity Supply Industry (ESI) was accompanied by the biggest industrial re-structuring in the world; the only comparable activity was the reform of AT and T in the US. The lessons learned by the privatisation of telecommunications and gas were the reason for the total transformation of the electricity industry. The government was determined to answer criticisms that it merely transferred monopoly power out of the public sector, where it was subjected to parliamentary control via ministerial accountability, to the private sector, where accountability was less obvious. To this end it appointed Professor Stephen Littlechild as its advisor, a post that led to his eventual appointment as the first Director General of OFFER.

Background to the Sell-off

The industry had remained virtually unchanged from the time of its post-war re-organisation under the 1957 Electricity Act (Massey, 1988). The Central Electricity Generating Board (CEGB) was the largest organisation to stem from this, being responsible for the generation of electricity in England and Wales and control of the National Grid. Regional distribution companies purchased current from the grid and sold it to consumers. Smaller boards were constituted for Scotland and Northern Ireland. An Electricity Council was established to try to coordinate the industry, but the major organisation was the CEGB, which came to dominate the ESI.

There existed within the CEGB a tremendous corporate spirit. It took its obligations under the Act, to supply constant electricity at the lowest price consistent with safety, to its logical conclusion and became preoccupied (perhaps obsessed) with production (ibid.). There was no competition and little incentive to control costs or consult consumers. Costs were passed on to customers and the industry was run by its engineers within the general directions laid down from time to time by ministers. Within the Department of Energy the CEGB became known as 'The Kremlin' and this not always affectionate sobriquet illustrated the often fraught relationship between government and the technical experts who ran the industry (various interviews). The latter saw their brief in terms of the Act which gave specific technical goals to which they addressed themselves to the best of their professional ability. It allowed them to evolve a producer-driven organisation which performed its function superbly, but at the expense of the other members of the policy process. By 1985 there was general agreement amongst those groups that the system had to be reformed. Because of the prevailing fashion for privatisation it became clear that re-organisation would take place at the same time as the industry was sold off.

As the foregoing sections have sought to explain, the experience of British Gas and British Telecom had convinced the government of the need to inject a degree of industrial re-organisation and competition into the privatisation of monopolistic utilities. A year of policy formulation led to the White Paper in 1988, *Privatising Electricity* (Cm 322) where the government showed its clear intention to introduce competition to the ESI. This was partly based upon its interpretation of the the the experience of utilities in the US who were required to enter the market to tender for new supplies.

Cm 322 reflected the fact that the grid and distribution system is a natural monopoly, but that the provision of new generating capacity is not necessarily similarly monopolistic. To remove the CEGB's monopoly would strike to the core of professional domination within the industry and reduce the power of the engineers and other technical experts, indeed it would transfer that power to 'the market', replacing technocratic decision-making with economic and/or political decisions.

The government was presented with a series of options by its advisers in Whitehall and the City. This placed ministers in their familiar role of policy arbiters, in that having set the strategic goals to be pursued they were now required to select the route by which those aims were to be realised. There were three main options:

1. the government could decide to keep the grid with the CEGB, re-organise the twelve area boards into one super-distributer and thereby create a powerful duopoly;
2. retain the CEGB within the public sector and privatise the twelve area boards;
3. break up the CEGB and privatise the whole ESI.

Whitehall found itself pressed to find answers for three questions when deciding which course to take:

1. How could competition be injected into the system?
2. How could natural monopolies be effectively regulated?
3. What was to become of nuclear power?

In a sense the problem here was one of personality and professional power, in that the CEGB's Chairman, Lord Marshall, was a person of great influence. He had access to the Prime Minister and could command a hearing with the Secretary of State; both abilities are of fundamental importance to the workings of Britain's informal and secretive political system. Marshall's firmly expressed preference was for keeping the CEGB as a single unit and retaining the influence of its engineers over the whole of the ESI. He felt that it would be too expensive to separate the grid and the CEGB, furthermore that the introduction of competition would hamper the expansion of nuclear power (*Financial Times*, 1/12/89). The Government decided that on balance it could live without Lord Marshall, but the electoral costs of another privatised monopoly abusing its consumers might not have been survivable. Ministers decided to break up the CEGB and take away the National Grid from the electricity producers.

The initial plan was to separate the CEGB into two generating companies, quaintly called Big G and Little G (later re-christened, 'National Power' and 'PowerGen'). Big G was to be the larger of the two, comprising seventy per cent of the CEGB's generating capacity, including the nuclear power stations. Whitehall felt that it required a company large enough to take on the financial costs (and risks) of de-commissioning nuclear power stations. The grid was to be transferred to the regional distribution companies, known for a short time as the DisCos. They were to maintain the pooling of supply and merit order, whereby the grid controllers call up the cheapest power stations to supply electricity first and then the next cheapest and so on as demand rises. Peak demand would see expensive old plant, gas turbines and oil-fired power stations contributing to the grid, plant which for the rest of the time would remain idle. There was to be light regulation of the new system, with price control using the RPI-x formula established for BT and gas. It was thought that there would be sufficient competition for the generators from France, Scotland and the new independents to ensure that Big G and Little G would not need price control.

The Secretary of State, Cecil Parkinson, had made it clear that he wanted full privatisation and competition for the ESI. His lead financial advice came from the City firm of Kleinwort Benson. They were of the opinion that if the government wished to maximise the recipts that privatisation would produce for the Treasury then competition ought to be avoided; this was advice that Parkinson ignored (*Financial Times*, 28/6/90). His technical advisors were also from the private sector. He sought their views on separating the grid from the producers, something the CEGB's engineers said could not be done. The consultants showed the Department of Energy a way, however, in which the brutal rending could be implemented.

Implementing the Policy

After a short debate in the Commons, and the announcement of an inquiry by the Select Committee on Energy, the government set about drafting the Bill that was to become the Electricity Act, 1989, an Act that was to lead to the signing of over 5,000 separate contracts to effect its implementation. The Act sought to:

1. define the future duties of the Secretary of State over the industry;
2. establish and define the duties of OFFER; create the new companies and enable the government to sell them;
3. establish the non-fossil fuel obligation mandating the distribution companies to supply a percentage of electricity produced from renewable or nuclear power stations;

4. enable the establishment of grants to pay for back-end (de-commissioning) nuclear costs;
5. consolidate electricity legislation.

The Bill was introduced to Parliament in 1988.

The Labour Party decided upon a bizarre method of opposing the Bill during its committee stage; they opted to release to the press a statement nearly every day which they calculated would embarrass the government. The Bill itself was not examined line by line and the Secretary of State was able to get his way without even having to apply for a timetable motion. Such an easy passage is most unusual given the controversial nature of the legislation. The few defeats the government did suffer were inflicted in the Lords; these were mainly in the field of renewable energy, where the government was forced to concede one or two environmentally-worded points of a fairly minor nature. The Bill became law in 1989.

The Act set in train a process whereby the Secretary of State for Energy became the sole owner of the new companies prior to privatisation. The sixteen new companies came into existence on 31 March 1990 (three generators, PowerGen, National Power and Nuclear Electric; the National Grid Company; and twelve Regional Distribution Companies). The Secretary of State then took possession. This unprecedented degree of power, total control of the ESI, was of vital importance as it allowed Whitehall to force through and establish the complex array of relationships within which the order would exist. The government was clear as to how that would be constructed.

The industry had not had a contractual relationship with itself or with its suppliers (such as British Coal) whilst it was in the public sector. Neither had it had formal detailed contracts with its large customers. This meant that a contractual structure had to be established, prior to privatisation, between the suppliers, the generators, the grid, the distribution companies and the larger consumers who would be allowed to deal directly with the producers (see for example, the *Daily Telegraph*, 13/8/90). The 'Pooling and Settlement' agreement was designed to draw all of this together and establish the new codes and relationships governing behaviour for those involved. The structure was heavily influenced by management consultants and the new regional companies. An insight into this is provided by one senior civil servant, who argued that:

I guess the more visionary and enterprising of the regional companies played a role and once the decisions were taken there was very loyal cooperation from people at the CEGB. The central ideas came from all over the place. There were quite a few outside people who wrote articles and books and were consulted in various ways. A good example is Stephen Littlechild, who began by being our adviser on regulation and wound up being the Regulator. (Interview)

The losers in this process, apart from the CEGB, were the private sector manufacturers of plant and equipment. An official noted that:

The manufacturers were not involved and I don't think the manufactureres are finding the outcome quite to their liking either ... [a company] came in to complain about it all. I'm afraid that I told them the Government believed in markets and they had better wake up to that. It's been a bitter blow to them to see National Power and Powergen out buying from foreigners and switching to turn-key contracting. They should have invested a bit more in research, but that's effectively back to the [old] structure of the industry which effectively squeezed that out to a large extent by doing research in-house at the generation end. (Interview)

A harsh conclusion, but one which reflected the newly dominant philosophy in Whitehall. That is, industry's problems were largely a result of feather-bedding by the public sector, the restructuring of the latter also meant that the former would suffer for previous misdeeds. Adjusting to market forces would correct this, but it was no business of government to intervene to save companies from the consequences of their own inadequacies. This may be a simplistic conclusion, but then the prevailing political tone of the last decade has been expressed in simplistic terms.

The Problem of Nuclear Power

Nuclear power did not fit easily into any of these provisions. In the Summer of 1989 the CEGB announced that it was unhappy with the figures allocated in its balance sheets for the costs of de-commissioning nuclear power stations. It wanted to virtually treble the money set aside for de-commissioning to over £10 billion (see for example, *The Guardian*, 1/12/89). This placed the government in the position of having to put a massive injection of cash into National Power, something which it had done for public sector industries in previous privatisations, but which it had decided to eschew with the ESI. One senior official argued:

We had decided at the end of July that the liabilities of the Magnox were too large and simply could not be carried forward into the private sector in a sustainable way. We had a lot of intense meetings with National Power in the Autumn about the form of contracts for AGRs and PWRs and the Sizewell PWR under construction. What began to emerge from that made it clear that you could either take an extremely radical decision, that is changing your previous plan and not have nuclear power, that is leave nuclear power out of privatisation. Or you could adopt a different form of privatisation for nuclear power from that which had previously been proposed. There could have been models where effectively the Government would have taken the liabilities and the private sector would have marched off with the assets and used them to best advantage. The view was taken that that really wasn't privatisation; to send people off into the private sector surrounded by guarantees of every possible kind is not privatisation in the form in which it should take place and it doesn't meet what the Government regard as the benefits of privatisation. The benefits of privatisation include the need for managements to take on assets and liabilities and make the most of what they've got. (Interview)

This is a view that constitutes a considerable change upon that prevailing during the earlier sell-offs.

In addition to the CEGB's new-found concern for the costs of nuclear power, new technology was coming on stream that was threatening to make both coal and nuclear plant uneconomic by comparison. For example, Combined Cycle Gas Turbine (CCGT) stations promised quick-build techniques for smaller and lower capital cost power stations, which could also be combined with district heating schemes. The new companies appeared reluctant to opt for the CEGB's traditionally large power stations of over 1 GW, especially when coal and nuclear stations were attracting strong opposition on environmental grounds (see, for example, *The Guardian*, 17/10/90). The market dictated small (300 MW) stations that could be built quickly to much lower capital costs and thereby allow a return on investment for shareholders in a fraction of the time large coal or nuclear plant promised. Short-termism had arrived within the ESI.

An additional problem was the back-end costs of setting aside monies for de-commissioning power stations and also insuring them on the money markets. On both counts the government's advisers pointed out that it would be extremely difficult to privatise the nuclear component of the ESI unless considerable state aid was provided to meet the cost of decommissioning and insuring; insurance also had to be combined with a statutory limitation on insurers' liability even in the event of an accident due to operator negligence. In the Autumn of 1989 it was decided by the new Secretary of State, John Wakeham, to drop nuclear power from the privatisation, reversing an explicit commitment given by his predecessor. The government retained the nuclear option, however, promising a review of nuclear construction in 1994.

The New Structure in Place

The new structure in England and Wales is unique, with the National Grid Company forming the guts of the system. Yet there was no trial run; that is, the industry was not given a year or two to settle down into its new structures. Implementation of a massive undertaking was forced through in a remarkably short time frame against opposition from many technical experts within the old order and under the explicitly ideological motivation of party politicians who cared little, if anything, for gaining a consensus other than for their own ideas. Achievement of all this was only possible because the Secretary of State owned all the shares in all the companies. There was a constant jockeying for position between the new companies, even breaking out in conflict on occasions (see, for example, *The Times*, 24/8/90). The Ministers would allow a short period of debate for each issue and then the department would make a ruling and all interested parties would be forced to abide by it.

When the structure was brought to the market the directors of the different companies began to negotiate with the government, trying to get the lowest possible price marked up for their respective companies. This was so that when they ventured out into the market an increase in the price of their shares would make their performance appear better than it really was. They also tried to negotiate away their debt, something the government again refused to countenance, reversing the practice of earlier privatisations.

The prospect of entering the private sector spurred the management of the companies considerably, a lot of entrepreneurial flair was released as the CEGB's strong conforming pressure was ended. A senior member of OFFER's management team argued that:

> I think one does observe that there is something about the cultural shock in moving to the private sector. The threat of take-over, having to raise your money in the market and to finance yourself, and service your own debt; not as it were laying off responsibility up the line to the Government, because you always could before, quite frankly ... [it is now] your assessment of how to do it and how to produce value for money and to keep yourself financed, and to look attractive to shareholders and to be perceived as a successful performer by the public at large ... it has to be sharper. (Interview)

Privatisation also forced a proper costing of all of the elements of the ESI and made the true costs of nuclear power apparent for the first time. In this respect it performed a valuable public policy function, far more effective than the public inquiries at Sizewell and Hinkley. In this sense privatisation is an example both of policy formulation and policy evaluation as it forced an evaluation, in purely market terms, of Britain's nuclear energy policy. A senior official summed it up by arguing that:

> Much of the debate about privatisation as a whole was about the relationship between the constituent parts of the industry, was about where risks should lie and about the definition and apportionment of risk. Now in the case of nuclear power, the risks are risks of a financial rather than a safety nature ... The financial risks were not easy to get hold of and not easy to quantify. The numbers moved very sharply while the process was going on, partly as a result of a more precise focus of risk. When you are a public sector entity expecting to exist for all future time and you have total cost passed through to the consumer, your attitude can be one attitude. If however, you are a private sector entity picking up similar responsibilities, but with a potentially shorter life span and exposure to commercial pressures of various kinds, you focus in much more clearly as to what the risks might be that you are asked to take and then you look for somebody else to take it. (Interview)

Some Lessons from Privatisation

With specific regard to the privatisation of the ESI, it can be argued in its favour that there is a greater diversity of producers leading to the stirrings of a new market. When this is allied to the break-up of the CEGB it can be seen that there is now the opportunity for the industry to change from being producer-led to being consumer-driven. In addition to this, the industry has had to scrutinise financial costs and benefits in a way never before forced upon it, something that has led to privatisation acting as a novel form of policy evaluation.

Yet there are some negative aspects highlighted by the experience of the ESI. As with previous privatisations there is no consensus regarding proof of benefits. Indeed, there is no evidence of any measurable benefit accruing to consumers whatsoever. Neither is there any evidence that the structure of the ESI is any more consumer oriented than before. To be sure, OFFER has prodded the companies towards being more responsive and there is a great deal of material published by the industry promising this, but there is a dearth of empirical evidence to support the claims. Indeed, with the loss of direct ministerial accountability and the lack of formal structured procedures for judicial review, along the lines of those which exists in other EC countries and North America, there is even less protection for the consumers/citizens than before the sell-off. Furthermore, there are considerable disbenefits, indeed hardships visited on coal mining regions of Britain as a result of the new contractual structures which allow the producers to import cheaper foreign coal. Whilst this may allow less expensive electricity (though this is doubtful) it will inevitably lead to further mine closures and therefore redundancies with all the attendant costs in social and financial terms that this entails (The Watt Committee on Energy; evidence to the HoC Select Committee for Energy, November 1991). There will also be more coal imports and therefore detrimental effects upon the balance of payments. In the long term the privatisation of the ESI may prove an expensive folly for which the nation will have to pay an excessive price.

At a wider level, the implementation of the policy of privatisation in both Britain and the US has provided policy-makers with a novel opportunity to inflict lasting cultural changes on the public sector and unprecedented structural reforms. It has also indirectly forced a complete and detailed costing of some policies that have not previously been subjected to this form of accountability, something of a boon for policy analysts and anti-nuclear groups. In Britain there is no general evidence that consumers as a group have benefited from the re-structuring of the public sector, or indeed that the companies involved are necessarily performing better than they would have within a reformed public sector. In short, the main lesson is that privatisation has been an ideological experiment imposed by one group of policy-makers, aided and encouraged by those for whom it is simply another management technique which promises improved methods of control and service delivery. It is from within this second group of parvenu executives that the putative benefits to consumers will be delivered.

NOTES

1. Various sources, but see, for example, Marquand, 1988; Veljanovski, 1987; and the statements of parties in the run-up to the 1992 General Election.
2. See, for example, the work of Kavanagh, 1987; Middlemas, 1979; Brittan, 1977; Gilmore, 1983; Blake, 1985; Gamble, 1974; Bulpitt, 1986.

7 Managing Sub-national Government: A Check and Balance?

If there be any intention to restore our Laws and Liberties and free us from arbitrary Government, it is fit that these Committees ... be laid down ... and that the old Form of Government by Sheriffs, Justices of the Peace etc., be re-established, and the Militia in each County settled, as before, in Lieutenants and deputy-Lieutenants or in Commissioners. (Clement Walker, 1648)

Local government has become a focus for some wider conflicts between Left and Right as well as an arena for political competition between business, trade union, environmental, community action, women's and ethnic minority groups. From being a quiet back-water of routine administration and parochial politics, local government has been pushed into the limelight. (Gerry Stoker, 1988, p.xv)

Federal government isn't participating, but isn't giving us the ability to participate either. A lot of problems that we deal with are national in scope, they can't be dealt with locally and shouldn't be a responsibility (from a financial point of view) of local government. [A senior officer of the government of the County of Los Angeles]

INTRODUCTION

It is not the purpose of this chapter to seek to advance the theoretical understanding of federalism or sub-national government, but rather to attempt to explain the impact of new managerialism upon the sub-national levels and the reactions to it. As such this chapter should be seen as a continuation of the themes explored in the previous chapters, not as a switch away from them. Because there is not the room for a lengthy introduction explaining the structures of sub-national government in the two countries, the contents of this chapter assume a working knowledge of the two systems. For those who need 'quick' introductions, Stoker's book (1988) is a useful guide to the UK, whilst Gerston and Christensen (1991) provide a good introduction to Californian government.

Sometimes the periphery's reaction to Republican and Conservative reforms has taken the form of a vigorous counter-attack, on other occasions responses have varied from studied indifference through to an embracing of approaches and attitudes that have 'come of age' (Walsh, 1990). The phrase 'sub-national government' is an attempt to show the limitations of theoretical ambition at this juncture, deliberately eschewing a debate along the lines of Rhodes, that is redolent in his description of sub-national government as 'sub-central government' (1988). The limitations on this chapter are not designed to ignore the debate, but acknowledge that an account of all the theoretical perspectives, levels of analysis, territorial and structural ensembles is beyond the modest aims of this book, let alone a single chapter.

It may help readers, however, to keep in mind Rhodes' definition of sub-central government in which he argues that in Britain it consists of (a) territorial representation and (b) inter-governmental relations, which are divided into the sub-sets of (1) central–local relations and (2) inter-organisational relations. According to Rhodes, 'territorial representation refers to the representation of ethnic–territorial units (e.g. Scotland, Wales and Northern Ireland) at the centre and the activities of territorially based political organisations' (ibid., p.15). Whilst the term 'inter-governmental relations' is applied to those 'relations between all forms of governmental organisations', his division into sub-sets reflects the links between central departments and local authorities ('central–local-relations') and 'inter-organisational relations' refers to other types of sub-central organisation such as government-owned industries or decentralised units of central departments (ibid.). Such a definitional perspective provides the foundation for a valuable analysis of sub-central government, although it requires some further evolution to adequately cope with the federal system of the US. Whilst it cannot be taken further in this chapter, it does inform some of the points made here.

The next section explores the relevance of the New Right's impact upon sub-national government in the UK and the US. There is a strong emphasis given to Barnekov, Boyle and Rich's account of privatism (1989), a perspective that helps to illustrate the implementation of liberal/conservative theory since 1980. There follows a case study of privatisation and liberalisation in the state of California, the County and the City of Los Angeles. This section may be read in conjunction with chapter 5, on privatisation at the federal level in the US, as it is a natural concomitant to the national scene. Finally, a contrast to a wealthy American county is provided by a short case study (almost a vignette) of the impact of liberalisation upon Hampshire, a wealthy British county.

PRIVATISM AND THE PROVINCES

Barnekov *et al.* have elevated the managerial techniques of the New Right to the status of an 'ism': 'privatism'. The term was originally used by Sam Bass Warner, Jr 'to denote the dominant cultural tradition influencing urban development in America. It is a tradition that has equal importance in Britain' (1989, p.vii). Urban development and re-development is important because in Britain and North America most people live in an urban environment (which includes suburbs). The political culture is that of an urban society, which probably accounts for the mythologising of the countryside in both countries. In Britain this often takes the form of a constant harking back to the past as a sort of bucolic 'merry' England, made 'real' by a rash of theme parks and centres infesting the more tourist riddled parts of the countryside, whilst in America, their atavistic tendencies lean towards those of the pioneer West. In both cases these are artificial constructions of history, fairy stories to impress the children. The modern reality is an urban one, and that is where political change is centred. As such, privatism as a tradition is one that

> encourages a reliance on the private sector as the principle agent of urban change. Privatism stresses the social as well as economic importance of private initiative and competition, and it legitimises the public consequences of private action. Its legacy is that both personal and community well-being are evaluated in terms of the fulfilment of private aspirations and the achievments of private institutions. (Ibid., p.1)

There are clear echoes in this definition of the analysis of (for example) Hanke, Veljanovsky, Butler and Savas, as discussed in the previous chapters. Privatism is no more than ideological liberalism. But for Barnekov *et al.*, it is the urban *modus operandi* in Britain and the US. Be that as it may, and there are clear indications that this is not the case in Northern Britain (Goldsmith, 1986; Blunkett and Jackson, 1987), they trace the history of privatism from the urban developments of these two countries since the Nineteenth Century, plainly showing the degree to which the New Right is rooted in the individualism of Victorian liberalism. Their analysis is apposite because it places the changes wrought upon the provinces within the context of the political culture responsible for those upheavals.

In seeking to ameliorate the perceived problems of urban areas, the New Right attempted to extend its prescriptions for government and bureaucracy down through the states and counties and into the town/city halls. The sub-national governmental constructions in the UK and US were subjected to

> a belief that the private sector is inherently dynamic, productive and dependable; a belief that private institutions are intrinsically superior to public institutions for the delivery of goods and services; and a confidence that market efficiency is the appropriate criterion of social performance in virtually all spheres of community activity. (Barnekov *et al.*, 1989).

Furthermore, this is firmly linked to the wider national agenda, so that the local perspective is a reiteration of the broader attempt at privatisation (or 'privatism') as 'the key to national recovery as well as local prosperity' (ibid., p.223). In Britain, because of the expansion of the Welfare State from 1945 to 1975, the attempt to reverse state intervention and bolster the private sector began from a level of public control and intervention that 'had no equivalent in either scope or magnitude, in the US' (ibid., p.4). Yet even in America the gradual accumulation of interventionary activity by national, state and local government, particularly during the era of Johnson's Great Society, meant that by the election of Ronald Reagan there was a complexity of official initiatives within the urban area. It was this public/private interface that the New Right sought to shift firmly into a more liberal camp.

The urban, or sub-national policy of the liberal/conservative governments of Britain and America has been to encourage 'a reliance on the private sector as the principal agent of urban change', which inevitably 'tied the fortunes of cities to the vitality of their private sectors and concentrates community attention and resources on economic development and private investment', whilst establishing 'market efficiency as the criterion for judging the appropriateness of any action, public or private' (ibid., p.11). Thus, according to Barnekov *et al.*, cities and ultimately citizens were viewed as economic entities. In the US this has been a part of the political culture since the Nineteenth Century. In Britain, however, this culture was interrupted by the era of corporatist intermediation brought in by the period of Welfarism (Saunders, 1985). Since 1979, successive Chancellors of the Exchequer and Secretaries of State for the Environment have sought to break the control of the 'planning regime' which grew during this period (Barnekov *et al.*, 1989, p.26). To this end they have used techniques such as Enterprise Zones and Urban Development Corporations to encourage and reward private sector investment in run-down inner cities, as an alternative to further public subsidies. The expertise most sought after was that of the business person, the 'professional' skills most lauded have been those of the private sector manager.

In both countries the 1980s saw governments turning to the business manager for solutions to the problems of the localities. Task Forces, Urban Development Action Grant programmes, and the whole panoply of new bodies were either led by businessmen and women, or were heavily influenced by them. Indeed, the business community often took the lead in, for example, establishing 'urban compacts' with inner city schools (in Boston and East London), or Task Forces to 'deal' with areas that had become economically unworkable (see for example, CBI, 1988). Yet there can be drawbacks from the point of view of the local governments that are the recipients of this 'aid'. The experience of some American city managers of programmes designed to use public funds as a leverage to entice private investment is that the process can work in reverse and 'private enterprise often leverages public funds to accomplish its own objectives' (Barnekov *et al.*, 1989, p.97). Perhaps more importantly:

> local economic development programmes remove significant actions of local government from public debate, reduce political accountability of local officials, and narrow the representativeness of local government. (Ibid.)

This is similar to the criticisms levelled at privatisation of the public sector generally (see the preceding chapters) and which have been voiced particularly strongly by the local community in London's Docklands, following the establishment of the London Docklands Development Corporation in 1982 (Docklands Consultative Committee, 1985).

With the election of President Reagan and an administration opposed to government *per se* there began an era of 'new' federalism. The President sought to give back to the states 'matters best left' to them (Barnekov *et al.*, 1989, p.100). His budget proposal for the fiscal year 1982 contained outline cuts of $44 billion from federal programmes, marking a determination to withdraw the central government from substantial fiscal intervention in the sub-national arena. One of Reagan's advisors in the urban policy area was Savas, whose commitment to liberalism has already been noted (chapter 5, above). The only interventionist policy the administration appeared to favour for its urban agenda was Enterprise Zones, an idea imported from the Conservative Party of Mrs Thatcher. Otherwise President Reagan, and also Mr Bush, opted to apply market principles to urban problems, relying on the private and voluntary sectors to break the cycle of deprivation and wean people away from a 'welfare mentality'. It is somewhat difficult to know what objective performance indicators to apply to evaluate the implementation of this policy.

In the UK the election of Mrs Thatcher meant a concerted effort to transform the culture of local government, and this involved importing from America the concept of leverage, mainly through Enterprise Zones and Urban Development Corporations (before the idea of the former was re-exported to the US). Yet, in contrast to the US, this did not lead to efforts to withdraw from the sub-national arena, although the rhetoric often implied this was indeed the Government's intention. To the contrary, there was a centralisation of control (Gamble, 1988; Barnekov *et al.*, 1989, p.191). The reason for the different approaches partly reflected the different political cultures; America has staunchly avoided compromising the separation of powers and the federal principle has always remained entrenched, if somewhat re-constructed. In Britain, however, the move to centralisation and executive dominance is almost a political reflex, so embedded has it become within the culture of the policy-making elites. Also underpinning the centralising propensities of Conservative ministers was the rise of the 'urban Left' in Britain, a challenging counter-culture that deliberately set out to subvert and undermine the New Right and indeed the concept of private property itself:

> activists called for fundamental changes in national politics that would reflect an understanding of the institutionalized economic sources of urban malaise and create a capacity for the disadvantaged to organise in opposition to dominant economic interests. (Ibid., p. 149)

Mrs Thatcher's governments were hostile and uncompromising. A series of reforms led to the control of revenue raising and expenditure being taken from local authorities and vested in the Secretary of State for the Environment. Wholesale reform of the structure followed on a sort of rolling programme, beginning with the abolition of the Greater London Council and the metropolitan counties, a process designed to weaken opposition to the government and bludgeon the recalcitrant local authorities into acquiescence, if not agreement (Stoker, 1988, pp.192–214; Blunkett and Jackson, 1987).

Comprehensive liberalisation was placed upon the agenda of British sub-national government. Successive Acts of Parliament implemented the policy of privatisation (Ascher, 1987; Stoker, 1988; Barnett and Knox, 1991), beginning with the 1980 Local Government, Planning and Land Act which gave the Minister powers to order local authorities to sell land and property. The process continued with the 1980 Housing Act which provided local authority tenants with the right to buy their own (rented) property at a substantial discount and proved one of the most far-reaching and popular privatisations in Britain. The Local Government Finance Act (1982), the Rates Act (1984), and the Local Government Act (1985) followed, increasing ministerial power over finance and expenditure, whilst 1988 saw the Local Government Finance Act, the Housing Act (1988), the Education Reform Act and another Local Government Act.

These all ensured an expansion of central control over sub-national government, whilst simultaneously forcing through a major policy of privatisation that saw the selling-off of much of the housing stock, the sale of other land holdings, the de-regulation of much of local transport, and the compulsory competitive tendering for and contracting out of services (Painter, 1991) leading to the ending of many council direct labour organisations. The Conservatives argued that all the reforms were carried out in order to empower consumers, free business from unnecessary bureaucracy, and force greater accountability onto local government. Another perspective saw the process as one which, whilst supporting private enterprise and devolving greater initiative down to individuals, also 'reduced the role and importance of the state as the guardian of community interests' (Barnekov *et al.*, 1989, p.168). Yet Mrs Thatcher and other advocates of the New Right did not recognise such a thing as 'community', much less argue that it was the state's role to protect it.

THE NEW ENTERPRISE STRUCTURES

As already noted, there was a wealth of new structures created in the form of task forces, partnerships, compacts and so on. In America many of these were localised, being confined to individual states and often to individual cities, although if they proved to be successful the professional structures of the city managers and such ilk provided a conduit through which a winning concept was quickly channelled throughout the nation. Two of the more abiding and lauded concepts were enterprise zones and (in the UK only) urban development corporations; both enshrined a partnership between government and the private sector as the motor for their success.

The concept of enterprise zones is traced to a proposal by the planner Peter Hall, in 1977 (Barnekov *et al.*, 1989, p.199) and more generally to a speech given by Sir Geoffrey Howe in 1978, whilst the Conservatives were still in opposition (Butler, 1991, p.27). Speaking in the depressed London Docklands, Howe argued for the establishment of a number of small areas in the most derelict parts of Britain, perhaps occupying one or two square miles each, in which taxes and government regulation would be suspended. The goal was to entice private enterprise to take advantage of the competitive edge this would provide, whilst simultaneously reviving the area (ibid., pp.27–9). Even before the election of the Conservatives in 1979, and Sir Geoffrey's elevation to Chancellor of the Exchequer, the American Heritage Foundation called for a similar strategy in the US (ibid.). Jack Kemp (then a Republican Congressman) and his Democratic colleague for the South Bronx, Robert Garcia, cosponsored legislation which sought to refine the British idea for the American context and 'thus set in motion what turned out to be an intense debate over urban policy in America' (ibid.). It was no less intense in Britain.

By the 1980s many American states were questioning their ealier efforts to attract heavy industry, known as 'smokestack chasing' (Hansen, 1991, p.15). It was felt that the experience of the 1970s suggested new jobs came from expanding existing plant and founding new small companies, rather than enticing large plant to relocate across state lines (ibid.). Clearly one of the ways of encouraging this form of economic activity is to provide tax holidays and other incentives of the type that are found in enterprise zones. Much of the legislation establishing the zones was federally inspired and it was this that supplied the 'template' for state legislation (Butler, 1991, p.37). Several states, including Connecticut, led the way by enacting state legislation which they reasoned was in line with a Reagan-supported federal Bill and would therefore attract federal support in the form of grants (ibid., pp.37–9). The legislation failed to pass through Congress, however, other than in an emasculated form in

1988. Thus most zones attracted very little federal funding and there evolved, therefore, a wide variety of different state-inspired zones. The bold plans have had a mixed success and it is not always clear whether the zones have actually helped re-generate run-down areas. This led one senior federal civil servant to comment:

> there are a variety of enterprise zones in this country now without a great deal of activity by the federal government, other than authorising legislation. That is the feds will permit tax-free or enterprise zones. ... The evidence to date on non-federal enterprise zones (that is zones that are federal only in that they have authorising legislation, they don't have active federal participation) suggests that they have more often than not been wilful flops. And that they are like a variety of more active federal activities, which were designed to effect the location of jobs. They have done a reasonable job for movement of new employment and new growth, but they have done a terrible job of speeding along growth that would not otherwise have taken place. (Interview)

That is, enterprise zones have merely re-located jobs, not created them.

Existing evidence suggests a similar experience for Britain (Tym *et al.*, 1984). Companies have tended to take advantage of the tax and regulation holiday to move within their own region; thus jobs have merely been transferred, often to the detriment of neighbouring loclities. Furthermore, few firms have been created because of the zones; what evidence there is suggests that new companies in the zones would have been established regardless of the concessions (ibid.). Finally, the tax haven acts as another form of public subsidy to the private sector and in Britain had cost the Treasury about £180 million between 1980 and 1985 (National Audit Office, 1986). Far from being a liberalising measure, in both countries enterprise zones appear to be a new form of state intervention, a modern type of regional policy. In America one Democratic member of Congress voted against them on precisely those grounds, arguing enterprise zones were no more than an extension of welfare en masse to the inner cities and other depressed areas, that is localities populated by 'the underclass' and low achievers. He said:

> I think enterprise zones are a big mistake. You are trading off special favours and consideration for a kind of pie in the sky hope that they will hire people that are unemployable. It doesn't make sense. If the idea is free enterprise, then make a good product at a low cost and get the best people. Then you don't want to hire the unemployable, and the purpose of enterprise zones is to hire those that in many cases are unemployable. (Interview)

This also tends to be the attitude of the employers themselves, at least in Britain. Those that have re-located within the UK have either been inclined to bring their existing staff with them, sought government-sponsored retraining schemes for the local population to upgrade the pool of skilled labour in the area, or hired people from the zone for menial positions (various interviews and evidence to CBI Task Force, 1988).

Enterprise zones represented an attempt at liberalisation that foundered on the need for government intervention and support to ensure its 'success'. In Britain 'the initiative that drew together privatisation and central control of policy was the Urban Development Corporation' (Barnekov *et al.*, 1989, p.192). Two UDCs were initially established by Heseltine during his first tenure as Secretary of State for the Environment using his new powers under the 1980 Act: the London Docklands Development Corporation and the Merseyside Development Corporation. They were given sweeping powers (which were taken away from the local authorities) for:

> land acquisition, environmental improvement, provision of infrastructure, land use planning, and control of development as well as responsibility for the marketing and promotion of their area. In many respects, the UDCs replaced the duties and responsibilities of the elected local authorities in that they were able to exercise a variety of powers including assistance to industry, building control, fire fighting, even public health. (Ibid.)

They were run by a Chairman and Board appointed by Heseltine and the day-to-day administration was by a Chief Executive supported by a team of administrative, professional and technical staff. The appointees were overwhelmingly from private sector backgrounds, as were the professional managers; this was reflected in the organisations' policy-making and its implementation.

Results have been mixed, with Merseyside doing far less well than the London Docklands. The latter consists of over 5,000 acres of derelict dockside which is in the process of being transformed. Although there have been some casualties amongst the developers the scale of the transformation is staggering, with, for example, the national newspaper industry locating almost entirely to the area. The UDC has exerted a respectable leverage of 5.5:1 private to public sector monies.

The details of the changes are beyond the scope of this book, but the manner of their implementation has important lessons for the implementation of privatisation and public sector management in the UK. In

short, the area was 'taken into care' (ibid., p.196). It was effectively nationalised by the central government, which then imposed its own private
sector prescriptons upon it. Whether or not the cure has been successful
is not relevant here. What is relevant is that the government saw fit to
disregard all but its own wishes. It imposed a solution using a mechanism
insulated from local accountability and held in check only via the tenuous
links of ministerial accountability. The reason there were no UDCs in
America is quite simple; they would have been unconstitutional and an
affront to that country's democratic traditions. Clearly that which exists
throughout most of Docklands is immeasurably preferable to that which
was there after the docks closed in the late 1970s/early 1980s, but it is
an imposed solution, not a negotiated one. It represents the exercise of
naked power, not the careful seeking of a consensus. It illustrates the
perfect flexibility of an imperfect constitution, and the lack of concern
for the individual shown by those ideologically committed by their
liberal philosophy to the cult of the individual. In these respects it is a
fitting flagship for many of the recent changes imposed upon the provinces
by central government.

British sub-national government exists at the pleasure of Parliament.
There are no official structures in the UK that exist as of right, other than
the Crown in Parliament. Britain may or may not benefit from adopting
a codified constitution which establishes the role of all elements within the
polity, although, as has already been noted, a reformed electoral system
would be more effective than the fluff of grand-sounding charters. The
British sub-national structures would benefit from a legal/administrative
framework that placed them beyond the day-to-day attentions of national
party politicians and ensured that reforms reflected national, rather than
partisan, requirements; it does not need federalism or major constitutional change to achieve this. The extent of Conservative antipathy towards
local government is illustrated by the UK's refusal to sign the Council of
Europe's European Charter of Local Self-Government. The Charter has

> an important symbolic significance in that it accords constitutional recognition to
> local government. The British view is that, while it supports the broad priciples set
> out in the Charter, it believes that the regulation of the role of local government is
> essentially a domestic matter and not one which should be subject to Treaty
> obligation. (Rao, 1991, p.7)

Whilst local government remains a domestic matter, the New Right will
continue to use central authority to transform the structures. In the UK

local government is less a check and balance on central government, as for example Jones (1983) argues it ought to be, but more a commissary of central power in the provinces.

It was against this degree of centralisation that the US Constitution inaugurated a system of federalism replete with separation of powers. Over two centuries of practice have led to a refinement of checks and balances, judicial review and negotiated compromise. This is not to say that the system has ossified into immobilism, indeed the corpus of work analysing the evolution of federalism is testament to the flexibility of the system, but it is flexibility within the rule of law, not the whim of Crown prerogative. To a certain extent the evolution of American federalism is continually addressing the issue of balance between the various levels of the Republic, although, of course, sub-national structures in the US are enshrined, protected and inviolate, within the political system. Peterson *et al.*, have argued that:

> Federalism works well when national, state, and local government together take the time to design and implement programs that meet broad social needs not easily addressed by local jurisdictions alone. (1988, p.216)

That is, the American approach to sub-national government, even following the attempted withdrawal from that arena by the Reagan and Bush Administrations, is one of negotiation and consensus. The centripetal nature of the American political system forces the dissident tendencies within it to meet each other in the middle ground. The following case studies are designed to contrast the two approaches of the UK and US, illustrating the very different political cultures that inform sub-national policy-making.

PRIVATISING THE STATES: THE EXPERIENCE OF CALIFORNIA

Clearly there is not the room to deal with the privatising activities of all fifty states in the Union, as each of them has its own approach to and experience of the process, reflecting its unique set of political structures and circumstances. For observers of the American scene who approach that nation from the perspective of a small centralised European country, it is often easy to forget the sheer size and diversity of political activity within the federal system, an oversight any attempt to review privatisation on a state-by-state basis will quickly remedy. For the purpose of this section, therefore, attention is mainly focused upon California, the largest and richest state in terms of population; indeed, were it to be an independent country, it would rank as the sixth largest economy in the world. The lively political culture of California has also ensured that it is often to the forefront of developments that are then adopted by the rest of the country. Privatisation has proved to be no exception and with its voter initiative process, which bequeathed to the world the taxpayers' backlash of Proposition 13 and the Gann Amendment (Gerston and Christensen, 1991; Ross, 1988, pp.207–10, 212–13), California has led the US in its pursuit of managerial techniques to deliver services demanded by a citizenry unwilling to fund them within the traditional mode of delivery.

The two dominant methods used throughout the US of facilitating the implementation of privatisation are enabling legislation 'that permits and encourages local governments to privatise their services'; and the privatising of services directly provided by the state itself (Fixler, undated, p.1). Fixler lists some of the different examples he has uncovered; they include privately operated local jails (for which enabling legislation already exists in Montana and New Mexico); contracting out 'homemaker and chore services' in Texas and Utah; workfare in Alameda County California; and the perceived need for large state-wide infrastructural investment:

> Privatisation of state infrastructure such as highways is becoming almost a necessity as the billions of dollars needed for new development or rehabilitation are often no longer available. Some states are already contracting out highway sweeping, clean-up, and maintenance. But why not provide for new highways or rehabilitation of existing highways by encouraging private financing, design, construction, operation and *ownership* of such highways? Private firms could 'rent' the highways to the state for a fixed amount or be paid according to usage. (pp.1–7)

Such novel and sweeping options are being given serious consideration in California and although there are, as yet, no plans to fully privatise the state's highway system, the two-term conservative administration of Governor Deukmajian reversed much of the policy of his predecessor, the regime of Governor Jerry Brown. Although moderate in Republican terms, Deukmajian's successor, Pete Wilson, is facing a fiscal crisis and will be forced to continue policies that reduce state expenditure. This inevitably will mean a continuing appraisal of schemes for privatisation.

Deukmajian emulated the federal example of Presidents Reagan and Bush in that he appointed people who shared his ideological perspective to positions of authority throughout the bureaucratic apparatus of Sacramento. The situation is complicated in California, though, by the fact that several other elected state officials belonged to the opposition (Democratic) Party, including the Deputy Governor, who becomes Acting Governor whenever the Governor leaves the state! Be that as it may, the penetration of the apparatus of government by ideological liberals has been thorough and although the State Assembly has also been controlled by Democrats, there is an awareness of the damage past spendthrift fiscal policies caused and as a result the members of the Assembly tend to compete with each other in forcing fiscal rectitude upon the administration. One senior Deukmajian appointee argued that in office she saw her task as being the Governor's representative within her department, but that:

> in our view the only reason we privatise is that they [the private sector] can do it cheaper than the government. You see we believe, the Department of ... strongly believe that we are the State's business manager and that we should get the best bang for the dollar. If the private sector can do it cheaper and better then they will do it. If we can do it better and cheaper then we will do it. In fact we have 23 different offices and 23 different functions and when we have our internal budget briefing in the Spring, when they come before our management team to get their budget, they have to show us what the private sector is doing in their area; if they're not doing it cheaper than the private sector then they're not going to be doing it anymore. So we're treating it like a business as near as I can tell, and that includes overheads so that there's nobody that's free and clear. (Interview)

Despite the emphasis upon privatisation that pervades much of the managerial ethos within Sacramento, there is an even greater emphasis upon public/private sector partnerships.

These partnerships exist within the penumbra of the public/private interface and blur the distinctions. State officers, however, are convinced of their efficacy for aiding the implementation of expensive public policies and for providing alternative sources of revenue for the government. A 1986 report by a Little Hoover commission argued that the state was a poor manager of its six million acres of land (Ross, 1988, p.140) and one of its recommendations was that the bulk of the real estate should be returned to the private sector. The administration did embark upon a programme selling off the land and property, but in recent years this has been amended to seek partnerships with the private sector. One senior official summed up the relationship under the Republicans by saying that:

> the Little Hoover commission has now changed its mind and part of the legislature in the State of California have changed their mind and are now looking at the privatisation aspect of it. The Chairperson indicated to me, in a private conversation, that maybe he was a little bit too emphatic in trying to get us to dispose of the property because it now seems that there is the opportunity to share in a partnership relationship with the private sector real estate assets. His commission has come out with a programme proposal that the legislature is looking at. We in turn are trying to develop within [his department] the concept of a partnership with the private sector in the development of real estate to make the best use of public real estate assets. (Interview)

Examples of where these partnerships have been implemented include new hospitals and nursing homes for people who qualify under the Veterans Schemes; other welfare programmes; urban renewal; and straightforward exploitation of state property in areas of rapid growth and high land values, the latter providing the state treasury with tenancy or leasehold revenue, whilst obviating development costs and at the same time (in some cases) providing the opportunity for local government to expand its tax base.

Another area of substantial private-public partnership at the state level, within a privatisation framework, is to be found within the Department of General Services Office of Energy Assessments. It has as its mission the aim of reducing the use and cost of energy at state facilities, which is accomplished through the 'development of projects that conserve energy, produce energy, or reduce rates' (programme summary, 1988, p.1). The 1980 Budget Act brought about Energy Assessments and Governor Deukmajian's Administration issued Executive Order D-50-86, which mandates that 'all state agencies reduce their energy use by 15% by 1989–90 and by 25% by 1992–93 (relative to a 1979–80 "base year")' (ibid., pp.1–2). The Office of Energy Assessments develops energy service agreements and leases and finances energy projects by selling revenue bonds through the Public Works Board.

The private sector is involved in a variety of ways, not least of which is via 'third party financing' whereby it helps to finance energy projects within the state sector and then shares in the benefits. Such projects involve private developers who lease property from state sites whereupon they construct and maintain cogeneration plants and the state organisations purchase the products. The structure of the ventures entail that the

> contracts provide for the State to share in project benefits with no ceiling. This financing approach results in placing most of the financial risks, and a share of the rewards during the repayment period, on private developers/builders. (Ibid., p.5)

Cogeneration projects include:

Correctional Training Facility, Soledad;
California Veterans Home, Yountville;
Metropolitan State Hospital, Norwalk;
University of California, Berkely;
Camarillo State Hospital;
California Institution for Men, Chino;
San Jose State University;
Caltrans Caples Lake Maintenance Station (ibid.).

These and other projects have the potential to provide substantial revenue benefits to the state. Other benefits that senior managers identify as accruing and which have a positive impact upon the governance of the state include improved energy reliability, state support for cogeneration and energy efficiency, infrastructural improvements and the recovery of state development costs.

At the state level, then, it appears that the dynamics toward privatisation, first identified at the federal level, are repeated, namely that there is an ideological commitment on the part of those in power that has an inherent tendency to view the private sector as the natural repository for the provision of goods and services which are currently provided by government. This ideological commitment, however, is aided in the implementation of policy by the managerial dynamic towards the provision of programmes by the bureaucrats themselves, who may or may not share the ideological commitment to New Right policies, but nonetheless see privatisation as a useful management tool allowing them to do their job effectively in a climate of budgetary constraint. This aid to the privatisation dynamic also acts to constrain it, preventing implementation of the pure form or ideal type which seeks a complete removal of state influence from many areas and a retrenchment to a minimalist stance. The heuristic nature of implementation has led instead to the establishment (or perhaps the re-establishment, given the nature of American development of the West) of public/private partnerships. As the next section will now seek to illustrate, this is a pattern repeated at the local level.

PRIVATISATION IN THE COUNTIES AND CITIES

As with the preceding section (and for much the same reason) the emphasis here will be on the situation pertaining to California. Because of constraints of space and the fact that California possesses a population in excess of twenty-five million people, the examples are confined to the county and the city of Los Angeles. An additional interest to British readers may be the fact that, like London, Los Angeles is suffering from a combination of the problems of growth which puts pressure upon land and resources and attracts economic migrants in their hundreds of thousands. There is a visible division of the city between those who are clearly the beneficiaries of the growth and wealth and those who are not. In short, like London, parts of the city and county of Los Angeles more closely resemble the Third World than the First. Sometimes, as in the Spring of 1992, this results in violent disorder and outbursts against the symbols of power, as well as more mundane acts of looting.

Within California, local government exists at four somewhat overlapping levels: the counties, cities, boards of education and special districts. The last can range from a little cemetery up to big multi-county agencies like the Air Quality Management District in Southern California. Los Angeles County is the social agent for the state and federal government, it runs the welfare system as the administrative agent and is responsible for the public hospitals, the mental health system, the courts, the Public Defenders and the District Attorney. With a population of over ten million people in over eighty cities (which themselves range in size from a few thousand to several million) it is the largest Urban County in the US. The economic statistics regarding the county and city of Los Angeles are impressive and although there is not the space to list them here, it is worth remembering that discussions regarding the privatisation of services and policies for infrastructural re-generation take place within a *local* economy that is greater than the GDP of the neighbouring Republic of Mexico.

The City of Los Angeles is responsible for Public Works and Public Safety, but in performing these functions it employs over 50,000 people, including one of the largest police forces in America, within a strict civil service merit system. At the apex of the bureaucracy, Department Heads are paid in excess of $160,000 per annum, considerably more than federal bureaucrats of similar rank and among the highest local government salaries in the country; indeed, for many jobs Los Angeles does pay better than any other sub-national government in America. For the financial year 1988–9, the City of Los Angeles budget consisted of total appropriations of $2,939,881,837, within a total City budget of $3,3321.6 million (City budget summary, 1989), considerably more than the national budget of many Third World countries.

Yet the twin squeeze of declining federal financial assistance (down from twenty-five per cent of the total City budget in 1978–9 to about five per cent in 1989/90) and the voter initiatives (proposition 13 and proposition 4) which slashed the local tax base have meant that politicians elected upon interventionist programmes or compelled (as in the case of the County) to carry out state and federally mandated activities have to do so within severe financial constraints. The situation is further complicated by the fact that the budget squeeze has fallen disproportionately upon the conservative controlled County, whilst the Democrat controlled City has been more fortunate in that its rapid economic growth has provided greater revenues and the division of responsibilities with the County have meant less of a drain upon those resources. The cuts, therefore, have fallen hardest upon the welfare functions of the County and it is these that have been subjected to the greatest level of privatisation.

In 1987 the County established an Economy and Efficiency Commission Task Force on Contracting Policy to revue current practice and make recommendations with regard to expanding the privatisation of County functions. The Task Force noted that the County is more advanced than most municipalities in the US in contracting out, with twenty per cent of its $4.2 billion operating budget being contracted out to the private sector. There followed a list of five recommendations to improve and expand the implementation of privatisation in the County; most of these are currently being implemented. As part of the goals for the County the Task Force recommended that the County:

- expand the scope of contracting to the mission functions of County Government;
- establish a clear priority on using contracting to improve County productivity through technology and organisational innovation;

- identify areas for full privatisation, including divestiture of County assets and operations to commercial enterprises. (Report, p.2)

Of great interest is the call made by the Report for the County to use external sources of expertise, information and advice to implement the privatisation of its activities, specific mention being made of the Reason Foundation, a Los Angeles liberal think-tank which has produced many proposals for reducing the role of government (ibid., p.3). One of the senior members of the Foundation argued that:

> I think the ideas for privatisation in this area came from this Foundation. We've not only provided the ideological basis, but we've tried to sell the idea in terms of being a good management option, so if some of these local governments in their perspective see it as originating strictly as a management option, then I think we've done our job well. (Interview)

This is a viewpoint which accords with the analysis of the preceding chapters and sections dealing with the formidable fusion of the ideological and the pragmatic in America's privatisation experience.

The second set of recommendations dealt with requests for contracting out proposals by the County, calling on the Board of Supervisors to direct the Chief Administrative Officer to work with departmental chiefs to revise the County's approaches to writing requests for proposals so that:

- contracting encompasses a large enough proportion of the function to lead to overhead reduction within five years of award;
- contracting focuses more on performance requirements of the work to be performed than on organisation, staffing and labour inputs of the contractor;
- where feasible, a contract can be used as a master agreement for purposes of expansion to additional bidders, departments, or workload without additional solicitations and proposals:
- proposals can include cost-plus as well as fixed price bids. (Report, p.3)

In short, the County was to focus its efforts on defining contracting programmes in terms of functions and outputs 'at a significant enough scale to reduce managerial and indirect costs, as well as direct labour costs' (ibid., p.4).

It has already been noted the County has adopted privatisation in many forms in order to meet its obligations; the Report provided the best and most recent comprehensive review of current practice and proposed future savings. The process accords fully with the ideological perspective of most, though not all, of the Board of Supervisors and as such it can be viewed as a plan of implementation. Areas already privatised include most refuse collection, most building and development, a degree of leaseback on buildings and a variety of welfare functions. At least one County Supervisor, however, is less than happy with the effect that privatisation has had on the former workforce, his aide argued that:

> when you have government employees that have worked ten or twenty years or so doing the best they could working for the County, devoting their lives to the County, I think that to turn around and cut their job and essentially replace them by a lower paid often less skilled worker is not only bad from the point of view of the quality of the service, but I think it breaks the good faith that the employees have had with you for a long period of time. (Interview)

It is precisely these manual workers, banded together in strong public sector unions, that in the past negotiated favourable pay and conditions and have subsequently sought to frustrate much of the programme of privatisation, a programme often implicitly aimed at achieving the political goal of breaking their power to veto change designed to usher in flexible management practices. Prior to 1978 the County Charter prohibited contracting out for services which were provided by the County employees, a prohibition policed by the courts which limited contracting out to examples 'where no civil service employee was presently qualified to perform the work' or where 'it was impossible to recruit such personnel over the period of time the County needed the service' (Edelman, 1988, p.2). In 1978 Proposition A was adopted by the County electorate and swept away these barriers to privatisation, allowing private contractors to replace County personnel 'in services when it is more economical or feasible to do so' (ibid., pp.2–3). Proposition A was passed in the period of tax-cutting initiatives and ushered in the storm of changes which were reviewed in the 1987 report. Yet these changes have not always met with approval in the City, or even with the voters.

The political elite of the City tends to take a slightly different view of privatisation from that found in the County. LA is a self-governing charter city with a weak mayor and a strong council system of administration; the charter explicitly allows contracting out if it is feasible or less expensive. Like thousands of cities across America, LA has indeed participated in privatisation; for example, large construction activities have always been carried out by the private sector and there is a $3 billion sewerage scheme currently being built by private contractors. There are limits to the extent to which the City will privatise, however, and that limit is governed by shrewd practical considerations and voter pressure. An example is the proposal to privatise the City's refuse collection service, emulating the County's move. On being asked why the City did not contract out its refuse collection a senior official said:

> You know what killed that one? It's interesting. One of the leaders of the Council wanted a pilot scheme in her District in the San Fernando Valley, which is a newer section of the City, relatively wealthy and moderately conservative. The Council member did a survey of her constituents and said here are the issues, here's what it'll cost and here are the gains. The responses came back that the quality of service from our refuse handlers was so good that compared particularly with the County area (some of them said) which the private sector did, our service was superior. They used examples where in the County sector 'they throw our trash cans on the street, they drive over them in the truck, they leave trash all over the place, your people do a nice job, they take anything we put out, they do it neatly and they are there on time all the time'. So the public sector guys won it on the service level, people in effect said 'we are willing to pay the extra buck or two, don't privatise', so that was one of the swing votes in the City. (Interview)

Clearly in a wealthy middle-class suburb cost did not dominate the consideration of the issue by the voters; it was service quality and accountability which decided the policy as those able to afford it asked for the maintenance of a superior, albeit more expensive service. Where the imperative to cut costs in order to maintain the minimum delivery of a service, as in the provision of welfare to the poor and indigent predominates, then privatisation appears to be the favoured option. Where service quality and accountability considerations count in the provision of services to the middle class, however, questions of consumer satisfaction are those which are of greatest importance. The shift to market solutions, so often presented by the New Right as a vote for choice, is ironically often the result of a specific lack of choice by those most vulnerable to the whim of government and least equipped to hold the bureaucracy accountable. This is the paradox of privatisation at local level.

It appears, therefore, that if privatisation at local level is to present a true choice and properly allow a competition of provision then it must be applied to those presently powerful enough to resist it. The real issue then is not the ideological or political worth of privatisation, but the ability of groups of citizens to opt for the type of service provision they will receive. The City runs its own airport and refuse collection, because a coalition of dominant groups gains benefit from this situation. The

County privatises welfare activities because that is one of the few ways, perhaps the only way those activities will be affordable for the public sector in the future. Utilities such as water and electricity are publicly run in LA for the same reason, it is in the interest of the ruling interests to perpetuate this situation. This is not to lapse into some puerile conspiracy theory. Politics in LA are so complex that the phrase 'ruling coalition of interests' means loose power groupings that vary over time and are so amorphous that it is difficult to dignify them with the description 'coalition'. It is easier to describe this coalition (admittedly simply, perhaps even simplistically) as those who are not recent immigrants, who mostly speak English, are not unemployed, are legally resident, do not claim welfare from the state, are politically aware and receive adequate regular income. In short, it excludes the 'underclass', however they may be defined.

A senior political appointee argued that the City, when compared to the County and the State, tended, therefore to be:

> more pragmatic and less ideological in our approach to privatisation, however there is one concern that might be considered ideological and that is that sometimes the cheaper price you pay for a service provided by some element of the private sector may defer the societal cost. What I mean by that is if a private entity can pick up and dispose of trash more cheaply in terms of dollars per ton than the public sector, then maybe they can do that because their employees are not given the same benefits and the same pay as those employed by the city. (Interview)

Concerns like this mean that compared to other cities in the US and the County of which it is a constituent part, the City of LA has gone relatively slowly along the road of privatisation. It must be recalled, however, that even this is considerably further than many European cities of comparable size. In LA there is a more radical political tradition than that found in other parts of the state and when reflecting upon privatisation activities elsewhere, particularly those relating to the emergency services, a senior political appointee remarked:

> there are some governmental things dealing with personal liberty that should never be contracted out to a private agency. There have been some experiments elsewhere in the United States about prisons being contracted out and that sort of thing, but if indeed personal liberty is the most precious thing we have I think it needs to be guarded very jealously; even at high cost. The truth of the matter is that a dictatorship of some sort or a kind of monolithic government could be more efficient than we are and the price we pay is that we do not justify the means by the end. (Interview)

Clearly this is an attitude from which most economic liberals would not disassociate themselves, the point of contention being that they would see liberalisation as the best defence against tyranny, whilst the political appointee saw a strong, respected and independent bureaucracy held properly accountable through clear governmental structures and operating under an explicit code of ethics as the best defence for the citizen against the excesses of government. The debate, therefore, is still about the nature of government as much as about its proper sphere of influence, a debate that can be traced back through a history far longer than that of the Republic.

PRIVATISING HAMPSHIRE

The privatisation with the biggest impact electorally in Britain has probably been the sale of council houses to their tenants. This was enshrined within the 1980 Housing Act, which gave tenants of three or more years the right to buy at a discount of thirty-three per cent of the market value, with a further one per cent for each year of tenency up to a maximum of fifty per cent (Stoker, 1988, p.178). This incentive was combined with large rent increases for those who declined to purchase their dwelling. Competitive tendering and contracting out of services has been the other area of privatisation that has had a major impact. This section will concentrate upon the latter because it has had a greater structural effect upon the management of local authorities and it also illustrates most clearly the role of professional managers in the process of attempting to reconstruct the counties in the image of the New Right.

Hampshire is a large south coast county with a population a little in excess of one and a half million people; but it should be placed within the context of London and the South East region generally, which has about one-third of the UK's population, and accounts, therefore, for about twenty million people, depending on where the boundaries are drawn. Furthermore, it is firmly within the so-called 'golden triangle', which comprises the most prosperous and powerful geographical region in the European Community. Although it has much rural acreage, Hampshire also contains the major cities of Southampton and Portsmouth, as well as the overspill town of Basingstoke. Much of the rest of the population is located in the 'growth-points' of Aldershot/Farnham, Waterlooville/Havant and along the M27 corridor. The majority of people are, therefore, urban dwelling.

The problems facing the county include those of excessive growth and development into the rural areas, which is the result of close proximity to the Continent via the Channel ports, as well as considerable commuter traffic into London. Successive governments' policy of locating overspill population and industry out of the capital has also led to the massive planned growth to the north of the county. At the same time the run-down in traditional industries and defence-related work has led to the more familiar urban problems of unemployment and dereliction in the cities in which they were situated. The recession of the early 1990s exacerbated this trend, as large defence contractors laid off workers, following the end of the Cold War, a factor that did not pertain during the last period of high unemployment in the 1980s, when the South's economy continued to expand. The defence industry was joined by the service sector in cutting back. Yet Hampshire's planners have eschewed attempts to persuade company relocations from outside of the county, seeking instead to consolidate existing development and fight attempts to further erode the rural landscape (various interviews).

Although the political history of the county can be traced back to Saxon times, its present form and responsibilities date from the 1974 reforms which established the two-tier structures outside of the metropolitan areas: county councils and district councils. These followed the series of centrally imposed changes heralded by the Maude, Malleby, and Bains reports, which reconstructed the internal management of the local authorities at about the same time as the Fulton Report attempted to reform central government in the 1960s and early 1970s. The 1991 announcement by the Secretary of State for the Environment, Michael Heseltine, that there will once again be comprehensive reform of local government, has put the future of counties in doubt. It is possible that the district councils will eventually assume the role of unitary authorities and the County of Hampshire, as anything other than a historical entity, will cease to exist. The quickening flow of recent reforms has in any case appeared to effect a return to an almost Nineteenth Century view of local affairs, when local boards were responsible for the implementation of statutory duties such as poor relief and education (Rao, 1991, p.1). The modern manifestation of this is professionally/managerially run authorities. The establishment of competitive tendering, local management in schools and other activities which have peeled off the functions of local authorities has turned them over to council officials, private sector managers and professional experts (Laffin and Young, 1990).

The experience is similar to that of the US with its concept of the city manager and the plethora of boards and authorities employing experts and managers to run a service. Unlike the US, however, there is a greater degree of de-politicisation as the checks and balances built into the American system are missing in Britain. Even the traditional obeisance of the New Right to consumers is tarnished by the reality of the inadequacy of lay people when confronted by professional power. One senior Hampshire County officer saw elected councillors becoming the conduit through which consumer response could be measured, but recognised its limitations. He argued:

> You can't just ask the recipients of existing services, you have to go on a wider basis. In a sense that is what the elected members are there for, that is their role. It is for them to be the champions of their electorates and to come forward and say what is needed. I think we need to spend a bit of time helping elected members to fulfil that role more effectively. That begs all sorts of questions about living in a democracy. We need to use the members more constructively, more fully to be the eyes and ears of the county council and to find ways of more formally and more fully feeding that information into the corporate planning process. (Interview)

In other words, the democratic part of the local government structure ought to function as a sort of sounding board for those professionally qualified to make policy. The officer recognised this when he said that so far as he was concerned the new role of local government meant that:

> a very significant area of work is being taken out of the [elected] member arena. Commercial judgements are being made by managers. The role of the members is increasingly being marginalised. (Ibid.)

For other officers the use of management consultants and market research could just as easily fulfil the role of elected members (various interviews). It is a de-politicising perspective that would accord with liberal think-tanks; for example the Adam Smith Institute argued that all services should be put out to tender and that even the monitoring of these services should be privatised (Ascher, 1987, p.39). Politics and political activity are reduced to a facet of consumerism, where demand and supply are to be met and managed using the sort of skills normally honed in retailing, not in public service.

THE STRUCTURAL RESPONSE TO PRIVATISING SERVICES

Walsh believes that the British experience of competitive tendering is 'now, probably the most systematic and comprehensive' in the world (1990, para 1). The 1988 Local Government Act:

> extended the statutory requirement for competition to a number of 'defined activities', namely refuse collection, street cleaning, schools and welfare cleaning, other catering (for example, staff canteens), buildings cleaning, vehicle maintenance, grounds maintenance, and the management of sports and leisure facilities. (Ibid., para 2)

All British local authorities were given until 1 August 1989 to start initial contracts in their area, with the full implementation of the policy by 1991–2. The introduction of competitive tendering brought with it the establishment of trading accounts for local government services, changes in committee systems, departmental strutures and the managerial roles of elected members and career officials. In many cases it meant the end to the local authority as a providing organisation and its replacement by new structures which effectively turned the council into an enabling authority (Rao, 1991, p.4); that is, authorities which formulate strategy for their locality and then provide the political impetus for the provision of goods and services via the private sector. In this type of organisation a greater provision is often made for the impact of consumer demand at the policy formulation and evaluation phases.

Walsh shows that preparation for the implementation of competitive tendering took several different forms, but was usually preceded by detailed committee planning, with some councils opting to phase in the process slowly, whilst others put large tranches of work out to tender at a time (1990). In Hampshire the slow, phased approach was favoured. This reflected the political culture of the county, which one senior officer described in the following terms:

> although we're Conservative controlled now, until the last election we were a hung council with no overall control, we haven't got a doctrinaire Conservative administration. Our response to the competition legislation has not been, as perhaps it has been with some local authorities, that we're going to privatise and we don't see any continuing role for in-house organisations. Our concern is to get value for money and our [elected] members played the legislation straight down the middle.

> They want to give our in-house organisations an opportunity to flourish ... I think that is one of the characteristics generally of Hampshire traditionally. If you were going to classify it at all then I would call it a rather wet sort of Conservatism, it's not actually hard right-wing Thatcherite at all. It's more a pragmatic type of value-for-money Conservatism. There are many areas where we've taken a stance of opposition to government policies because we think they are bad for local government. (Interview)

Another officer, with considerable private sector experience, put great emphasis on the influence of the officers to formulate policy in counties like Hampshire that were of a more traditional shire orientation than a Tory flagship local authority like, say, the London borough of Wandsworth (interview). He pointed out that Hampshire, although Conservative controlled, exercised its independence by not being allied to Conservative Central Office:

> and most initiatives have come from the officers. Providing it makes good general business and management sense, then the politicians will go along with whatever the officers are proposing, providing they see the bureaucracy being rolled back in the process. In other words, that more of our resources go towards direct delivery and less towards keeping the bureaucracy running. Any proposal that comes up from the officers which appears to put more people at the centre of the organisation will be turned down. (Ibid.)

There are clear similarities here with the attitudes and experiences of American career officials, as discussed in the foregoing sections of this chapter.

These political considerations influenced the officers when they established a Business Services Group, in 1988, in anticipation of the legislation. The County also divided itself into fifteen geographically separate areas in which competition would be phased in and within which tendering would be contained. This was in contrast to counties like Avon who introduced the process in a single tranche throughout the unified structures of the county. Hampshire then set up Direct Service Organisations (DSO) within each of the departments that were to be transformed into a service organisation, for example, vehicle maintenance.

The Business Services Group (BSG) was intended to be a temporary organisation that was designed to establish and then facilitate competition policy within the county; to this end it acted as a bridge between the Treasurer's department and the service/user departments. It evolved:

because the County Treasurer basically knew that we had to create something, but didn't know what. So therefore it's a bit like creating a think tank group. It was set up to introduce two things; to get services established so they could prepare themselves to win tenders and once they'd won the tender to actually set their organisation up in such a way that they made it a going concern. (Interview with a former member of the group)

The BSG sought to inculcate service departments and the new DSOs with a managerial expertise. The aim was to ensure that they retained the contracts, keeping the employees in work and maintaining an in-house expertise, whilst operating according to best private sector management practices.

Many of the innovations reflected those that had been introduced into Whitehall. For example, the BSG established a shared data base system that created a client-based framework to aid management, something that at times appeared to closely resemble the MINIS of central government departments. The influence of motivations similar to those which provoked the FMI was also at work:

When you look at the kind of changes that we're accommodating at the moment, well a lot of them have their immediate spur from legislation, such as education and so on, but I have a feeling that even if it hadn't been for the legislation we would still have been moving in this general direction. The general direction being a concern with having a smaller, leaner centre that is much more concerned with setting standards and monitoring quality and output and devolving downwards responsibility and accountability, that is decentralising. A lot of structural change is all concerned with getting power down the system and actually giving managers a lot more freedom to manage, with the centre retaining responsibility for setting the strategy and goals and monitoring performance and quality. (Interview with a senior official)

This is precisely the motivation and perspective which informed the FMI and Next Steps in Whitehall. It reflects the depth of cultural change over the last decade, but not necessarily the victory of New Right ideology *per se*. This officer, in common with others, applauded the managerial advances the changes were making. It was a policy that was emancipating managers, especially those who adopted private sector attitudes. It was an expression of the advance of the professional (personnel/financial) manager, one that would not necessarily be welcomed by other, narrower, professional occupations, for example teachers and social workers. Indeed, many within the county forsaw the end of schools run by head-teachers, predicting their replacement by general (accountancy/personnel based) managers.

The implementation of competition policy in Hampshire was a success from the perspective of the council and senior officers, in that most of the contracts were won by the in-house DSOs. They were transferred to a new Commercial Services Directorate (CSD) which has the job of nurturing them. To a large extent the DSOs have been 'lucky' in that for much of their business the private sector competition has been knocked out because of low quality (Hampshire imposed a level of quality assurance that insisted upon British Standards Institution accreditation), or uninterested in the level of profit that can be extracted from the services put out to tender, especially in rural areas. Yet Hampshire has had to be careful to avoid rigging the competition unfairly, as 'this is a permanent revolution, you can't stop the tide' (interview with senior officer in Client Services department). Furthermore, councils that have been identified as being in breach of the spirit of the legislation by the Secretary of State have already been informed that under the Act the Minister alone can decide what is unreasonable:

> he has got total powers under the Act to decide whether a local authority is in breach of the Act, so he can decide whether something has to be re-tendered. (Ibid.)

Where the private sector has met the quality and profit levels dictated by the county the DSOs have lost the contract. As a result there is a slow haemorrhaging of work out of the public sector and into the private sphere. In time the county will more nearly become an enabling authority. The elected members and a core of senior officers will formulate and evaluate policy, with the private sector providing most of the goods and services. The county will be left with a rump of services impossible to privatise due to cost or other (equality/justice) considerations. These latter activities might include some social service, police and probation services, as well as road maintenance.

In conclusion, this snapshot of Hampshire has illustrated that many of the elements that the broad cultural shift the New Right has wrought in the UK and US are clearly identifiable at a micro level in the English shires. The changes originate through legislation, professional power, influence and national political parties implementing policy. These changes are of a kind that are essentially de-politicising. The beneficiaries are those located within the hierarchies of sub-national government as general managers. Men and women who seek to implement private sector management techniques within the public sector are those who have inherited the local authorities. This is not to say that they are ideologically committed to the New Right's prescriptions. The lesson of Hampshire is that they often seek to manipulate the changes in such a way that the goal of liberalising legislation is thwarted in its implementation, great pains being taken to retain sizable workforces within the auspices of the local authority. Control and autonomy are passing to the professional managers, not elected politicians or consumers.

CONCLUSION

Privatisation as practised in the US has come of age and grown old. It is informed by a long line of managerialist innovations that stretch back into the post World War Two administrative tradition, a tradition that has always borrowed freely for its ideas from the private sector. It is not a new development, but a re-structuring of bureaucratic worldviews to take account of political developments that threaten the ability of government to deliver programmes voted for by the electorate, an electorate that perversely insists on the simultaneous need to cut taxes.

The new development is the extent of the ideological shift that has taken place within the upper reaches of the American polity since the election of President Reagan, although, as Pfiffner (1988) shows, it is a shift that really began with Nixon and so should not be deemed a novel development at all. What is innovatory is the degree of ideological commitment demanded of and by Reagan's political appointees to the administration, the infrequency with which they 'went native' and the impact this ideological coherence has had at all levels on the governance of the US. Neither the ideology nor the managerial activities are all that new, what is new is the vigour with which they are implemented. It is this vigour which has pushed privatisation to the forefront of many of the changes taking place within the different levels of American political society, but as Morgan and England attempt to show, it can emphasise private interests at the expense of community interest (1988, pp.979–86), a perennial topic of discussion within the American polity.

The advance of the liberal Right has been aided by the taxpayers' revolt and its distaste for interventionist government has contributed to the crisis of programme delivery by insisting on the need to cut budgets in real terms. A large proportion of the cuts have fallen upon welfare programmes and upon support for those programmes in the states and localities, reflecting political fashion in favour of the devolution of responsibility back to its lowest level, that is to the locality and the individual. There are barriers to these developments within the political system, most obviously within the Congress, which is the focal point of the competition between a myriad of interests: ideological, parochial, commercial, trade union, ethnic, and others. These have used the American political system to check the full-blooded advance of liberalism, although whilst the electorate remains resistant to tax increases, particularly if they are to be used for welfare purposes, the greatest check will remain consumerist self-interest. The coalition in favour of privatisation, therefore, reflects that which is in favour of liberalism *per se*, a movement within which privatisation remains a managerialist tool.

For the British, the culture of liberalism, or 'privatism', as Barnekov *et al.* have called it, is of a different kind. The experience of the UK since 1945 is that of Welfarism and the notion of the state's care for its citizens from the cradle to grave is one that became deeply ingrained. Even the Conservative Party, pragmatic as ever, adopted Welfarist slogans and policies between 1945 and 1975; indeed, there were corporatist propensities within the party for most of this century. Like most converts (or apostates) Mrs Thatcher's zeal in demolishing the old verities was unbounded. Carrying her party with her throughout the 1980s she and her ministers unleashed a torrent of reform upon the sub-national governments of Britain. Most of it was inspired by New Right ideology and as such there are considerable similarities with that which occurred in America, especially the move toward greater professional management techniques and, of course, privatisation.

Unlike America, however, Britain lacks the constitutional checks and balances to prevent the proverbial baby being tipped out with its bathwater. Change in the US has been designed to withdraw the federal authorities from sub-national involvement; in Britain it has been fundamentally centralising. In the US liberalisation has been designed to aid devolution, protect local government and defend the provision of goods and services. In the UK it has been imposed upon most local authorities through the device of central government decree. Such devolution as has occurred has merely been a transfer of functions from the public to the private sector and of power from citizens and elected officials to private sector managers and public sector professionals/managers. The enabling authority in Britain may herald a new age of responsiveness to citizen/consumer demands, replete with management techniques that ensure efficient, effective and fair delivery of goods and services; but the manner of its birth provided a hard lesson in power politics, underlining the strength of the Crown in Parliament, personified in Her Majesty's Secretaries of State.

8 Not A Seamless Web: Bureaucrats, Managers and Markets

A double minded man is unstable in all his ways. (James 1.12)

ADMINISTRATION IS NOT A MARKET

The past decade has seen a fundamental re-definition of the role of the state across the world. Much of the momentum for this has come from the New Right, which has sought to reclaim for liberalism the territory lost this century; slowly, often haltingly, even the East is being privatised. The newly emergent democracies of Eastern Europe and the former Soviet Union are bowing to fashion, the failure of communism and the liberalising actions which precondition aid from the International Monetary Fund and World Bank. Romania's Law No. 58 envisages the privatisation of that country's 6,000 state-owned enterprises, whilst in Hungary twenty organisations were identified in 1990 as being available for privatisation. The triumph of liberalism appears complete, there are few parts of the world where command economies remain, and those that do are crumbling. It remains to be seen whether the political structures which eventually take root in these countries also emulate the West in terms of the separation of powers and other checks and balances. This book has concentrated upon Britain and the US, but the issues relating to the proper boundaries between the public and private sectors, the protection of liberty and the role of the public service, are being aired afresh across the globe.

Despite their bias and rhetoric, it would have been a foolish act for the New Right governments of the UK and the US to supplant the entire public sectors of their respective countries with managerialist replacements, merely to satisfy the requirements of ideology. Although there has been a fundamental questioning of the role of bureaucracy, all but the most die-hard ideologues have recognised that the accumulated practice and wisdom of generations is not something to be lightly discarded in a fit of nostalgia for a laissez-faire phantasm. Yet the force of the New Right critique demanded that something be done to redress the drag exerted by Welfarist baggage upon the economy and policy-makers. That 'something' included a managerialist onslaught upon the public sector, denigrating its norms and structures and seeking to replace its dominant culture with that of the private corporation. Both East and West have had to address the proper role of the public sector in a democracy, but the US and the UK have had the luxury of a decade-long experiment in moving the boundaries away from interventionism and back towards a laissez-faire ideal. This book has attempted to show that the results have been mixed. There have been major reforms, to be sure, even cultural transformations, but the public sector remains powerful within the two countries. This is as it should be in democratic countries governed under a legitimate constitution (however that may be defined to include mass support); it is the public sector (the state) which legitimately exercises or licenses coercion and thereby protects the private interests of its citizens.

It has been argued throughout this book that there is a difference between the private and public sectors that is both qualitative and quantitative. Baber's list (1987) is a useful expression of those dissimilarities, and some New Right political appointees (like Paul Volker, 1987) are themselves also critical of attempts to belittle the work of the public sector by casting it within the same light as routine (generic) management. The lessons from Britain and America suggest it would be wrong to conclude that the shift in emphasis from 'administration' to 'management' is entirely the product of New Right iconclasm, it is not. The assault upon the public service began in the US with Nixon, but continued under the Democratic President Carter. In Britain there are clear traces of it in the Labour Party of Wilson, Callaghan and Kinnock. T. Smith (1985) has identified in this a trend in Britain towards 'constitutional erosion' whereby the 'twin pillars of nineteenth-century constitutional rectitude', the doctrines of collective Cabinet responsibility and ministerial responsibility have all but collapsed. He argues that they have been replaced by managerialism with its goals of efficiency, effectiveness and economy. The latter, he argues, is incomparably weaker than those Victorian stalwarts of rectitude; indeed, they may not even be considered analogous. Chapter 3 showed how ministers have grasped greater control over policy and their officials, whilst simultaneously reducing the level and quality of accountability to which those officials are subjected. *Next Steps*, for example, re-defines accountability, making it more distant from Parliament.

The depth of change implemented throughout the British public sector has not been repeated in America. The separation of powers (or more correctly, the sharing of power by separate institutions) has prevented the wholesale reform of the civil service. Yet, whilst the intransigence of Congress has prevented the Presidency from reducing the size and pro-grammatic scope of the federal service, it has also prevented any effective modernisation of its structure and function. The service thus limps on into the Twenty First Century a refined and much larger imitation of its Nineteenth Century self: an historic compromise between the legislature and the executive, never truly belonging to either, but prey to the myriad powerful interest groups which inform the American polity.

In both these pluralist countries it may be academically useful to view politics as a market (Lindblom, 1977), but market solutions to the problems of the public sector are not only often irrelevant, they can be harmful in that they reduce the effectiveness of the state to meet the requirements of the citizenry, thereby lessening the legitimacy of the state itself. The major objection to market solutions comes when natural monopolies such as water, telecommunications, gas and electricity are considered. Questions of equity and access, as well as pricing, are to the forefront. In both the US and the UK the New Right has sought to privatise that which was in the public realm. In America this was accom-panied by de-regulation, whilst in Britain there was an increase in the number and scope of regulatory bodies. Where there is a natural monopoly, governments have a limited number of options from which to choose. They may either:

1. allow the monopoly to continue unfettered, something which in democracies is politically unacceptable;
2. control the monopoly in the public sector;
3. control the monopoly through regulation in the private sector; or
4. seek to use technological and managerial innovation to construct a market.

In both countries, New Right governments have tended towards options 3 and 4. It was the perceived failure of the collective process to be either democratic or efficient in 2, that is the imperious exercising of power over people by bureaucrats, that supplied the impetus for managerialist reform (Flynn, 1990, p.186). Yet in opting for a market-inspired managerialist reform the reformers have overlooked the special role of public administration. In doing this they have failed to build upon the need for a national constituency and a concept of the public interest, an underrated aspect of the US political system, with its seamless enmeshing of the public and private sectors. The American academic, McConnell, called for recognition of this constituency as far back as 1966.

Pollitt argues that there has been a near total omission in all the reforms of the distinctive ethical and legal basis of the public services (1990, p.112); a similar criticism is levelled by Baber against the Grace Commission (1987). Furthermore, there is rarely any attention given to the issues of fairness, re-distribution or democratic participation, much less the service ethic of the staff who run the public services (Pollitt, 1990). The concern to emulate the private sector overlooks the role of accountability, specifically in failing to produce a counterpart to the elected representative within the ordinary company. Referring to electors as 'shareholders' and their representatives as 'directors' is all very well, but when there is a clash between efficiency and accountability constitutional propriety demands that accountability wins. The contrast with the private firm is marked at this juncture, though sadly many of those involved in the reforms have affected not to notice (see examples in chapters 3 to 7, above), although the reforms of an earlier private sector managerial revolution had also curtailed the power of individual shareholders over company boards.

The firm is a weak and stunted analogy for public administration; high officials are not tradesmen. Politicians and senior officials have to set priorites and objectives, but often these are unclear, confused and even contradictory (ibid., pp.120–2). This is not inefficient or poor management; it is the stuff of political compromise, the meat and drink of servicing a pluralistic, sophisticated and complex electorate, the seamy side of politics. The sort of clear goal-setting expected in the private sector would provide an inflexible handicap to the public sector. This is not to say that politicians should not have goals (for example, throughput in NHS hospitals or units of public housing built), but to note that any such goals can often prove to be necessarily contradictory and the cost of their implementation (or non-implementation) must be measured in social and political terms, rather than purely monetary ones. Furthermore, as Pollitt notes:

> In price-driven markets the more goods or services a manager supplies the more the supplying organization's income grows. This is the standard business model. In most public services, however, supplying more services increases costs without any corresponding growth in income ... Even when charges are made ... they are often symbolic or only weakly related to actual costs incurred. This is not an incidental feature of public services, alterable by some improvement in cost accountancy. Rather it is fundamental, for many public services are public precisely because there is little prospect of being able to finance them through direct consumer payments. (1990, pp. 123–4)

Clearly the state does not 'manage' these things, it administers them according to constitutionally approved principles of justice, equity and access. To do otherwise is to invite a measure of alienation which threatens the legitimacy of the system. Tinkering around with pseudo-markets run by parvenu executives may help to improve service and product delivery in the short term, and it is to be applauded for that, but the state cannot simply abrogate its responsibilities and return to some Victorian ideal. New administrative methods may be required, but the old concepts and notions of government intervention, fostered by over forty years of welfare provision and state/industry corporatism, will remain. People are citizens first, and mere consumers a poor second; if governments are to be held accountable, this relationship of the individual to the state must remain.

THE LEGACY OF THE NEW RIGHT

The Wilsonian dichotomy between politics and administration was re-opened by British and American governments. Often presented as the legitimate division between policy formulation (which is the preserve of elected politicians) and policy implementation (which is reserved for career bureaucrats), it amounted to an attempt to resurrect Wilson's prescriptions for good government. The essential caveat here, however, is that the governments themselves were not mechanistic enough to see it in those terms. Moe's belief (1987) (as quoted in chapter 4) that the modern

White House is profoundly uninterested in management re-structuring is probably correct. In both Britain and America the New Right governments were simply concerned with controlling the public sector and especially in controlling the permanent civil service. Reagan's administrations did not allow the career officials to engage in policy formulation because they were not to be trusted with the manifesto; only the ideologically pure were given the job of planning its implementation. Career officials were there to be given their orders. In Britain the degree of loathing never reached that pitch, but there was a manifest distrust of the civil service by Mrs Thatcher and her ideological cohort. There was a clear signal given after the appointment of Rayner that officials were to do as they were told. In both countries the attempt at re-inventing this most absurd of dichotomies (politics/administration) merely served to emphasise its artificiality.

The goal of the New Right was to re-assert the dominance of politicians, to proclaim that they were breaking free from the shackles of Welfarist compromise and re-negotiating the social contract anew on their terms. It was, as Jessop (1988) saw, a resurrection of the role of politics and the proposition that electoral victory carried with it the right to implement a swingeing series of economic and political reconstructions. The lasting legacy, therefore, was that the post-war verities were dead. It does not matter that in the long term a reformed consensus will emerge, as seems probable, the spell of the Welfare State and (to use the American term) the 'administrative state' was broken. That is the lesson of resurgent politics; there was to be no return to the periodic re-negotiation within fixed boundaries to which the electoral process had been reduced. This represented an opening up of the democratic process with the previously unthinkable being placed upon the agenda; it made the politics of the 1980s a kind of political zero-based budgeting.

In Britain with its centralised executive-dominated polity it was easier for the New Right to implement its reforms, for the checks and balances inherent to a federal system primed with the separation of powers are lacking. Yet that does not mean there is a need for such a system to be grafted onto the constitution. Certainly it would be of great benefit and must be a long-term goal, but the first priority is a simple electoral reform ensuring a more representative Parliament. This would be the foundation upon which reform of the party system and thence executive accountability could be built. The lesson for the New Right in Britain is that although it won the elections it did not win the arguments and never succeeded in capturing a majority of votes cast. Nor, according to the opinion polls taken during the 1992 General Election, did it manage to gain more than a minority support for the propositions engendered by the ideology. In short, the advance of the New Right within the Conservative Party and in Britain was halted because a credible social democratic alternative at last presented itself to the electorate and the Conservatives knew that the promise of another dose of 'Thatcherism' would have certainly lost them that election. Such a realisation would have come sooner under proportional representation, without the aid of any charter or bill of rights, vital though these may eventually prove to be. In America, the New Right never captured a majority in Congress, although it managed a working majority for its compromise policies. It never managed a majority in the states either and the advances made in the early 1980s were held and slowly reversed as Congress sought to contain rampant liberalism. The election of George Bush signalled the end of New Right occupancy in the White House. He is, as various American observers have perspicaciously seen, more a pragmatic High Tory than anything else (Aberbach, 1991).

There have been other legacies, the full force of which are yet to work through. In Britain the combined effect of the New Right years has been somewhat contradictory: a move towards greater political centralisation (often in order to impose a market solution, for example in local government) and a greater degree of depoliticisation. This is not as incoherent as it at first seems, for as Gamble has shown (1988), in order to ensure the full transformation of sections of the economy and polity, the Conservatives had first to centralise in order to de-centralise in a way that ensured their policies would be implemented. Examples here include local government reform, the establishment of Urban Development Corporations, and much of the privatisation programme. The NHS reforms, with the purchaser/provider split and the establishment of internal markets, have begun a process of forcing medical accountability through budgets (Pollitt, 1990), whilst local management in schools, ushered in through the 1988 Education Act, has forced education authorities and the teaching profession to take account of the wishes of parents. Both of these reforms are examples of deep structural change bringing accountability to citizens through managerialism. It is not, however, a collective accountability or one that is exercised through Parliament. It further atomises society and leaves it to individuals to seek redress. Paradoxically, customers when faced with the need to take individual action may find themselves worse off as the reforms free organisations and institutions to pursue a managerial logic, not a public service ethic.

When these activities are combined with the reforms of the central civil service it can be argued that Britain has been left with a public sector which is less accountable than before the election of Mrs Thatcher's first government in 1979. This is not to say that civil servants are less answerable to ministers, to the contrary, but that the effects of privatisation, opting out and *Next Steps*, amongst others, have conspired to place managerialist performance indicators above social and ethical ones. In the case of executive agencies and important national, but privatised, utilities, this has led away from strategic planning for the national good and towards the kind of short-termism that has bedevilled British industry, dominated as it is by the demands of the City. Furthermore, the role of Parliament and elected representatives generally has been further removed from the business of holding the executive accountable. As in the past, all too often Parliament has connived in its own emasculation.

For America, the legacy is harder to fathom. Because the US did not introduce such a comprehensive welfare system, or nationalise so much industry, its path to liberalisation was shorter and less nationally traumatic. The de-centralised nature of the polity, however, ensured that path was strewn with more hazards than in Britain. Most of those hazards were put there by a recalcitrant Congress which adamantly refused to implement Mr Reagan's programmes after the mid-1980s, and states which felt the effects of 'new federalism' and decided that they preferred the old type. The nub of the New Right programme in the US has been to further politicise the civil service and roll back as many federal programmes to the states as possible. If, as appears to be the case, the states remain reluctant to accept their new-found freedom to levy higher taxes in order to replace federal funds (funds which, in any case, Congress has continued to deliver, albeit with conditions attached (Bingham *et al.*, 1991)) then the attempt will ultimately be seen to have failed. With regard to the civil service, Mr Bush appeared to renounce the hard-line stance of his predecessor upon assumption of office, and Congress itself has also sought to improve the lot of the bureaucracy. Yet the New Right remains strong throughout the US and probably enjoys more, and more fervent, support than in Britain. Its influence will remain powerful for the foreseeable future, providing a counterpoint to whatever political style succeeds the pragmatic Bush White House.

CONCLUSION

All of the important conclusions are contained within the body of the text, but there are some points which merit emphasis. In constitutional democracies possessing many generations of political wisdom and experience, a properly ordered bureaucracy is an essential defence of liberty. It quite properly forms the interface between the personal and the political, it operates on the seamy side of politics and as such it requires a degree of probity and ethical behaviour greater than that found in most other spheres of public life. Public administration cannot be judged by the standards reserved for retailers, nor can it be run along the same lines. There are no generic laws of management that apply equally to the public and private sectors.

The series of administrative reforms launched in both countries by anti-state political parties has shown the degree to which modern government is dependent upon its public administrators for the implementation and also the formulation of its policies. To seek to exclude them from the policy process is facile. But the citizenry is also dependent upon its public officials, it depends on their efficiency and skill and it trusts in their integrity. If the New Right's reforms have improved efficiency, effectiveness and economy without harming the integrity of the public services, then they will have been worthwhile. The lesson of prolonged periods of one-party rule, however, is that intellectual, political and financial probity are harder to sustain without the periodic loss of power which a fully functioning democracy provides. Japanese experience suggests that successive governments of the same party are racked by continuing waves of corruption. The lesson of machine politics in the US and the Poulson affair in the UK underlines this concern. Managerialism is a very weak bulwark to defend democratic government against malpractice, however many citizens' charters may be invented. The difficulty for observers in assessing the worth of the New Right's reforms is that of timescale and information. Government's own performance indicators have changed, becoming more managerial, whilst questions regarding morale, integrity and public service will take years to answer. Preliminary indications suggest the cultural changes in both Britain and America are not as deep as the New Right sought.

There are new threats to the status quo on the horizon. In Britain, the gradual absorption of Europe's nation states by the European Community will have a profound effect. The assimilation of European administrative law and practice will establish a different constitutional propriety of administrative law and oversight, making clear the role and function of the bureaucracy. This will not be easy. The very constitutional system which the British sought to avoid for generations (see chapter 1, above), now properly reformed in the democratic mould, will transform the manner of administration and its relationship both to the citizenry and the politicians, unless the European momentum is slowed. The discussion of this, however, must be the preserve of another book. It must suffice to argue, successful implementation of the European administrative system will require careful and incremental execution; the lessons of reform in Britain illustrate the difficulty of grafting new procedures onto the body politic.

The American political system remains as robust, following its experiment with the New Right, as it was before. The flexibility and pluralism of the polity accepts change, but channels it, dissipates it and re-moulds it over a long period. The New Right never commanded majority support, but it had enough support to matter up to a point. The system took due cognisance of this, shivered, and then continued. There has been no systematic dismantling of America's welfare system or its civil service, nor will there be. The likelihood is that the welfare benefits of social security, housing and medical care will be extended. Certainly, the case for comprehensive health care is becoming irresistible because of an ageing population and deepening poverty. America's civil servants will meet the challenge and implement the policies.

Privatisation has had the biggest impact. This is not because of the power of the New Right, but because new technology and a realisation that Gross Domestic Product could not grow exponentially (and therefore neither could public expenditure) combined to make all concerned realise that structural change had to occur. For most of those involved, privatisation was simply a management tool, not a crusade. It allowed national and sub-national administrators to manage the re-structuring of service provision made inevitable by economic circumstances. It also allowed them to exercise their professional power less fettered by politicians. As such privatisation was an idea that had come of age, it suited policy makers of all persuasions, other than the Far Left, to make use of the benefits it could bestow. It would be a mistake, therefore, to see privatisation as merely an aid to liberalisation. As a management tool it has allowed for the de-politicisation of many areas of service provision, and the devolution of decision-making. It has not, on the whole, greatly contributed to the growth of markets; the case study of electricity generation (chapter 6) demonstrated that point.

It is ironic that an 'arms' length' approach was also a goal of Morrison when he established the post-war nationalised industries in the UK. Nationalisation and privatisation are simply alternative methods of attempting to secure the benefits from industry for society. The advocates of both believe that their option releases the greatest benefit. Under privatisation, however, even major industries are supposedly allowed to go bankrupt or pass into foreign ownership (notwithstanding the use of a golden share by the government), something that would have been anathema to Morrison and his belief in the need to put 'strategic' industries at the service of the country as a whole.

One of the main lessons of this book is with regard to the issue of political accountability, or (to complete the circle of the book) liberty. Macaulay's concerns were also those of the English, French, American and Russian revolutions. Yet it is only in the US and the UK that for the most part liberty and freedom have been continually protected for generations of uninterrupted political development. The reason for this is accountability. The emphasis of the New Right has been on management and control as a way to ensure the accountability of the state, devolving power out to the market and individual consumers. In short it has been an attempt to get the state to wither away. This is not the way to protect liberty. The wisdom of America's Founding Fathers was clear upon this point: only if men were angels could we do away with government. The Americans and their English cousins did not prescribe markets to govern people, but layers of administration and legislators accountable to each other and to the people, imbued with the practice and wisdom of centuries. In America the New Right have attempted to claim as their own the myth of the young America as a land of independent Jeffersonian yeoman farmers, but it is only a myth and one that Jefferson himself would not have recognised, acutely aware as he was of the need for vigilance and accountability. It is not through accident that liberty has flourished best in those countries where separation of powers and the accountability of government have been most insisted upon. To the New Right and their obsession with efficiency, accountability may appear like Aristo's serpent, 'a hateful reptile' that hisses and stings. Yet it is the foundation upon which the two countries have avoided overbearing government; accountability may be inefficient, 'but woe to those who in disgust shall venture to crush her'.

References and Bibliography

Aberbach, J.D. (1991), 'Public Service and administrative reform in the United States: the Volker Commission and the Bush administration', *International Review of Administrative Sciences*, Vol. 57, pp.403–19.

Aberbach, J.D., and Rockman, B.A. (1988), 'Mandates or Mandarins? Control and Discretion in the Modern Administrative State', *Public Administration Review*, Vol. 48, pp.607–12.

Aberbach, J.D., Putnam, R.D., and Rockman, B.A. (1981), *Bureaucrats and Politicians in Western Democracies*, Cambridge, Mass., Harvard University Press.

Agranoff, R. (1991), 'Human Services Integration: Past and Present challenges in Public Administration', *Public Administration Review*, Vol. 51, No. 6.

Albrow, N. (1970), *Bureaucracy*, London, Pall Mall Press.

Alexander, A. (1982), *The Politics of Local Government in the United Kingdom*, London, Longman.

Allison, G. (1971), *The Essence of Decision: Explaining the Cuban Missile Crisis*, Boston, Little Brown.

Alt, J., and Chrystal, K.A. (1983), *Political Economics*, Brighton, Wheatsheaf.

Arnold, R.D. (1979), *Congress and the Bureaucracy: a theory of influence*, New Haven and London, Yale University Press.

Ascher, K. (1987), *The Politics of Privatisation: contracting out public services*, London, Macmillan.

Ashford, D. (1981), *Policy and Politics in Britain*, Oxford, Basil Blackwell.

Baber, W.F. (1987), *Privatizing Public Management: The Grace Commission and Its Critics*, in Hanke.

Bacon, R., and Eltis, W. (1976), *Britain's Economic Problem: Too Few Producers*, London, Macmillan.

Ban, C. (1984), 'Implementing Civil Service Reform: Structure and Strategy'; pp.42–62, in Ingraham, P.W. and Ban, C. (eds), *Legislating Bureaucratic Change: The Civil Service Reform Act of 1978*, New York, State University of New York Press.

Ban, C. and Ingraham, P.W. (1988), 'Retaining Quality Federal Employees: Life after PACE', *Public Administration Review*, Vol. 48, pp.708–18.

Ban, C. and Redd, H.C. (III), (1990), 'The State of the Merit System: Perceptions of Abuse in the Federal Civil Service', *Review of Public Personnel Administration*, Vol. 10, No. 3.

Barker, A. (1982), *Quangos in Britain*, London, Macmillan.

Barnekov, T., Boyle, R. and Rich, D. (1989), *Privatism and Urban Policy in Britain and the United States*, Oxford, Oxford University Press.

Batley, R. (1989), 'London Docklands: an analysis of power relations between UDCs and local government', *Public Administration*, Vol. 67, No. 2, London, RIPA/Basil Blackwell.

Bartlett, R. (1973), *Economic Foundations of Political Power*, New York, Free Press.

Beaumont, E. (1991), 'Enterprise Zones and Federalism', in Green.

Beer, S.H. (1982), *Britain Against Itself: the political contradictions of collectivism*, New York and London, W.W. Norton and Company.

Beetham, D. (1987), *Bureaucracy*, Milton keynes, Open University Press.

Behan, R.W. (1983), *The 'Privatization' Alternative for the Future of the Federal Public Lands: A Penultimate Comment*, Paper presented to the annual meeting of the Western Political Science Association, Seattle, Washington.

Bekke, H. (1987), *Public Management in Transition*, in Kooiman and Eliassen.

Benn, T. (1981), *Arguments for Democracy*, London, Johnathan Cape.

Bennett, J.T. and DiLorenzo, T.J. (1987), *The Role of Tax-funded Politics*, in Hanke.

Bennett, J.T. and Johnson, M.H. (1981), *Better Government at Half the Price: Private Production of Public Services*, Ottowa, Caroline House.

Bingham, R.D. et al. (1991), *Managing Local Government: Public Administration in Practice*, London, Sage.

Bingman, C. (1985), *The Bureaucrat*, Summer edition.

Bingman, C. (1986), 'Sound and Fury – Signifying Nothing', *The Bureaucrat*, Spring, pp.43–4.

Blake, R. (1985), *The Conservative Party from Disraeli to Thatcher*, London, Fontana.

Blunkett, D. and Jackson, K. (1987), *Democracy in Crisis: The Town Halls Respond*, London, Hogarth.

Boyle, L.L. (1991), 'Reforming Civil Service Reform; Should the Federal Government Continue to regulate State and Local Government Employees?', *Journal of Law and Politics*, Vol. 7, pp.243–88.

Bretschneider, S. (1990), 'Management Information Systems in Public and Private Organizations: An Empirical Test', *Public Administration Review*, Vol. 50, pp.536–45.

Brittan, S. (1973), *Capitalism and the Permissive Society*, London, Macmillan.

Brittan, S. (1977), *The Economic Consequences of Democracy*, London, Temple Smith.

Bryner, G.C. (1987), *Bureaucratic Discretion: Law and Policy in Federal Regulatory Agencies*, New York and Oxford, Pergamon Press.

Buchanan, J.M. and Tullock, J. (1962), *The Calculus of Consent*, Ann Arbor, University of Michegan Press.

Buchanan, J.M., Niskanen, W.A., Roberts, P.C., Minford, P., Stelzer, I. and Budd, A. (1989), *Reaganomics and After*, London, Institute for Economic Affairs.

Bulpitt, J. (1983), *Territory and Power in the United Kingdom*, Manchester, Manchester University Press.

Bulpitt, J. (1986), 'The Thatcher Statecraft', *Political Studies*.

Burch, M. and Wood, B. (1983), *Public Policy in Britain*, Oxford Martin Robertson.

Butler, S.M. (1987), *Changing The Political Dynamics of Government*, in Hanke.

Butler, S.M. (1991), 'The Conceptual Evolution of Enterprise Zones', in Green.

Caiden, G.E. (1991), 'What really is Public Maladministration?', *Public Administration Review*, Vol. 51, No. 6.

Caiden, G.E., Loverd, R.A., Sipe, L.F. and Wong, M.M. (eds) (1983), *American Public Administration: a bibliographical guide to the literature*, New York, Garland Publishing.

Carroll, J.D. (1987), 'Public Administration in the Third Century of the Constitution: Supply-side Management, Privatization, or Public Management?', *Public Administration Review*, Vol. 47, pp.106–14.

Carter, N. (1991), 'Learning to Measure Performance: the use of indicators in organisations', *Public Administration*, Vol. 69, No. 1.

Case, H.M. (1986), 'Federal Employee Job Rights: The Pendleton Act of 1883 to the Civil Service Reform Act of 1978', *Howard Law Journal*, Vol. 29, pp.283–306.

Chapman, L. (1978), *Your Disobedient Servant*, London, Chatto and Windus.

Clarke, L. (1975), *The Grand Jury; the Use and Abuse of Political Power*, New York, Quadrangle/The New York Times Book Co.

Cm 525 (1988), *Civil Service Management reform: The Next Steps, London*, HMSO.

Cm 1261, Mellor, D. (1990), *Improving Management in Government: the Next Steps Agencies, Review 1990* (a presentation to Parliament by the Prime Minister and the Minister for the Civil Service), London, HMSO.

Cmnd. 8610 (1982), *The Future of Telecommunications in Britain*, London, HMSO.

Cmnd. 9058 (1983), *Financial Management in Government Departments*, London, HMSO.

Conant, J.K. (1988), 'In the Shadow of Wilson and Brownlow: Executive Branch Reorganization in the States, 1965 to 1987', *Public Administration Review*, Vol. 48, pp.892–902.

Confederation of British Industry (1988), *London Life: Special Report of the CBI London Region Urban Regeneration Task Force*, London, CBI.

Cox, A. and O'Sullivan, N. (eds) (1988), *The Corporate State*, Aldershot, Edward Elgar.

Dahl, R. (1982), *Dilemmas of Pluralist Democracy*, New York, Yale University Press.

Davies, A. and Willman, J. (1991), *What Next? Agencies, Departments, and the Civil Service*, London, IPPR.

Dawson, S. (1986), *Analysing Organisations*, Basingstoke, Macmillan.

Department of Energy (1987), *Privatising Electricity*, Cm 322, London, HMSO.

Derlien, H-U. (1987), *Public Managers and Politics*, in Kooiman and Eliassen.

Downs, A. (1967), *Inside Bureaucracy*, New York, Wiley.

Drewry, G. and Butcher, T. (1988), *The Civil Service Today*, London, Basil Blackwell.

Dunleavy, P. (1986), 'Explaining the Privatisation Boom: Public Choice versus radical approaches', *Public Administration*, Vol. 64, No. 1, London, RIPA/Basil Blackwell.

Dunleavy, P. (1989a), 'The architecture of the British central state, Part 1: Framework for analysis', *Public Administration*, Vol. 67, No. 3., London, RIPA/Basil Blackwell.

Dunleavy, P. (1989b), 'The architecture of the British central state. Part 2: Empirical findings', *Public Administration*, Vol. 67, No. 4, London, RIPA/Basil Blackwell.

Dunleavy, P. (1990), 'Core Executive Studies in Britain' (with R.A.W. Rhodes), also 'Reinterpreting the Westland Affair: theories of the state and core executive decision making', *Public Administration*, Vol. 68, No. 1, London, RIPA/Basil Blackwell.

Dunleavy, P. (1991), *Democracy, Bureaucracy and Public Choice: economic explanations in political science*, London, Harvester Wheatsheaf.

Dunleavy, P. and O'Leary, B. (1989), *Theories of the State: the Politics of Liberal Democracy*, London, Macmillan.

Dunsire, A., Hartley, K. and Parker, D. (1991), 'Organisational Status and Performance: summary of the findings', *Public Administration*, Vol. 69, No. 1, London, RIPA/Basil Blackwell

Dunsire, A., Hartley, K., Parker, D., and Dimitriou, B. (1988), 'Organizational Status and Performance; a conceptual framework for testing public choice theories',Public Administration, Vol., 66, No., 4, London, RIPA/Basil Blackwell.

Eades, G.C. and Fix, M. (1984a), *Relief or Reform? Reagan's Regulatory Dilemma*, University Press of America.

Eades, G.C. and Fix, M. (eds) (1984b), *The Reagan Regulatory Strategy: An Assessment*, University Press of America.

Efficiency Unit (1985), *Making Things Happen: a report on the implementation of government efficiency scrutinies*, London, HMSO.

Efficiency Unit (K. Jenkins, K. Caines and A. Jackson) (1988), *Improving Management in Government: The Next Steps*, London, HMSO.

Efficiency Unit (1991), *Making the Most of Next Steps: The Management of Ministers' Departments and their Executive Agencies*, London, HMSO.

Elcock, H. (1991), *Change and Decay?: Public Administration in the 1990s*, Harlow, Longman.

Fesler, J.W. (1987), 'The Brownlow Committee Fifty Years Later', *Public Administration Review*, Vol. 47, pp.291–5.

Fixler, Jr, P.E., and Poole, Jr, R.W. (1987), *Status of State and Local Privatization*, in Hanke.

Flynn, N. (1990), *Public Sector Management*, New York, London, Harvester Wheatsheaf.

Fry, G.K. (1988), 'The Thatcher Government, The Financial Management Initiative, and the "New Civil Service"', *Public Administration*, Vol. 66, No. 1, London, RIPA/Basil Blackwell.

Fry, G., Flynn, A., Gray,A., Jenkins, W., and Rutherford, B. (1988), 'Symposium on improving management in government', *Public Administration*, Vol. 66, No. 4, London, RIPA/Basil Blackwell.

Gamble, A. (1974), *The Conservative Nation*, London, Routledge and Kegan Paul.

Gamble, A. (1988), *The Free Economy and the Strong State; The Politics of Thatcherism*, Basingstoke, Macmillan.

Gerston, L.N. and Christensen, T. (1991), *California Politics and Government: a Practical Approach*, Pacific Grove, Brooks/Cole Publishing Company.

Gilmore, I. (1983), *Britain Can Work*, Oxford, Martin Robertson.

Goldsmith, M.J. (ed.) (1986), *Essays on the Future of Local Government*, West Yorkshire Metropolitan County Council.

Goldsmith, M.J. and Page, E.C. (eds) (1987), *Central and Local Government Relations: a comparative analysis of West European Unitary States*, London, Sage.

Goodin, R. (1982), 'Rational Politicians and Rational Bureaucrats in Washington and Whitehall', *Public Administration*, Vol. 60, No. 1, London, RIPA.

Goodman, J.C. (1987), *Privatizing the Welfare State*, in Hanke.

Government Executive, *The Civil Service: A Statistical Profile*, April 1991, pp. 28–32.

Grace, P. (1984), *Report of The President's Private Sector Survey on Cost Control*.

Graham, C. and Prosser, T. (1991), *Privatizing Public Enterprises: Constitutions, the State, and Regulation in Comparative Perspective*, Oxford, Clarendon Press.

Gramsci, A. (1971), *Selections from the Prison Notebooks*, London, Lawrence and Wishart.

Grant, W. (1989), *Government and Industry: a comparative analysis of the US, Canada and the UK*, Aldershot, Edward Elgar.

Gray, A. and Jenkins, W.I. (1985), *Administrative Politics in British Government*, Brighton, Wheatsheaf.

Gray, A., Jenkins, W. with Flynn, A. and Rutherford, B. (1991), 'The Management of Change in Whitehall: the experience of the FMI', *Public Administration*, Vol. 69, No. 1, London, Basil Blackwell.

Gray, J. (1986), *Liberalism*, Milton Keynes, Open University Press.

Gray, J. (1989a), *Liberalisms: Essays in Political Philosophy*, London, Routledge.

Gray, J. (1989b), *Limited Government: a positive agenda*, Hobart Paper 113, London, IEA.

Green, R. (ed.) (1991), *Enterprise Zones: New Directions in Economic Development*, Newbury Park Ca, and London, Sage.

Greenleaf, W.H. (1987), *The British Political Tradition; Vol. III, A Much Governed Nation*, London and New York, Methuen.

Greenwood, F. (1965), 'Attributes of a Profession', in M. Zaid (ed.), *Social Welfare Institutions*, London, Wiley.

Gunn, L. (1987), *Perspectives on Public Management*, in Kooiman and Eliassen.

Hailsham, Rt Hon. Lord (October 1976), 'An Elective Dictatorship', The Annual Dimbleby Lecture, *The Listener*, London, BBC.

Hall, J. (ed.) (1986), *States in History*, Oxford, Oxford University Press.

Hambleton, R. (1988), 'Consumerism, decentralization and local democracy', *Public Administration*, Vol. 66, No. 2, London, RIPA/Basil Blackwell.

Hanf, K. and Scharpf, F.W. (1978), *Interorganizational Policy-Making*, London, Sage.

Hanke, S.H. (ed.) (1987), *Prospects for Privatization*, Proceedings of the Acadamy of Political Science, Vol. 36, No. 3, New York, APS.

Hansen, S.B. (1991), 'Comparing Enterprise Zones to Other Economic Development Techniques', in Green.

Harris, R. (1988), *Beyond the Welfare State*, IEA Occasional Paper 77, London, IEA.

Harte, M. (1988), 'The Introduction of Commercial Management into the Royal Dockyards', *Public Administration*, Vol. 66, No. 3.

HC 496 (1991), *Seventh Report of the Treasury and Civil Service Committee: The Next Steps Initiative*, London, HMSO.

Heald, D.A. (1983), *Public Expenditure*, Oxford, Martin Robertson.

Heclo, H. and Wildavsky, A.V. (1974), *The Private Government of Public Money*, Basingstoke, Macmillan.

Hellinger, D. and Judd, D. (1991), *The Democratic Facade*, Pacific Grove, Brooks/Cole.

Henkel, M. (1991a), 'The New Evaluative State', *Public Administration*, Vol. 69, No. 1, London, Basil Blackwell.

Henkel, M. (1991b), *Government, Evaluation and Change*, London, Jessica Kingsley Publishers.

Hennessy, P. (1989), *Whitehall*, London, Fontana Press.

Heyman, P.B. (1987), *The Politics of Public Management*, New Haven and London, Yale University Press.

Hirschman, A.O. (1983), *Exit Voice and Loyalty*, Cambridge, Mass., Harvard University Press.

Hoffman, J. (1984), *The Gramscian Challenge*, Oxford, Blackwell.

Hoffman, J. (1988), *State, Power and Democracy*, Brighton, Wheatsheaf.

Hofmann, J.L. (1988), 'Productivity and Privatization', *The Bureaucrat*, pp.17–18, Winter 1988–9.

Hood, C. (1976), *The Limits of Administration*, London, Wiley.

Hood, C. (1986), *Administrative Analysis: An Introduction to Rules, Enforcement and Organizations*, Brighton, Wheatsheaf.

Hood, C. (1990), *Beyond the Public Bureaucracy State? Public Administration in the 1990s*, Inaugural Lecture, London School of Economics and Political Science.

Hood, C. (1991), 'A Public Administration for all Seasons?', *Public Administration*, Vol. 69, No. 1, London, Basil Blackwell.

Hood, C. and Dunsire, A. (1981), *Bureaumetrics*, Aldershot, Gower.

House, P.W. and Shull, R.D. (1986), *Regulatory Reform*, University Press of America.

Huddleston, M.W. (1988–9), 'Is There a Higher Civil Service?', *Policy Studies Journal*, Vol. 17, No. 2.

Illich, I. (1972), *Deschooling Society*, London, Calder and Boyars.

Ingraham, P.W. (1987), 'Building Bridges or Burning Them? The President, the Appointees, and the Bureaucracy', *Public Administration Review*, September/October 1987.

Ingraham. P.W. and Rosenbloom, D.H. (1988–9), 'Symposium on the Civil Service Reform Act of 1978; An Evaluation', *Policy Studies Journal*, Vol. 17, No. 2.

Ingraham, P.W. and White, J. (1988–9), 'The Design of Civil Service Reform: Lessons in Politics and Rationality', *Policy Studies Journal*, Vol. 17, No. 2.

Jessop, B., Bonnett, K., Bromley, S.M. and Ling, T. (1988), *Thatcherism*, Cambridge, Polity Press.

Johnson, R.N. and Libecap, G.D. (1989), 'Agency Growth, Salaries and the Protected Bureaucrat', *Economic Inquiry*, Vol. 27, pp.431–50.

Johnson, T. (1972), *Professions and Power*, London, Macmillan.

Jones, G.W. and Stewart, J.D., (1984), *The Case for Local Government*, London, Allen and Unwin.

Jowell, J.L. (1975), *Law and Bureaucracy: Administrative Discretion and the Limits of Legal Action*, New York, Dunellan and Kennikat Press.

Jowell, J.L. and Oliver, D. (eds) (1988), *New Directions in Judicial Review*, London, Stevens and Sons.

Karl, B.D. (1987), 'The American Bureaucrat: A History of a Sheep in Wolves' Clothing', *Public Administration Review*, Vol. 47, pp.26–34.

Kass, H.D. and Catron, B.L. (eds) (1990), *Images and Identities in Public Administration*, London, Sage.

Kavanagh, D. (1987), *Thatcherism and British Politics: the end of consensus?*, Oxford, Oxford University Press.

Kellner, P. and Crowther-Hunt, Lord (1980), *The Civil Service: An Inquiry into Britain's Ruling Class*, London, Macdonald.

Kinkaid, J. (ed.) (1988), 'State Constitutions in a Federal System', *The Annals of the American Acadamy of Political and Social Science*, Newbury Park, Beverly Hills, London, Sage Publications.

Kooiman, J. and Eliassen, K.A. (eds) (1987), *Managing Public Organizations*, London, Sage.

Laffin, M. (1986), *Professionalism and Policy: the rise of the professions in the central–local relationship*, Aldershot, Gower.

Laffin, M. and Young, K. (1985), 'The Changing Roles and Responsibilities of Local Authority Chief Officers', *Public Administration*, Vol. 63, pp.41–59.

Laffin, M. and Young, K. (1990), *Professionalism in local Government*, London, Longman.

Lane, J-E (1987), *Public and Private Leadership*, in Kooiman and Eliassen.

Lee, M. (1990), 'The Ethos of the Cabinet Office: a comment on the testimony of officials', *Public Administration*, Vol. 68, No. 2, London, RIPA/Basil Blackwell.

Letwin, O. (1988), *Privatising the World*, London.

Lewis, N. (1990), *Happy and Glorious: The Constitution in Transition*, Milton Keynes, Open University Press.

Lindblom, C.E. (1977), *Politics and Markets*, New York, Basic Books.

Littlechild, S. (1984), *Regulations of British Telecommunications Profitability*, London, HMSO.

Loomis, B. (1988), *The New American Politician: Ambition, Entrepreneurship, and the Changing Face of Political Life*, New York, Basic Books.

Luneburg, W.V. (1989–90), 'The Federal Personnel Complaint, Appeal and Grievance Systems: A Structural Overview and Proposed Revisions', *Kentucky Law Journal*, Vol. 78, No. 1.

Lynn, N.B. and Vaden, R.E. (1980), 'Federal Executives: Initial reactions to Change', *Administration and Society*, Vol. 12, No. 1.

Macaulay, T.B. (1854), *Historical Essays*, London, Longman, Brown, Green, and Longman.

McCurdy, H.E. (1991), 'Organizational Decline: NASA and the Life Cycle of Bureaus', *Public Administration Review*, Vol. 51, No. 4.

McGill, M.E. and Wooton, L.M. (eds) (1975), 'A Symposium: Management in the Third Sector', *Public Administration Review*, No. 5, 443–508.

Mannheim, K. (1940), *Man and Society in an Age of Reconstruction*, London, Routledge.

Mannheim, K. (1954), *Ideology and Utopia*, London, Routledge and Kegan Paul.

March, J.G. and Olsen, J. (1984), 'The New Institutionalism: organisational factors in political life', *American Political Science Review*, No. 78: pp.734–49.

March, J.G. and Simon, H.A. (1958) *Organizations*, New York, Wiley.

Marquand, D. (1988), *The Unprincipled Society*, London, Jonathan Cape.

Marsh, D. (1991), 'Privatisation under Mrs Thatcher: a review of the literature', *Public Administration*, Vol. 69: No. 4, pp.460–80, London, Basil Blackwell.

Massey, A. (1988), *Technocrats and Nuclear Politics*, Aldershot, Gower.

Massey, A. (1990), *New Public Management Grows Old: current views of privatization in the USA*, paper presented to the Political Studies Association of the UK, University of Durham, April.

Metcalfe, L., and Richards, S. (1987), *Evolving Public Management Cultures*, in Kooiman and Eliassen.

Metcalfe, L. and Richards, S. (1990), *Improving Public Management* (2nd edition), London, Sage.

Middlemas, K. (1979), *Politics in Industrial Society*, London, Deutsch.

Miller, T.C. (ed.) (1984), *Public Sector Performance: a conceptual turning point*, Baltimore and London, The Johns Hopkins University Press.

Milne, R. (1987), 'Competitive Tendering in the NHS', *Public Administration*, Vol. 65, No. 2.

Moe, R.C. (1987a), 'The Brownlow Report: A Timeless Message', *The Bureaucrat*, Fall, pp.45–8.

Moe, R.C. (1987b), 'Exploring the Limits of Privatization', *Public Administration Review*, Vol. 47, November/December, p.458.

Moe, R.C. (1991), 'The HUD Scandal and the Case for an Office of Federal Management', *Public Administration Review*, Vol. 51, No. 4.

Moore. J. (1986), *Britain's Privatisation Programme Sets World Example*, HM Treasury Press release 51/86, London.

Morgan, D.R. and England, R.E. (1988), 'The Two Faces of Privatization', *Public Administration Review*, pp. 979–87, November/December.

National Commission on the Public Service (Volker Commission), (1989), *Leadership for America: Rebuilding the Public Service* (also Task Force Reports), Washington DC, National Commission on the Public Service.

Nelson, M. (1986), 'The Irony of American Bureaucracy' in Rourke.

Neustadt, R. (1980), *Presidential Power*, New York, John Wiley and Sons.

Niskanen, W.A. (1971), *Bureaucracy and Representative Government*, Chicago, Aldine Atherton.

Niskanen, W.A. (1973), *Bureaucracy: Servant or Master?*, London, IEA.

Noll, R.G. and Owen, B.M. (1983), *The Political Economy of Deregulation: Interest Groups in the Deregulatory Process*, University Press of America.

Nordlinger, E. (1988), 'The Return to the State: critique', *American Political Science Review*, Vol. 82, No. 3.

OECD (1987), *Administration as Service, The Public as Client*, Paris, OECD.

Office of the Minister of the Civil Service (1991), *Setting up Next Steps*, London, HMSO.

O'Leary, R. and Wise, C.R. (1991), 'Public Managers, Judges and Legislators: Redefining the "New Partnership"', *Public Administration Review*, Vol. 52, No. 4.

O'Toole, B. (1990), 'T. H. Green and the ethics of senior officials in British central government', *Public Administration*, Vol. 68, No. 3, London, RIPA/Basil Blackwell.

O'Toole, L.J. Jr (1987), 'Doctrines and Developments: Separation of Powers, the Politics-Administration Dichotomy, and the Rise of the Administrative State', *Public Administration Review*, Vol. 47, pp.17–24.

Olson, M. (1982), *The Rise and Decline of Nations*, Newhaven, Yale University Press.

Page, E.C. (1985), *Administrative Authority and Bureaucratic Power*, Brighton, Wheatsheaf.

Painter, J. (1991), 'Compulsory competitive tendering in local government: the first round', *Public Administration*, Vol. 69, No. 2, London, Basil Blackwell.

Perrow, C. (1970), *Organisational Analysis*, London, Tavistock.

Perry, J.L. (1988–9), 'Making Policy by Trial and Error: Merit Pay in the Federal Civil Service', *Policy Studies Journal*, Vol. 17, No. 2.

Perry, J.L. and Kraemer, K.L. (eds) (1983), *Public Management: Public and Private Perspectives*, CA, Mayfield Publishing Company.

Peters, T.J. and Austen, N. (1985), *A Passion for Excellence: the leadership difference*, Glasgow, Fontana/Collins.

Peters T.J. and Waterman, R.H. (1982), *In Search of Excellence: lessons from America's best run companies*, New York, Harper and Row.

Peterson, P.E., Rabe, B.G., and Wong, K.K. (1988), *When Federalism Works*, Washington DC, The Brookings Institution.

Pfiffner, J.P. (1988), *The Strategic Presidency: Hitting the Ground Running*, Chicago, The Dorsey Press.

Pitt, D.C. and Smith, B.C. (1981), *Government Departments*, London, Routledge and Kegan Paul.

Pitt, D.C. and Smith, B.C. (1984), *The Computer Revolution in Public Administration*, Brighton, Wheatsheaf.

Pliatzky, L. (1984), *Getting and Spending: Public Expenditure, Employment and Inflation*, London, Blackwell.

Pollitt, C. (1990), *Managerialism and the Public Services: the Anglo–American experience*, Oxford, Basil Blackwell.

Ponting, C. (1985), *The Right to Know*, London, Sphere.

Price, D.K. (1983), *America's Unwritten Constitution*, Baton Rouge, Louisiana State University Press.

Price Waterhouse (1991), *Executive Agencies: Facts and Trends*, London, Price Waterhouse.

Rao, N. (1991), 'Developments in Local Government', *Politics Briefing Note No. 15*, London, Constitutional Reform Centre.

Rhodes, R.A.W. (1981), *Control and Power in Central–Local Relations*, Aldershot, Gower.

Rhodes, R.A.W. (1988), *Beyond Westminster and Whitehall: The sub-central governments of Britain*, London, Unwin Hyman.

Robson, W.A. (1951, reprinted 1970), *Justice and Administrative Law*, Westport, Greenwood Press.

Ross, M.J. (1988 edition), *California: Its Government and Politics*, Pacific Grove, Brooks Cole Publishing Company.

Rourke, F.E. (ed.) (1986), *Bureaucratic Power in National Policy Making* (4th edition), Boston, Little Brown and Company.

Salamon, L.M. (Panel Chairman) (1989), *Privatization: The Challenge to Public Management*, Report of a panel of the National Academy of Public Administration, Washington DC, NAPA.

Saunders, P. (1985), 'Corporatism and Urban Service Provision', in W. Grant (ed.), *The Political Economy of Corporatism*, London, Macmillan.

Savas, E.S. (1987), *Privatization: the key to better government*, Chatham, New Jersey, Chatham House Publishers.

Schachter, J. (1988), 'Volker's Target: A Flagging Federal Service', *Government Operations*, Washington DC, Congressional Quarterly.

Schlozman, K.L. and Tierney, J.T. (1986), *Organised Interests and American Democracy*, New York, Harper and Row.

Schmidtz, D. (1991), *The Limits of Government: an essay on the public goods argument*, Boulder, San Francisco, Oxford, Westview Press.

Seldon, A. (1990), 'The Cabinet Office and coordination, 1979– 1987', *Public Administration*, Vol. 68, No. 1, London, RIPA/Basil Blackwell.

Seldon, A. (1977), *Charge*, London, Temple Smith.

Self, P. (1970), 'Nonsense on Stilts: Cost Benefit Analysis and the Roskill Commission', *Political Quarterly*, July.

Self, P. (1977), *Administrative Theories and Politics*, London, Allen and Unwin.

Simon, H. (1945), *Administrative Behaviour*, New York, Free Press.

Smith, B.C. (1985), *Decentralisation: the territorial dimension of the state*, London, Allen and Unwin.

Smith, H. (1988), *The Power Game: How Washington Works*, New York, Ballentine Books.

Smith, T.A. (1972), *Anti-Politics*, London, Charles Knight and Co.

Smith, T.A. (1979), *The Politics of the Corporate Economy*, London, Martin Robertson.

Smith, T.A. (1985), *British Politics in the Post-Keynesian Era*, Inaugural Lecture, London, The Acton Society.

Stahl, O.G. and McGurrin, J.J. (1986), 'Professionalizing the Career Service', *The Bureaucrat*, Spring, pp.9–21.

Stockman, D. (1986), *The Triumph of Politics*, New York, Harper and Row.

Stoker, G. (1988), *The Politics of Local Government*, Basingstoke, Macmillan.

Storing, H.J. (1986), 'Reforming the Bureaucracy', in Rourke.

Swann, D. (1988), *The Retreat of the State: Deregulation and Privatisation in the UK and US*, London, Harvester Wheatsheaf.

Taylor, J.A., and Williams, H. (1991), 'Public Information and the Information Polity', *Public Administration*, Vol. 69, No. 2, London, Basil Blackwell.

Thomas, R.M. (1978), *The British Philosophy of Administration*, London and New York, Longman.

Tomkys, R. (1991), 'The Financial Management Initiative in the FCO', *Public Administration*, Vol. 69, No. 2, London, Basil Blackwell.

Touche Ross (1987), *Privatization in America*, New York, Touche Ross.

Tym, R. (and partners) (1984), *Monitoring Enterprise Zones: Year Three Report*, London, Department of the Environment.

United States Merit Systems Protection Board (1989a), *Delegation and Decentralisation: Personnel Management Simplification Efforts in the Federal Government*, USMSPB.

United States Merit Systems Protection Board (1989b), *The Senior Executive Service: Views of Former Federal Executives*, USMSPB.

United States Merit Systems Protection Board (1989c), *Working for America: A Federal Employee Survey*, USMSPB.

United States House of Representatives, Subcommittee on Civil Service of the Committee on Post Office and Civil Service (1989a), *Contracting at Environmental Protection Agency and its Effect on Federal Employees*, Official Record, Congress, February 23.

United States House of Representatives, Subcommittee on Civil Service of the Committee on Post Office and Civil Service (1989b), *Improving the Public Image of Civil Servants*, Official record, Congress, June 28.

Vaughn, R.G. (1988–9), 'The Performance of the United States Merit Systems Protection Board: The Foundation for Future Regulation', *Policy Studies Journal*, Vol. 17, No. 2.

Veljanovski, C. (1987), *Selling the State: Privatisation in Britain*, London, Weidenfeld and Nicolson.

Volker, P.A. (1987), *Public Service: The Quiet Crisis*, Washington DC, American Enterprise Institute for Public Policy Research.

Waldo, D. (1984), *The Administrative State*, New York, Holmes and Meier.

Walsh, K. (1990), *Competition for Local Government Services*, Birmingham, INLOGOV.

Wass, D. (1983), 'The Public Service in Modern Society', *Public Administration*, Vol. 61, No. 1, London Basil Blackwell.

Wilding, P. (1982), *Professional Power and Social Welfare*, London, Routledge and Kegan Paul.

Williams, S.F. (1985), *The Natural Gas Revolution of 1985*, University Press of America.

Williams, W. (1988), *Washington, Westminster, and Whitehall*, Cambridge, New York, Cambridge University Press.

Williamson, P.J. (1989), *Corporatism in Perspective*, London, Sage.

Wiltshire, K. (1987), *Privatisation: The British Experience*, Coventry, Longman Cheshire.

Wilson, J.Q., (1986) 'The Rise of the Bureaucratic State', in Rourke.

Wood, W.C. (1983), *Nuclear Safety: Risks and Regulation*, University Press of America.

Young, K. (1986), 'The Justification of Local Government', in Goldsmith.

Young, K. and Mason, C. (eds) (1983), *Urban Economic Development: New Roles and Relationships*, Basingstoke, Macmillan.

Index